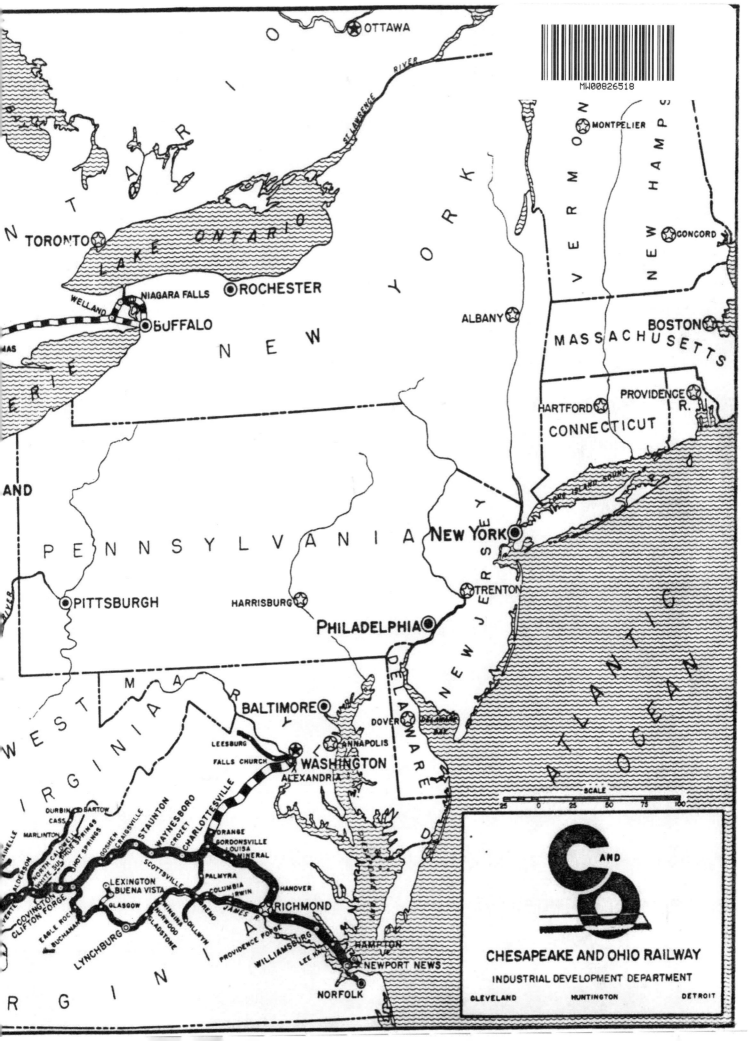

MW00826518

OTTAWA

MONTPELIER

VERMONT

NEW HAMPS

CONCORD

TORONTO

LAKE ONTARIO

NIAGARA FALLS
WELLAND
BUFFALO

ROCHESTER

NEW YORK

ALBANY

BOSTON

MASSACHUSETTS

ERIE

HARTFORD

PROVIDENCE
R.

CONNECTICUT

AND

PENNSYLVANIA

NEW JERSEY

NEW YORK

TRENTON

PITTSBURGH

HARRISBURG

PHILADELPHIA

ATLANTIC OCEAN

WEST

MARYLAND

BALTIMORE

DELAWARE

DOVER

ANNAPOLIS

LEESBURG
FALLS CHURCH
WASHINGTON
ALEXANDRIA

SCALE
25 0 25 50 75 100

VIRGINIA

DURBIN BARTOW
CASS
MARLINTON
NORTH CALDWELL
WHITE SUL SPRINGS
HOT SPRINGS
COVINGTON
CLIFTON FORGE
EAGLE ROC
BUCHANAN
LYNCHBURG

STAUNTON
WAYNESBORO
CROZET
CHARLOTTESVILLE
ORANGE
GORDONSVILLE
LOUISA
MINERAL

GOSHEN
CRAIGSVILLE

SCOTTSVILLE
LEXINGTON
BUENA VISTA
GLASGOW

PALMYRA
COLUMBIA
IRWIN
PREMO
WINGINA
NORWOOD
GLADSTONE
DILLWYN

HANOVER

JAMES R.
RICHMOND

PROVIDENCE FORGE

WILLIAMSBURG

LEE HA
HAMPTON
NEWPORT NEWS

NORFOLK

C and O

CHESAPEAKE AND OHIO RAILWAY

INDUSTRIAL DEVELOPMENT DEPARTMENT

CLEVELAND   HUNTINGTON   DETROIT

Chesapeake & Ohio
Super Power Steam Locomotives

by Eugene L. Huddleston

© 2005
The Chesapeake & Ohio Historical Society, Inc.
P.O. Box 79,
Clifton Forge, VA 24422

During a work session in 2002, author Gene Huddleston confers with artist and retired railroad machinist Allen Hickman at headquarters of C&O Historical Society, Clifton Forge. Gene's preparation as writer started with an A. B. from Marshall University, Huntington, following two years at Ashland Junior College in Kentucky. An M. A. from Ohio University, Athens, 1956, and courses at Indiana University, Bloomington, concluded with the Ph.D. from Michigan State University, East Lansing, 1965. Gene's article, "Topographical Poetry of the Early National Period," adapted from his dissertation, won the Norman Foerster Prize for 1966.

Preparation as railroad photographer and historian was less formal but no less intense. Strongly influencing his early development was Horace W. "Jack" Pontin, founder of Rail Photo Service in Boston. J. D. Bennett, C&O route clerk at Russell, inspired with toughness and good humor. Roy W. Carlson, co-founder of the Railway and Locomotive Historical Society, opened his Fort Wayne home to a young Tri-State College instructor. To Herbert W. Harwood, Jr., and Thomas W. Dixon, Jr., recognized national leaders in railroad publishing, he owes profound gratitude. Gene's major books, in terms of length, are a reference guide to Thomas Jefferson and a history of locomotives of the United States Railroad Administration in World War I.

Front Cover:
C&O H-8 2-6-6-6 No. 1636 is seen upgrade rounding the curve just west of the Hawks Nest Dam on the New River. This is from a painting done expressly for this book by D. A. J. Bunce of Surrey, England.

Digital Image Production: Debbie Paxton
Copy Editor: Lars Lemburg
Layout Design: Mac Beard
Printed in U.S.A. by Walsworth Publishing Company

The Chesapeake & Ohio Historical Society, Inc. is a non-profit organization dedicated to the collection, preservation, and interpretation of the history of the Chesapeake & Ohio Railway, its predecessors and successors.
The Society may be contacted by writing:

The Chesapeake & Ohio Historical Society
P.O. Box 79,
Clifton Forge, VA 24422

or calling toll free 800-453-COHS (Monday-Saturday 9am-5pm), or by e-mail at: cohs@cfw.com. The Society maintains a history information Internet site at www.cohs.org, and a full service sales site at www.chessieshop.com.

Library of Congress Control Number: 2005927174
International Standard Book Number 0-939487-75-6

TABLE of CONTENTS

Preface

Chapter 1
Super Power: The Big Picture 1

Chapter 2
C&O and Super Power 11

Chapter 3
Designing C&O Super Power 23

Chapter 4
C&O Texas Type T-1 33

Chapter 5
C&O Greenbriers 53

Chapter 6
C&O Hudsons 67

Chapter 7
C&O's 2-6-6-6 Alleghenies 87

Chapter 8
C&O K-4 Kanawhas (2-8-4) 103

Chapter 9
Improving, Maintaining and Repairing C&O Super Power 121

Chapter 10
C&O Super Power Suitability 143

Preface

Kids liked toy steam locomotives because their side rods made them move rhythmically down the "track, track, track, track," and "the little red caboose behind the train" intrigued them. Real locomotives had big bells that went "ding, dong", smoke stacks that emitted real smoke, and whistles that could play melodies mechanically, whether toy or real, they had the same fascination for small boys as steam shovels, fire trucks, and dump trucks. Though boys were the biggest fans of "choo choo" trains, girls could like them too. Lionel Trains, around 1958, advertised a special model for girls, with engine and tender done in pink -- that's right, pink! Today toys function with electronic interiors that are quiet and mysterious. Even a "buzz" from within is often missing. And real trains are not nearly as much in view as they used to be. Historian George Drury, in *Railfan & Railroad*, says that in order to get children interested today, they must be given books to read like Thomas the Tank Engine.

Adults liked steam locomotives, in Lucius Beebe's words, for pretty much the same reasons as children: "the hiss of escaping steam, the drum roll of the exhaust, the smoke that whips from the stack, the hot breath of the fire–box." These delights, even though they evidenced, said Beebe, "the steam locomotive's inefficiency," also pointed to its "beauty, simplicity, and utility." It was this combination in a single machine that has given rise to a popularity today of the steam locomotive that extends beyond fascination with its role in transportation history. People — mostly men, looking for a hobby on which to focus their "feel" for complex and visible mechanical detail and big machines housing it — find in the modern steam locomotive fulfillment for these needs. ("Modern" means roughly 1925 to 1960.) They can pursue their interest, through specialized historical investigation, such as exemplified in this book, or they can become modelers. A scale model locomotive embodies delicate detail, compact form, and precisely proportional measurements.

After boarding passengers from Norfork, across Chesapeake Bay the "Sportsman" leaves Newport News for Detroit early in 1952. Shorter train and lighter coaches mean 4-6-4 can replace 4-8-4 for run over Piedmont. "Elephant ears" smoke lifter was retrofitted to Hudson 301. (photo by H. Reid, from the collection of the California State Railroad Museum.)

A firebox so big it needed support of a six-wheel truck came in 1941 with the 2-6-6-6 type. C&O 1604 (Lima, December 1941), on permanent display B&O Museum, Baltimore, heads east with Tidewater loads near NC Cabin, Ky., August 1955. (E. L. Huddleston)

Modeling it requires concentrated attention to carrying through the prototype's actual appearance. Completion or acquisition of a model introduces into a devotee's life form and harmony that few other pursuits can bring. That feeling of everything coming together - especially when the engine is made to run through scenery imitating real scenes – accounts for the wide interest in big steam (primarily American) today. Devotees of the hobby want to make their model accord with its prototype. Thus they study every detail of the steam locomotive's design and appearance, in order to "get it right." There are so many designs of steam locomotives that have survived in photos and scale drawings that every modeler can be an individualist. Variety of form and detail on a steamer was almost always guaranteed, on even the most modern steam locomotives. Standardization was never really achieved; railroads wanted customized designs. Finally, with the adoption of diesels, locomotive manufacturers forced standardization on the railroads.

Obviously some one who gets interested in a particular type of steam locomotive, for whatever reason, wants to give that locomotive a personality by getting facts about its place in American steam technology. This book capitalizes on this interest, and tries to give the reader his money's worth by concentrating on one railroad's stable of modern freight and passenger locomotives known as Super Power. Defining the one railroad is easy enough. It's the Appalachian coal carrier Chesapeake & Ohio, connecting Chesapeake Bay not just with the Ohio river but with — most tellingly for the Super Power story — the Great Lakes at Toledo (and by 1947 after merging with the Pere Marquette Railroad, serving the industrial heart of Michigan). Because the C&O hauled long coal trains across mountainous Appalachia, it is a good road to examine for outstanding examples of Super Power. And because it had a long tradition of high-class passenger service, principally between Washington, and Cincinnati , and Detroit and Norfolk, it sought the finest in passenger power.

In Thomas W. Dixon's published summary of the status of the C&O in the mid-1940s, one finds a lucid statement of the condition of the C&O during the Super Power era: "Historically the C&O was a strong road based solidly in the large coal traffic from West Virginia and Kentucky to the Great Lakes and to Tidewater Virginia. During the Great Depression, the C&O not only avoided debilitating financial problems but inaugurated 'The Sportsman' (1930) and 'The George Washington' (1932) which [along with the 'F. F. V.'] became the leading trains of its fleet. Also, during the Depression, the C&O seized the opportunity to use its plentiful money when material and labor were cheap, to enlarge its tunnels, do signal work and generally upgrade its physical plant while other roads were forced to reduced and deferred maintenance. At the beginning of World War II, the C&O continually showed good profits and demonstrated the very best in operating practices."

Pinning down the term Super Power is harder than identifying the railroad. C&O was a corporate name. Super Power was a publicity ploy. What exactly was meant by Super Power will occupy a large portion of this book. The easiest definition of Super Power is any American steam locomotive with a four-wheel trailing truck. The reason of course for going from no trailing truck to a two-wheel, then four wheel, and finally to a six-wheel trailing truck, was to permit an ever larger fire box with the grates located below the level of the driving wheels in order to provide more firebox volume for more complete combustion As to the four-wheel "rule" for Super Power, there are always exceptions These exceptions show that it was grate area in square feet more than the existence of a four wheel truck supporting the fire box that defined Super Power. For example, the New York Central from 1925 to 1944 purchased several hundred of the very successful class L-2, L-3, and L-4 4-8-2 Mohawk type (called the Mountain type on most roads). The fire box above these classes' two-wheel trailing truck was 75.3 sq. ft. in area, whereas the Northern type (4-8-4), class U-4b, purchased from Lima Locomotive Works in 1938 by the Grand Trunk Western, had less grate area - 73.7 sq. ft. over its four-wheel trailing truck. (Average grate area for the 4-wheel truck was 90 to 100 sq. ft.)

Once the four-wheel trailing truck had been accept-ed as the norm on American railroads, it was only a matter of time until a freight engine was built that required a six-wheel truck for 135 sq. ft. of grate area. This development came in 1941 with the construction of C&O's Allegheny type. This articulated was quite successful on both the C&O and Virginian Railways. However, the diesel-electric locomotive revolution, which started on the eve of World War II, resumed its inexorable march afterwards, and all sixty-eight 2-6-6-6s were out of service permanently by October, 1956.

This book will first explain how Super Power came into being, how and why C&O adopted it, what it meant in terms of steam locomotive development, and who designed it. Subsequent chapters will cover the design, performance, and mechanical details of each Super Power type that C&O (and after 1947, the Pere Marquette) owned, from 1930 to 1948. Final chapters will elucidate how C&O Super Power was improved, maintained and repaired and will evaluate the adaptability to service of each type.

Offering invaluable encouragement and assistance with the text, photos, and other illustrations are Thomas W. Dixon, Jr., Gary E. Huddleston, Donald Leach, Rod Crawford, Phil Shuster, Don Riel, Terry Seaks, Jerry Ballard and Richard Burlingame.

Cab forward view of Grand Trunk 4-8-4 No. 6405 (at Detroit in 1959) shows why 4-wheel trailing truck is not needed to support the 73.7 sq. ft. of grate area. Woodard created Super Power by using 4-wheel truck for 100 sq. ft. of grate area. (E L. Huddleston)

Chapter 1

Super Power: The Big Picture

"Speeding up operation without reducing train tonnage (which is the same as an increase in gross ton-miles per train-hour) can only be accomplished with higher horsepower."
– Lima brochure cited in Richard Cook's *Lima Super Power Steam Locomotives*

2-8-4 L&N #1952 in northern Kentucky southbound.

Super Power: The Big Picture

The time was ripe in America for Super Power, a term originated by advertisers, not mechanical engineers. "Super" took advantage of interest in Nietzsche's "superman" and in the increasing enthusiasm of Americans for high speed and horsepower in automobiles. "Super" was in the public consciousness because of the introduction of supercharging to automobile engines in the early 1920s. As autos developed, people wanted more and more speed. Standing out in the public consciousness in the 1920's, when Super Power locomotives first appeared, was the American made Stutz Bear Cat auto. In 1925, Stutz introduced an improved Bear-Cat model with a straight-eight engine developing 92 hp. The new model proved an immediate success with more than $3 million of orders taken in a single day at the dealers' convention in December 1925.

That same year came the first Super Power locomotive. What is Super Power? A too easy definition is any steam locomotive with a four wheel trailing truck. The reason for going from no trailing truck, to a two-wheel, then four-wheel, and finally to a six-wheel, was to permit an ever larger firebox with grates located behind the driving wheels in order to have more firebox volume for more complete combustion. As to four wheels being the "rule," there are always exceptions, which show that it was grate area in square feet more than a four-wheel truck that defined Super Power. For example, the New York Central from 1925 to 1944 purchased several hundred of the very successful class L-2, L-3, and L-4 4-8-2's, called Mohawks on NYC but named the Mountain type on most roads. The fire box resting on the Mohawk's two-wheel trailing truck was 75.3 sq. ft. in area, whereas the Northern type (4-8-4), class U-4b, purchased from Lima Locomotive Works in 1938 by the Grand Trunk Western, had less grate area-73.7 sq. ft. over its four-wheel trailing truck.

In 1925 American motive power design was in need of some fresh thinking. The steam locomotive was still king, for diesel technology had not advanced beyond use of diesel electrics as single unit industrial switchers, and electric locomotives powered from overhead wires or by "third rail" contacts which were being put to work on high-density routes, trackage with long underground passages, and mountain divisions handicapped by steep adverse grades. Yes, steam was still king but in technical development had not advanced beyond the "standard-

New York Central H-10 class Mikado at Elkhart, Indiana, in 1940's. The 1922 original of this successful line of heavy Mikes provided the principal dimensions for Lima's experimental A-1 2-8-4 of 1925. Though alike in many ways, a main difference was 66.4 sq. ft. of grate area for the H-10 and 100 sq. ft. for the Lima A-1. (E. L. Huddleston collection.)

ized" designs adopted by the United States Railroad Administration in World War I, when this agency took over operation of the nation's railroads during the breakdown in railroad transportation on the eve of America's entry into that war. Designed by committees representing the railroads and the builders, the locomotives were built by venerable Baldwin Locomotive Works of Philadelphia, busy American Locomotive Company of Schenectady (and its other eastern and southern plants), and smaller Lima Locomotive Works of Lima, Ohio. Partly because of cut-backs in production caused by the Great Depression and the shortages of World War II, these locomotives mostly lasted into the 1950's. The twelve designs agreed to (and later copied after dissolution of the USRA) included freight, passenger, and switching types. The most popular wheel arrangements, as it turned out, were the light and heavy Pacific types, the light and heavy Mikado types, and the 8-wheel switcher, and heavy Mallet. The engines are defined as popular because they were copied over and over again. Granted they were "safe" designs, not daring to "push the envelope."

Take either a light or heavy USRA Mikado (2-8-2) and put a four-wheel trailer under it and you have, superficially, a Super Power locomotive. The first Super Power engines were for freight hauling, but soon the demand for faster overland speeds and the growth in length and weight of passenger trains made development of Super Power passenger engines a certainty. The key to improved performance by both passenger and freight engines was boiler capacity (the term "boiler" includes both fire box and boiler assembly).

As demonstrated by the popularity of the Stutz Bear Cat, America in the 1920's was no longer in the horse and buggy days. But steam locomotive designers were slow to think in terms of horsepower-admittedly an odd term to describe the work of machines! Locomotive power was conventionally measured by a formula for tractive effort; that is, starting power. Lucius Beebe has stated clearly the problem with tractive effort as a measurement of a locomotive's power. "Although the pressure of the steam in the boiler is an important factor in the formula [steam pressure times cylinder diameter, squared, times piston stroke divided by driving wheel diameter], there is nothing in it which appraises the ability of the boiler to keep up that pressure. If one of the (Super Power) New York Central Hudson-types, for instance, were fitted with a boiler half the regular size and everything else left the same, its theoretical starting tractive force would still be the same, even though its real power would be reduced by half. As a matter of fact, its starting tractive force would be the same."

In order to increase tractive effort, designers usually increased cylinder size and reduced driver diameter. This approach worked, but the designers often neglected to increase the boiler's capacity to supply steam to the larger cylinders. Thus would locomotives literally run

out of steam at moderate speeds. In spite of this disparity between starting power and running power, rated tractive effort continued to be the standard against which all locomotives were compared, and tonnage-rating charts were based on tractive effort. Boiler capacity, the true key to locomotive performance, was completely ignored.

Enter here Will Woodard — originator of Super Power — born in Utica, New York, and educated at Cornell University. His sixteen years with American Locomotive Works at Schenectady ended when he was lured to small but innovative Lima Locomotive Works as vice-president in charge of engineering. His obituary (1942) in *Railway Age* sums up his achievements there: "In 1925 Mr. Woodard designed the Lima A-1 locomotive, with 2-8-4 wheel arrangement, which is a prototype of the modern steam locomotive, combining high speed with high horsepower capacity. It was largely through his work . . . that the horsepower has superseded the tractive-force pound as the unit in terms of which steam locomotive capacity is customarily measured."

Woodard, then, saw that (in George Drury's words) "sustained power output depended not on boiler pressure, weight on drivers, and driver and cylinder dimensions, but on the capacity of the boiler to generate steam." And that required grate area –so much, in fact, that more than one trailing axle was needed to support the additional weight. Of course, some locomotive designers thought the weight of the boiler firebox should rest entirely on the driving wheels to add more traction. They thus were against redistributing weight to the trailing truck. Woodard answered them by putting the rear axle of the trailing truck to work. Thus the A-1 had a "booster" — a small self contained steam engine that would add power in getting the train moving, when there was steam to spare, and that would cut out at 15 mph, before steam production became critical to horsepower output.

Before putting all his bets on the A-1 's new 2-8-4 wheel arrangement, Woodard experimented with a Mikado type. The 2-8-2 wheel arrangement was so well proven and accepted for "drag" freight service that it would be safe to put to work some of Woodard's pet ideas on it — like a booster on the 2-wheel trailing truck. Brian Solomon has recorded how under Woodard's directions, "Lima built a series of experimental 2-8-2 Mikados for the New York Central with greater boiler capacity. The best of these were the H-10's, which could haul more tonnage than just about any other comparable locomotive on the railroad." Lima labeled the H-10s "the Wonder Locomotive." The lessons learned from adapting a "drag era" Mikado design to incorporate Woodard's favorite innovations were applied to the next project — Lima's experimental "A-I." It would add to the Mikado type wheel arrangement another axle to the trailing truck, creating a 2-8-4.

That extra axle would support the weight of the

huge fire box that Woodard designed for the A-1. It would have, for a two-cylindered locomotive, an unprecedented 100 square feet of grate area. A four to six-inch fire spread evenly over the grates by a mechanical stoker would create the heat to make the steam, and limited piston valve cut-off would permit more economical use of the steam in the cylinders as the engine accelerated to running speed. An increase in steam pressure within the boiler would permit greater steam expansion at the shorter cut-off, and a trailing truck booster would compensate for the power lost in starting through limiting the valve cut-off. A feedwater heater would take some of the exhaust steam (before it entered the smoke box) and heat the cold water from the tender prior to its being pumped into the boiler. Feedwater heaters were, in 1925, just coming into general acceptance.

A-1 2-8-4, numbered "1" under the cab window and with "Lima Locomotive Works, Inc." on the tender sides went to work, upon completion, on test trains over the Boston and Albany (NYC subsidiary) main line between Albany, New York, and Boston. This route was pretty much a straight line, but its directness was achieved only by crossing the Berkshire Range in extreme western Massachusetts. Hence the name "Berkshire" for the new type. Tests were conducted on the 100-mile division between Albany and Springfield, in central Massachusetts. Nine test runs proved that the A-1 could maintain high speed "while lifting heavy tonnage up a long steep grade." And it did this while consuming less fuel than the very successful NYC H-10 Mikado. Richard Cook, in his *Super Power Steam Locomotives*, (1966), has documented this success: "Unquestionably the most dramatic test occurred April 14, 1925. At 10:57 that morning, No. 190, a class H-10 2-8-2, steamed eastbound from the Selkirk yard [at Albany] with a manifest consisting of 46 cars aggregating 1,691 tons. Almost one hour later, at 11:44 A.M., the A-1 with dynamometer car in tow led a string of 54 cars from the same yard with a total of 2,296 tons. As the A-1 passed the yard limit sign, she put her shoulder to the hard eastbound climb through the Berkshires. Not far ahead, No. 190 with a lighter train made good time without any undue delays. Steadily the A-1 narrowed the gap. At Chatham, No. 190 was switched to the outside track, and moments later, the A-1 came into the block. In a matter of minutes, the A1 pulled up to the caboose and was running side by side .... Between East Chatham and Canaan, the most difficult portion of the line came into view. This didn't hold back the A-1; she kept pace with the No. 190, then overtook her car by car." The 2-8-4

Eastern Railroads Exhibit at huge 1948 Railroad Fair in Chicago showcases the latest in motive power-steam, diesel, and electric. New York Central (middle) displayed one of its 4-8-4s of 1946. Designated "Niagaras" instead of "Northerns," these passenger engines had 79-inch drivers for high speed and 100-inch (BMOD) boilers for high horsepower. Tight clearances in passenger service kept height to little less than 15 ft., 3 inches. (E. L. Huddleston)

ended its run ten minutes ahead of the Mikado.

On this run horsepower had triumphed over the tractive effort. Horsepower, or power at speed, was difficult to measure. Lucius Beebe, in *High Iron* (1938) pointed to the New York Central's Super Power 4-6-4 of 1927 — a new wheel arrangement originating at Alco — for its, "steaming capacity at high speed." He claimed that a big reason for the neglect of horsepower before the mid-1920s, was difficulty of measurement," . . .figuring horsepower wasn't easy. There was a cylinder horse-power formula which didn't concern itself with boiler size, and invariably underestimated the capacity of a modem engine; and there was a boiler horse-power formula which was of practically prohibitive complexity. About the most trustworthy way of estimating horse-power was to test the engine in actual service [a measurement called drawbar horsepower]."

In spite of the success of the A-1 and the spate of Super Power designs appearing in 1926 and 1927, some leading motive power designers still thought an added trailing wheel would detract from the tractive effort of the locomotive by lessening the weight on the drivers needed to keep the drivers from slipping. For example, Leonor F. Loree (1858-1940) wrote in 1922, "It is very desirable to carry on the driving wheels all the weight possible in order to utilize it as adhesion. For that reason four-wheel leading trucks and trailing wheels should be avoided if possible." So much for adding grate area to the locomotive! J. Parker Lamb in *Perfecting the American Steam Locomotive* (2002) emphasized how the formula for tractive effort worked against increasing horsepower; from the formula it follows that "starting tractive effort is inversely related to driver size."

Thus thinking of the power of an engine to move a load —that is, its tractive effort— as its most important characteristic means selecting drivers of small diameter. (Fifty-seven inches was about standard for "drag" power of this period.)

The Erie and Virginian Triplexes (2-8-8-8-2 and 2-8-8-8-4) of 1914 and 1916 respectively illustrate the absurdity of emphasizing tractive effort over all else. The designers must have thought that mechanical stokers (which had just been proved practical a couple of years earlier) would enable these giants to keep up steam to supply three sets of cylinders (one set under the cab). The principle of the "Mallet" would apply — using steam twice — but using it twice, twice over. "In operation," Parker Lamb wrote, "each of the high-pressure, center cylinders exhausted to a pair of the low pressure cylinders," front and rear. In both cases, the fire boxes were unable to keep enough steam coming, despite boilers of huge girth. Low steam production, then, doomed both locomotives.

The impression should not be left that only Lima was interested in improving the steam production rate and increasing the locomotive's drawbar horsepower or

that Lima did everything right and the other builders made mistakes. Lima was the first to hire an innovative designer and to have the foresight to construct a working model embodying an unproven concept. But not all innovations Woodard applied to the A-1 worked out in practice, and he was quite conservative about size potential. Also, limited valve cut-off did not attain widespread acceptance. His articulated trailing truck, made part of the frame, proved impractical. And though he knew the need for burning completely all the coal in the fire box, he did not immediately see that a forward extension of the fire box called the combustion chamber would improve combustion. (In this chamber unburnt gases mingled with air and ignited before entering the narrow tubes and flues.) Another shortcoming was drivers too small in diameter. They were kept to 63 inches, the standard height for the heavy and light Mikados built by the government in World War I. The best of the Super Power Berkshires would have 69 or 70 inches, for improved speed and better riding quality. Woodard soon corrected the absence of a combustion chamber, for the first 2-10-4 (named the Texas type) of 1925 for the Texas and Pacific had the chamber, as well as siphons for improved water circulation in the fire box. (The first freight Super Power with high drivers came in 1927 with 70 inch diameter for Erie 2-8-4s.) Many roads preferred 2-8-4s with 63-inch drivers because of clearance problems. The Erie, originally laid out for broad gauge, had no clearance problems.

Though Lima pioneered the Berkshire and Texas types, American (Alco) originated the enlargement of the 4-8-2 Mountain type into a 4-8-4 and of the 4-6-2 (Pacific) into the 4-6-4. In 1927, two years after completion of Lima's A-1, the first Super Power freight locomotive, Alco turned out the first passenger locomotive with a four-wheel trailing truck- the New York Central's famous "J" class. Because these 4-6-4s originated for service on the NYC's "Water Level Route" between New York and Chicago, they were named Hudsons. Clearance restrictions kept these stately engines from being noticeably "Super Power' in size, but the streamlined jackets on some of the nearly 200 of the Hudsons that NYC eventually owned make them the most famous of Super Power designs. Another factor making them well known to the general public was that Lionel and American Flyer made "electric train" models of them in the 1930's and 1940's.

American (Alco) built the first 4-8-4 for Northern Pacific for passenger service, though later it and most other 4-8-4 designs (of which there were a great many despite having the same wheel arrangement) would be for dual service and in such capacity would become the dominant wheel arrangement among Super Power types until the end of steam. Because the Northern Pacific Railway received the first 4-8-4s in early 1927, the new type was dubbed "Northern". As for the oldest locomotive manufacturer, Baldwin, its engineering staff had also seen the need for innovative improvements to "drag era" designs which had become dated by the quickening pace of American life. George Drury, in his *Guide* (Kalmbach, 1993), well summed up how Samuel Vauclain (1856-1940), president of Baldwin, aimed to make Baldwin the leader in the horsepower and steam efficiency race: "Baldwin's 60,000th locomotive was a three-cylinder 4-10-2... The middle cylinder was high pressure; the outside cylinders were low pressure. The locomotive was sent out on a demonstration tour, but the combination of water tube fire box, three-cylinder running gear (which was expensive to maintain), and compound working were too exotic for the railroads. The locomotive returned to Philadelphia and was placed on display in the Franklin Institute, where it remains today."

Vauclain's innovations were not as radical in practice as they might sound. Three cylinders had the advantage, according to Drury, of dividing power among three pistons and main rods instead of two, and six power impulses produced more even torque than four. Also the water tube fire box produced higher steam pressures and was more efficient than the conventional fire tube boiler. Further, compounding was the principle that made the Mallet an outstanding design concept. J. Parker Lamb attributes the failure of No. 60,000 to the conservative mind set of the locomotive design fraternity. After all, Will Woodard's ideas for the A-1 and its successors were more evolutionary than revolutionary.

Baldwin started building Super Power at about the time Alco did. In 1927, nearly two years after after Lima built the first 2-10-4s for the Texas and Pacific, the Chicago, Burlington, and Quincy received from Baldwin ten (with two more following the next year) 2-10-4s that were intermediate in size between the T&P 2-10-4s of 1927 and the C&O 2-10-4s of 1930. The CB&Q 2-10-4s were powerful indeed for their time and had boilers of 104 inches maximum diameter, a 54-inch combustion chamber, and 107 square feet of grate area. The new 2-10-4s for the Burlington were so close in major dimensions to the huge Erie 2-8-4s under construction at Lima and American at the same time that historian Don Leach wonders if the Burlington design was "copied" from the Erie design.

As for Super Power articulateds, there was no way a true Mallet (that is, a double expansion, compound, "hinged" locomotive) could be considered Super Power. Hardly any true Mallets had drivers over 58-inches, and that alone would keep them from making much speed regardless of how much steam was supplied to the cylinders. Only simple articulateds (single expansion types) could be Super Power. The first simple articulateds were ponderous machines with low drivers and 2-wheel trailers. A practical resolution of when the first Super Power articulated appeared need not concern us. Lima itself built only two simple articulated types. Its first,

a 2-8-8-4 in 1939 for the Southern Pacific, appeared eleven years after the first Super Power articulated (assuming one considers a 4-wheel trailing truck sure evidence of Super Power) for the Northern Pacific, which had introduced the Yellowstone type. Lima's second, a 2-6-6-6, came in 1941 for the Chesapeake & Ohio (with copies in 1945 for the Virginian Railway.) It was logical that if the 4-wheel trailer was to evolve into a six-wheel trailer, it would be for an articulated. The C&O's Allegheny type was designed for horsepower, and the longer truck was needed to support the weight of a fire box with 135 sq. ft. of grate area. One needs keep in mind that this fire box rested entirely behind the driving wheels, not the case with most simple articulated designs.

Lima is associated in the popular mind more with Super Power than the other two builders, mainly because Lima originated the concept and because of the success of the C&O 2-10-4 in 1930, which was so advanced as a steam design that the Pennsylvania Railroad in 1942 built 125 copies, which became that road's finest heavy steam locomotive. Adding to Lima's reputation were 2-8-4s for the Nickel Plate, designed by the Advisory Mechanical Committee of the Van Sweringen empire and copied so often it became the "standardized" 2-8-4 modern design. However, Lima's total steam locomotive production since the mid-1920s consisted of more "drag era" types than Super Power types. The reasons for this were two. First, the Great Depression discouraged purchase of new locomotives, because many serviceable locomotives were stored "for the duration." Second, during World War II Lima had contracts for government and foreign locomotives in great numbers, none of which were Super Power. And many railroads put off purchases because they wanted diesels instead of steam.

The preference of the Advisory Mechanical Committee for contracts with Lima contributed to Lima's reputation for quality, high horsepower steam power from the late 1920s to the end of orders in 1949. One might assume because Lima built among the most impressive of the Super Power designs that Will Woodard, who pioneered the concept, was in charge of the best designs. However, Woodard had made a condition of his employment that he work out of New York, not Lima, Ohio. There he became a restless experimenter, being awarded ninety-two patents on various mechanical features of steam and electric locomotive design. Among achievements that led to his honoring by the National Association of Manufacturers in 1940 were development of lateral motion driving boxes and "constant resistance" engine and trailing trucks. At his death in 1942, he was working on poppet valves for Franklin Railway Supply Company (of which Lima was a subsidiary).

From 1930 for nearly a decade Woodard's genius was held hostage by the weakness of Lima's financial condition and to the absence of significant locomotive orders. Eric Hirsimaki wrote that "Lima lost $2,533,211 between 1930 and 1939 with only 1930 ($1,382,318) and 1937 ($1,019,983) showing a profit." Obviously Lima had little money for research and development. If it had, Woodard might have come up with actual production of some novel ideas he had floating around. One of these ideas did reach an article stage in *Railway Age* for April 1929, on the eve of the Depression. Titled "Modern Locomotives for Secondary Service," its sub-head was its thesis: "The author proposes a design for all-around service to replace the accumulation of misfits handed down through the years." The design was for a medium sized 4-6-4 to replace "older and lighter" locomotives that had been relegated to branch lines from mainline service. Interestingly, drivers for this standardized model would be 69 inches, the height that became standard for heavy duty freight Super Power. Woodard's most convincing case for this "light weight" Super Power design was the savings which Super Power in service had already demonstrated, plus the savings that would accrue in reduced parts inventory and uniform repair procedures. Another of his novel ideas that never saw production was his 1934 proposal for a 4-4-4 equipped with poppet valves.

Woodard's prescience about the need for standardized motive power anticipated what American railroads belatedly learned from diesel electrics-that one design could serve the needs of practically all American railroads. Woodard specifically anticipated the design of the "Geep" at the Electro-Motive Division of General Motors some twenty years later. Woodard aimed to keep the axle load of the 4-6-4 at a low 52,000 lbs. and the maximum height at fifteen feet and width at ten feet This would permit its use on low maintenance branch lines; its generous heating surfaces would at the same time permit use on main lines. Woodard wrote: "It would be a general utility locomotive which could be used on branchline freight, main-line fast freight, or in passenger service if needed." Woodard's words would be the same that designer Dick Dilworth of EMD could use twenty years later in describing his highly popular General Purpose locomotives, for the famous GP7 and GP9 models handled all three assignments well.

The closest that Lima got to a standard model for a steamer was the Berkshires Lima built for the Nickel Plate, Pere Marquette, Chesapeake and Ohio, Virginian, and Richmond, Fredericksburg and Potomac. (The federal government during world War II encouraged standardization but ended up enforcing it only for locomotive orders of ten and under.) This commonality was prompted by the Advisory Mechanical Committee, headquartered in Cleveland's Terminal Tower, home of the Van Sweringen brothers holding company, until succeeded by Young's Alleghany corporation. The AMC standardized designs for the four Van Sweringen roads — C&O,

2-8-4 C&O #2735 on #97 in southern Ohio

Erie, Nickel Plate, and Pere Marquette. (C&O officials who went to the Virginian in 1943 as Chairman of the Board and as President were responsible for copying the C&O 2-8-4 for the Virginian.) The AMC 2-8-4 design was so popular that it was copied by other Eastern railroads not part of the Van Sweringen empire, like the Louisville and Nashville. "Committee" is a misleading term, for it implies a relatively small group making recommendations. The paper trail the AMC left behind in its work on locomotive orders suggests a fully staffed organization of draftsmen, technical writers, mechanical engineers, and even a lawyer.

One might think that with the example of the Advisory Mechanical Committee's work and with advertising campaigns waged in trade journals for modern Super Power, thoughtful executives within the industry would have made some move toward standardization. However, few American railroads believed that standardization of design would improve efficiency, costs, or performance, for most locomotive orders at the three major American builders were customized. Each road believed it had special needs that only custom designs could meet. During the last twenty years or so of steam in America, designs proliferated for the Northern type 4-8-4, which ended up as the most popular of the Super Power wheel arrangements. Two studies have documented variations in the 4-8-4 designs. (Space prohibits listing how even the name "Northern" for the 4-8-4 was ruled out by any number of American railroads.)

The first was a practical project in 1943 for the Office of Defense Transportation, by Charles D. Young, Deputy Director, and the second was a historical study in 2000 by Robert A. LeMassena. (Both accounts are cited in *Uncle Sam's Locomotives.*) Brig. General Young, a former Vice-President of the Pennsylvania Railroad, examined how mass production would lower first costs. He studied 4-8-4's ordered from October, 1942, through September 1943. He found that the Northerns, "built to ten different designs, could have been narrowed to two and still have met the requirements of all the railroads involved." He even intended for standardization to extend to specifications for materials and to manufacture of specialties and appliances.

2-8-4 NKP #742 east of Fort Wayne, Indiana

2-8-4 VGN #506 leaving Roanoke, Virginia

The 2-8-4s pictured are basically the same locomotive. First designed for the Nickel Plate Road in 1934 by the Advisory Mechanical Committee for the Van Sweringen roads, they served well in central Ohio (NKP 742), in southwestern Virginia (VGN 506), in northern Kentucky (L&N 1952), in southern Ohio (C&O 2735), and in eastern Kentucky (C&O 2694, originally PM 1210). Actually only NKP, C&O, and PM were Van Sweringen roads. L&N and Virginian, plus RF&P and Wheeling & Lake Erie (not pictured), appropriated this Super Power general purpose heavy freight locomotive.
(all Eugene L. Huddleston)

The other study, in *Railroad History*, was more extensive than Gen. Young's. Between 1926 and 1963 there were sixty-three models of Super Power 4-8-4's built in the United States, Canada, and Mexico. This absurdity, LeMassena believed, was the result of "steely individualism," for all Northerns could have been made to three sets of principal dimensions. But even assuming, he added, that the railroads could agree on the principal dimensions of the three standard locomotives, "bitter arguments" over the details would have persisted – for example, over Baker vs. Walshaerts valve gear, single vs. double crosshead guides, or over Boxpok vs. spoked driving wheels. The seeming fickleness in locomotive orders is illustrated by the Detroit, Toledo, and Ironton Railroad buying several modern, but light 2-8-4 Berkshires from Lima, which was followed by orders to Lima for some modern and heavier 2-8-2 Mikados.

The Advisory Mechanical Committee of the C&O, Erie, Nickel Plate, and Pere Marquette did introduce "standard" designs for the roads under the Van Sweringen umbrella. These included designs that could serve on all four roads; namely the famous Berkshires. But the committee also designed "standard" models that could only go in service on roads – namely C&O – with the highest bridge ratings and maximum horizontal and vertical clearances, which came to C&O in the line improvements made during the Depression of the 1930s, but which did not come to the other Van Sweringen roads because they had not the tonnage demands or the mountain territory that Chesapeake and Ohio had.

2-8-4 C&O #2694, originally Pere Marquette #1210

New York author and sportsman S. Kip Farrington listed his favorite locomotives in *Railroading Coast to Coast* (1976): "For the Mikado 2-8-2 type my favorites would be the Chesapeake & Ohio K-3 and the Baltimore & Ohio Q-4. While the Great Northern had the largest and heaviest with the highest drivers, I ... would put it in third place."

K-3 1257 (Alco, Richmond, 1924) opens up after "slow orders" over the Richmond viaduct on way to Gladstone yard, September 1947. The same class heavy Mikado was tested against Lima demonstrator A-1 in 1925. (CSPR, collection. COHS)

Chapter 2

C&O and Super Power

"The Chesapeake and Ohio, with a huge mineral traffic from the so-called 'Coal Bin of America,' in East Kentucky and West Virginia northwards to Toledo and eastwards for export at Newport News, had a long-established tradition of excellent freight locomotive practice of which the 'H8' was merely one manifestation. "
— *O. S. Nock, English locomotive authority of Bath and official of the Westinghouse Air Brake Co.*

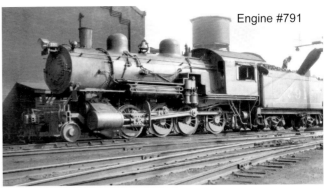

Engine #791

C&O did not get involved with Super Power immediately because during the "roaring twenties" the road had purchased some 250 new locomotives of original design to meet the demands from increased long distance passenger travel and from tonnage coming out of rapidly developing coal fields like the Logan and Coal River. (This did not even include some 60 new switchers.) The biggest individual order during these years was for one hundred heavy Mikados between 1924-26 from American Locomotive's Richmond Works. These were bigger than the heavy Mikados designed by the United States Railroad Administration in 1918-1919, which had set the standard for heavy Mikados of the 20s. Tractive effort for the C&O engines was 67,700 lbs. vs. 60,000 lbs. for the USRA and many of its copies. For making steam, the C&O had grate area of 80.8 sq. ft. vs. 70.8 for the USRA. C&O was definitely well fixed in its "level land" freight power. And this was the service for which A-1 demonstrator at Lima had been designed.

Engine #1085

To show how well fixed C&O was, consider the late Don Ball's statistics (in *Portrait of the Rails*) on the dominant type of locomotive during the Great Depression at the start of the turnaround in business: "In mid-1934 . . . the most prevalent type of locomotive was the 2-8-0 Consolidation, of which 11,266 were in service — roughly 47% of all locomotives on the nation's rails. Their average age was almost 26 years and the repair costs alone were enough to dictate a need for new power." By contrast, in 1934 C&O had 126 Consolidations vs. 214 Mikados and 178 compound 2-6-6-2 Mallets, plus well over 200 other steam locomotives of various types. Lucius Beebe, writing from the perspective of 1957 in his *The Age of Steam*, summed up C&O's achievement in steam power quite well: "Once, in a time when railroading possessed style and breeding, the Chesapeake and Ohio, a carrier of honors and antiquity, had [in the 1940s] twenty different wheel arrangements on its motive power roster."

Engine #972

It's not that C&O failed to test Super Power or failed to do it soon. The testing did come at an odd time, however. Lima demonstrator A-1 arrived on C&O July 12, 1925, for two weeks of tests. C&O's first order for fifty heavy Mikes already being in service, it appears the sec-

Engine #1037

Typical of the Consolidations (2-8-0) C&O relied on in the twentieth century were these four, which together illustrate a lack of uniformity in retrofitted details but a sameness in basic dimensions. The major external variation on the four is the Stevenson (inside admission) valve gear on G-7 791 (taking water at Covington, Ky.) with the rest having Walshaerts. The most recent of the four is G-9 No. 1037 (Alco, Richmond, 1909), in mine shifter service at Danville, W.Va., in 1953. (972 from Staufer collection; 791 from Ray Curl collection.; 1085, Henry Steams; 1037, E. L. Huddleston)

ond order for fifty — to arrive December 1925 through March 1926 — had just been placed. (Typically it took nine months to complete a locomotive). So it would seem C&O was not in the market immediately for any more "level land" freight power. Probably justifying the tests was that representatives of the mechanical departments of the Van Sweringen controlled roads — C&O, Erie, Nickel Plate, and Pere Marquette — all witnessed the tests. C&O went ahead with the tests, using a borrowed Nickel Plate dynamometer car. (C&O would receive its own state-of-the-art test car in 1930.) The majority of the tests took place over the summit of the Alleghenies, between Hinton, W.Va., and Clifton Forge, Va., territory to which C&O regularly assigned powerful articulated locomotives. Testing over the "level land" Cincinnati Division was reported on only in an appendix. This seems odd, for the "CD," between Russell and Stevens yard near Cincinnati, was standard operating territory for the new class K-3 heavy Mikes of 1924.

Seemingly C&O did not take the tests very seriously. For example, the 37-page report seldom expressed its findings clearly and directly, and the main conclusions were hidden in the body of the report. (This lack of clarity is in contrast to the incisive reports issued on C&O Super Power by the Advisory Mechanical Committee in the 1930s and 1940s.) When C&O motive power officials looked at the Lima A-1 they did not see that much improvement over the practically brand new K-3 Mikes. For one, driving wheel diameter was unchanged at 63 inches, and boiler maximum diameter and cylinder bore were not even as large as on the C&O. The one big improvement was the huge firebox (100 sq. ft.) resting on a two-axle trailing truck (actually a rear extension of the frame) instead of a single axle. More direct heating surface resulted in the A-1 making more steam than the K-3.

Actual comparison tests revealed to the engineers a draw, though this conclusion had to be dug out of the depths of the report: "It is ...evident from the general overall results of the tests that neither of the engines showed any marked advantage over the other, the extra speed of the Lima in getting tonnage over the road being offset by the K-3's economy in coal." Given that there was so little fundamental difference between the two

At Handley, March 1956, H-8 1627 is on ready track awaiting trip to Hinton. H-6 Mallet at right has been in mine shifter service since mid 1920s when class H-7 2-8-8-2s arrived to relieve them of the mainline Allegheny crossing. (E. L. Huddleston, COHS collection.)

freight locomotives, it was easy for the C&O men to find faults in the Lima A-1. Specifically, they seem to discount any real benefit from the trailer booster on the A-1, probably because the C&O K-3 had no booster. This is ironical in light of the fact that the AMC, beginning in 1930, would equip with boosters all C&O road locomotives until the end (with exception of the 2-6-6-6 articulateds). Another fault was slipperiness. The A-1, having considerably lower factor of adhesion than the K-3, was less sure-footed. Also faulted was the extremely high back pressure of the steam exhaust, which interfered with the power stroke of the piston. As T. W. Dixon has written in *Chessie's Road*, "The results of the dynamometer tests were so close that the C&O concluded that its conventionally designed 2-8-2s were quite sufficient for its immediate future needs." Another feature unpopular with C&O authorities was the "articulated rear end" of the A-1 in contrast with the K-3's well balanced Delta type trailing truck. Further, C&O did not go for limited cut-off as a way to preserve steam and prevent slipperiness. C&O preferred "full gear," which was about 80% cutoff. (Of course, C&O engineers were instructed to "hook her back" to near center when running at speed.)

Although C&O in the late 1920s was under Van Sweringen control, the Vans did not form the Advisory Mechanical Committee until 1929. Thus C&O's Mechanical Department in Richmond was still in control of motive power designs and orders. Once the AMC took over in 1929, it determined designs, based on the road's needs, but not necessarily timing of the orders. The Depression took care of that. Meanwhile, C&O knew it had a fine fleet of switchers, road freight, and road passenger engines. They were big engines, too. The class K-3 heavy Mikes could take 160 loaded coal cars down two divisions along the James through Virginia to Richmond, and after the Russell yards enlargement could take an equal number down the Ohio to Stevens near Cincinnati. "Level land" passenger engines equaled in quality the "level land" freight. In *C&O Power* Phil Shuster targets the famous F-19 heavy Pacifics, received from Alco's Richmond Works in 1926 and numbered 490-494, "When one thinks of C&O power in the pre-war era, it is almost always the picture of the F-19 which is visualized. The F-19's used the same boiler design as was originated on the F-17 in 1914 (and slightly larger than the U.S.R.A. Heavy Pacific's boiler) but used 73" drivers (later 74"), 14" piston valves and Baker valve gear, features which were later duplicated on both the F-17 and F-18 classes. The F-19's compared quite closely to the Pennsy's K-4, the B&O's P-7 and Southern's PS-4 Pacific types, being most like the latter 4-6-2's which also had 73" drivers." (One of Southern's heavy 4-6-2's now resides permanently at the Smithsonian Institution in Washington.)

For "mountain territory" big power for coal trains was obviously needed, but a problem – which would per-

Ironically, the last C&O steam and last built in U. S. for domestic use by a locomotive builder was not Super Power but a World War I era H-6 Mallet. Nothing illustrates better the suitability of 2-6-6-2 Mallets for switching at coal mines than the delivery in 1949 of H-6's 1300-1309 (an order that had been cut from 25) for shifter service only. Here, in 1951, H-6 1301 has backed six miles from Peach Creek with about 60 empties to head up Rum Creek toward two big mines. The lack of wye tracks at Rum Jct. and up the hollow required backing. (E L. Huddleston, collection COHS)

sist until the 1930's — was tunnel clearances that prevented heights over fifteen feet. C&O and Alco were able to overcome this problem in 1924 by designing an articulated that kept the centerline of the boiler low through use of high pressure cylinders for both engines. (Articulateds' front engines usually had low pressure cylinders that were of necessity quite large.) The low slung frame, plus drivers of only 57 inches diameter, permitted a boiler with an impressive 104 inches in maximum outside diameter and — the longest yet made by American — yet keeping within the fifteen foot vertical clearance. Prior to the 45 2-8-8-2's that C&O received first from Alco and then from Baldwin from 1924 to 1926, the only "single expansion, simple articulated" ever built had been an experimental 2-8-8-0 for the Pennsylvania Railroad in 1919. The C&O 2-8-8-2s (class H-7 and H-7a) were adept at taking tonnage up Allegheny Mountain. Prior to the PRR's and C&O's, all articulateds had been "compound" in steam distribution, steam first used in the rear and then over again in the front engines. With its big boiler the C&O 2-8-8-2 could supply high pressure steam directly to both engines. About their only faults were a lack of speed over the road and a shallow fire box that caused cinders (unburned fuel) in profusion from the twin smoke stacks when the engine was working hard.

Because C&O originated the Mountain type in 1911 (class J-1, final numbering 540-542) for its "mountain territory" passenger trains, most casual observers think C&O had no problem powering its named passenger trains over the Alleghenies and the Blue Ridge. True, C&O had "invented" the new type – the 4-8-2 by replacing a Mikado's two wheel lead truck with a four wheel truck to gain more stability at high speeds. And the new type was powerful, so powerful that to fire the engine properly required an automatic stoker, a new invention. However, C&O never bought more than three of them, probably because their small drivers and heavy main rods made them into rough riders. In 1914 C&O tried to make a Pacific type serve its mountain territory. Let Phil Shuster in *C&O Power* tell about these outstanding 4-6-2s: "'Six exceptionally large and powerful Pacific type locomotives have been delivered to the Chesapeake and Ohio by the American Locomotive Company. They have a maximum tractive effort of 46,600 lbs. and are believed to be the most powerful Pacific type locomotive ever built. ...[They] are not only exceptional in having such a large tractive effort, but also have a boiler large enough to sustain it.' That is how the *RAILWAY AGE GAZETTE* of December 1914 described the new F-17 4-6-2's which Richmond had delivered to the C&O in September and October of the same year... " Interestingly, to make a Pacific powerful enough for mountain territory hauling, C&O equipped the F-17 class with 69-inch drivers. When the F-17 class was removed from mountain service in the early 1930's, driver diameter was increased to 74 inches. (About that time, the F-17's were renumbered 470-476.)

As passenger cars got heavier during the teens — with steel replacing wood — the six F-17 Pacifics , all with 69-inch drivers, were taxed at performing well on mountain grades, several of which were over one percent. Luckily for C&O, the federal government solved its mountain passenger engine problems in 1918-1919 when the United States Railroad Administration allotted C&O five Mountain types of a new design that was part of a plan to standardize motive power when the government took over the nation's railroads during World War I. The committee charged with the standardized designs produced light and heavy versions of each type. C&O, which got its heavy 4-8-2s from Baldwin and American, told stock holders in its 1918 annual report that these engines (plus 20 2-6-6-2 Mallets) had been forced on the road. They were, the Directors announced, "not necessary," "unsuited" to the company's purposes, and "the purchase of such equipment . . . was inadvisable." When C&O changed its mind and bought two copies of this design in 1924, it need not have been embarrassed, for seemingly all railroads allotted USRA locomotives (from six designs, with

light and heavy versions of each) complained as much or more about their unsuitability to their particular needs. The real problem with these railroads was ill feelings toward the federal government's takeover of the railroads, which lasted until 1920.

The USRA heavy Mountain design, as delivered, and as updated by C&O around 1930, was outstanding for its beauty (e.g., its "flying pumps.") and its ability to start trains rapidly and to keep them running at speed. The J-2's had 69-inch drivers and boiler and fire box identical in size to the boiler and fire box used on the USRA light Santa Fe type (2-10-2) freight locomotive. Clearly, with a locomotive of this size and power C&O needed no Super Power for its mountain area passenger service. (The Super Power version of the Mountain type would be the 4-8-4, a wheel arrangement, which though introduced in 1926, did not get a real start until the 1930s.)

By 1926, shortly after the introduction of Super Power by Lima and then by Alco, C&O seemed to have modern steam locomotives covering all its needs. However, C&O had just recently solved a major problem in its efforts to have the "long haul" on coal moving west out of C&O's coal fields. True, C&O had a line westward to Cincinnati and Chicago, but the main trend was for the trans-shipment of coal across the Great Lakes, and C&O was a long time getting together direct access to a Great Lakes port. It was not until 1927 that C&O completed the last link through Ohio con-

C&O's principal "level land" freight haulers from 1924 until 1943, when the K-4s started arriving, were 100 K-3 heavy Mikados. K-2 1252, in 1949, here crosses the two-mile long Richmond viaduct eastbound toward Fulton yard. K-3s regularly hauled 160 loaded coal cars, up to 14,000 tons, down the James River from Clifton Forge to Richmond, following most of the way the tow path of the R&A Canal. (S. Morrill, collection COHS)

necting the old Hocking Valley Railroad's line (which C&O had purchased) with its own newly constructed line. Thomas W. Dixon has explained the climax to this endeavor: "A massive new... terminal... at Presque Isle, at the mouth of the Maumee River in Toledo... was completed in 1930, with two coal dumpers and dock space, as well as an ore dock with three Hewlett unloaders. It was the most modern coal/ore dock in the world. Coal business was on the rise as never before, and the time was ripe for a new innovation in Lake coal hauling... " That innovation would be a locomotive — the T-1 2-10-4 — that could take heavy tonnage over rolling

topography straight through, from Russell, Ky., on the edge of the coal fields, to Toledo Docks.

For this haulage Super Power was in order, but so far Lima had been overly cautious and was not "thinking big." Perhaps this conservatism arose from Lima's practical recognition that most of Lima's potential customers had not removed the restrictions of height, width, and weight recognized by the USRA in World War I. Despite the booming 1920s, comparatively few roads had been wealthy enough to replace 1890-era wooden trestles with fills or light girder bridges with heavier truss bridges, or to drill wider and higher tunnels or replace overpasses

The C&O 2-10-4 of 1930 was tailored to a specific need — a locomotive that would, without change, take 160 cars of coal from northeastern Kentucky, across the state of Ohio, to the Lake Erie car dumpers at Toledo without assistance (except for grades over .40%) and at speeds that would deter pay for overtime or for exceeding the hours of service law. T-1 3007 opens up , circa 1948, after the rear end has cleared the 160-car capacity yard track from which the loaded train is pulling at Russell, in northeastern Kentucky. (E. L. Huddleston)

and underpasses. As late as 1942, Lima stressed its conservative approach in a lengthy ad promoting Super Power; it stated that the use of a four-wheel trailing truck was not so much for bearing the increased weight of a large fire box as for redistributing locomotive weight. While the ad did emphasize higher horsepower with a four-wheel truck, it implied that the horsepower could be attained without increasing weight on the rails: "It was obvious to the designers that high speed necessitated larger boiler capacity which in turn demanded larger grate areas to avoid excessive fuel rate. It was obvious, too, that the higher speeds would increase the stress on track structure unless a new design could possess the desired high horsepower without extending the limits of axle loads. This combination of requirements pointed to a redistribution of locomotive weight and the use of a 4-wheel trailing truck."

RIGHT - The passenger engines on C&O that really clicked for mountain service were the heavy Mountains (4-8-2) of the United States Railroad Administration. Though C&O had originated the Mountain type in 1911, C&O's J-1 class had neither the driver height nor boiler capacity for highballing heavy passenger trains across the Blue Ridge and the Alleghenies. But the USRA heavy 4-8-2 of 1919 did. J-2 No. 547, resting at Charlottesville in the 1930s, exhibits the "flying pumps" on the front end that were the trade mark of heavy C&O freight and passenger power before the Super Power era. (E. L. Huddleston collection.)

F-17 Pacific 474 had been delivered as a "mountain land" passenger locomotive in 1914, pioneering the heavy Pacific type along with the famous Pennsylvania K-4 Pacifics. The big 4-6-2 was an attempt to use Pacifics for mountain service by equipping them with 69-inch drivers. By 1935, when 474 posed at Huntington with the F.F.V., the class had been given 74-inch Boxpok drivers so that they could be used in "level land" service, as on this premier train headed down the Ohio to Cincinnati. (William Monypeny)

Roster of C&O Superpower Locomotives

Road No.	Type	Class	Builder	Date Built
3000-3009	2-10-4	T-1	Lima	1930
1600-1609	2-6-6-6	H-8	Lima	1941-42
1610-1619	2-6-6-6	H-8	Lima	1942
1620-1629	2-6-6-6	H-8	Lima	1944
1630-1644	2-6-6-6	H-8	Lima	1944
1645-1659	2-6-6-6	H-8	Lima	1948
2700-2739	2-8-4	K-4	Alco	1943-44
2740-2749	2-8-4	K-4	Lima	1945
2750-2759	2-8-4	K-4	Lima	1947
2660-2784	2-8-4	K-4	Alco	1947
2785-2789	2-8-4	K-4	Alco	1947
600-604	4-8-4	J-3	Lima	1935
605-606	4-8-4	J-3	Lima	1942
610-614	4-8-4	J-3a	Lima	1948
300-307	4-6-4	L-2	Baldwin	1941-42
490-494	4-6-4	L-1	Huntington Shop	1946-47
310-314	4-6-4	L-2a	Baldwin	1948

In 1925 Lima had developed a 2-10-4, the next step upward in size of Super Power beyond the 2-8-4, but, while successful, the Texas and Pacific (hence the name "Texas" for the type) 2-10-4s had only 63-inch drivers, no different from the Lima A-1 and its copies. True, the T&P 2-10-4s were seven inches taller than the A-1 (which had gone to the Boston and Albany). It was appropriate for a Western road to get such big engines first, for construction west of the Mississippi was newer than in the East and clearances were more liberal. They were an advance in design over the Lima A-1 in that they had Nicholson Thermic Syphons and combustion chambers, both of which features increased the direct heating surfaces of the fire box. In 1927 came Baldwin's entry into the Super Power race — another 2-10-4, this one for a Midwestern road — Chicago, Burlington and Quincy. The CB&Q class M-4 was 16 ft., 2 inches above the rails, but its drivers were only 64 inches in diameter, and until higher drivers came along, the 2-10-4 type's ability to develop its horsepower would be held in hostage by drivers that could not be counterbalanced sufficiently to prevent pounding of the rails.

The really big advance in Super Power freight engines came with the adoption of 69-70 inch drivers. This advance came first not from a Western or Midwestern road but from one of the oldest Eastern roads — the Erie. The explanation was that the Erie had been originally laid out for six-foot gauge, and that meant generous vertical and horizontal clearances and weight limits for bridges. As Chief Mechanical Officer for the Erie in 1927, A. G. Trumbull took advantage of this situation and designed a Super Power 2-8-4 that was 16 ft., 4 inches from rail to stack and that had a boiler with maximum outside diameter of 100 inches, unprecedented at that time for an eight-coupled locomotive. They were so successful in service that Erie purchased 105 of the Berkshires from Baldwin, Alco, and Lima. In 1928 Trumbull moved from New York to Cleveland in order to take charge as Chief Mechanical Officer for the newly established Advisory Mechanical Committee for the four big roads under the Van Sweringen brothers umbrella. The committee's first assignment (made before the Stock Market crash of October 1929) was to design a powerful and fast freight locomotive to take long coal trains (from a new yard at Russell, Ky., with tracks holding 160 cars) across Ohio to the rail-to-freighter transfer on Lake Erie. The result was, of course, the famous C&O T-1, Nos. 3000-3039. This new two cylindered engine was quite in contrast with the big four cylindered articulateds C&O had purchased only four years before. Because of mountain district tunnels, the big boilered 2-8-8-2 had to be kept at fifteen feet in height. That turned out to be a ridiculous restriction on the new Russell to Toledo route, for the new 2-10-4 could and would go up to 16 ft. 7 inches in height!

The AMC in Cleveland worked closely with the C&O

mechanical officers in Richmond on the new T-1. They could not ride roughshod over the C&O officials if they wanted to, but Trumbull , who had moved to Cleveland after 29 years as a mechanical officer with the Erie, put the Erie stamp on the new engine by giving it an Erie appearance. J. Parker Lamb in *Perfecting the American Steam Locomotive* tells how the new C&O 2-10-4 "became the prototype for all future Texas-type engines (in particular those for AT&SF and the Pennsylvania Railroad)". The C&O T-1 was "as much ahead of the original T&P Texas type as that locomotive had been ahead of the first Berkshire [the A-1]. The engine's boiler expanded from 100 inches at the smokebox to 108 inches at the rear flue sheet (beginning of the firebox). A 66-inch combustion chamber [lacking in the Erie 2-8-4] gave the firebox a total volume of 825 cubic feet. The result was a steaming rate of 100,000 pounds per hour translated into 5000 drawbar horsepower." In late 1930 Lima began delivering the first of the forty class T-1 2-10-4s.

Thus was C&O sold on Super Power. T. W. Dixon summed up the influence of this C&O Texas type of "monumental proportions": "C&O's Super Power Lima Locomotives of the next two decades made the road famous in the annals of steam design and performance. The T-1s seemed to have unlimited power, and with their huge boilers could supply enough steam to haul the heaviest trains at sustained high speeds. . . Their design was epochal for the C&O because it ushered in the modern locomotive era... But the Great Depression loomed just as the T-1 fleet arrived, and many of these great machines were stored... until business improved."

The year 1930 marked the end of Super Power being ordered in large quantities for some time. The next design by the Advisory Mechanical Committee would be in 1934 for fifteen of the famous Nickel Plate Berkshires, which were scaled down from the major dimensions of the C&O T-1, an order that would eventually total eighty. Kevin J. Holland in his book on the NKP 2-8-4s gives some interesting facts about the number of 2-8-4s built between the Lima A-1 and the first NKP 2-8-4: "By the time Alco began work on Nickel Plate order S-1736, there were already 282 Berkshires in service on American railroads, as well as two in Canada." Kevin includes a table breaking down the total into nine different railroads. Only two of the roads — the NKP and Erie — used 69-inch drivers, which became the standard by which real Super Power freight engines were measured. The other Berkshires were mostly copies of the original Lima A-1. By 1930, of course, besides the 2-10-4 Texas type, there had been introduced the 4-6-4, or Hudson type, for the New York Central, and the ever popular 4-8-4 type by the Northern Pacific (hence the name Northern for that type).

Some big railroads never ordered any Super Power designs. For example, the Southern Railway, which in the early 1950s operated 6,344 miles of road, purchased its last steamers in 1928 — 2-8-8-2 Mallets — and thus after World War II started dieselizing rapidly so that by 1950 624 diesel units were performing about 50% of all gross ton and passenger miles, and more than 60% of all yard switching hours. (See R. G. Lewis, *Handbook of American Railroads*.) C&O completely dieselized in 1956 and it ordered its last steamers — 2-6-6-2s — in 1949. From 1930 to 1948 C&O, under supervision of the Advisory Mechanical Committee, received a total of 220 Super Power units (defined as locomotives with four or six wheel trailing trucks and drivers 67 inches or higher). Broken down into wheel arrangements — 2-10-4, 4-8-4, 4-6-4, 2-8-4, and 2-6-6-6 — C&O possessed more different types of Super Power than any other railroad. Only the union Pacific and Santa Fe would come close to this achievement.

The 4-8-4s that arrived in 1935 (class J-3) were supplemented by repeat orders in 1942 and 1948. They were designed as passenger locomotives only and for only the portions of the road with steep grades. (In 1952, after dieselization of mainline passenger service, the 1948 4-8-4s did serve in freight service on the "level" portions of the C&O, and again in locomotive shortage of 1955-56, they once again went in "pool" freight service with some of the remaining Van Sweringen Berkshires.) They were C&O's biggest Super Power locomotives other than the T-1 2-10-4 and the H-8 2-6-6-6-both freight engines. The first of the tremendous class H-8 Allegheny type simple articulateds, No. 1600, was completed at Lima, Ohio, almost on the day that Japan attacked Pearl Harbor on December 7, 1941. These engines could handle the war load of traffic, in both mountain territory freight and passenger service. The 1941 need for mountain freight engines would have been an order for more T-1 2-10-4's were it not for the success in the late 1930's of high speed articulateds on both the Norfolk & Western and Union Pacific.

In 1942 came from Baldwin in Philadelphia seven Hudsons (class L-2) , which were the world's heaviest. These engines had the highest drivers of any C&O steam locomotive (78 inches), and the AMC designed them as passenger versions (in low-land territory) of the Berkshires first designed for the Nickel Plate and Pere Marquette before World War II started. With the U.S. heading into war with the Axis powers, it looked like the AMC would recommend more T-1's as supplements on the busy "arsenal of democracy" line from the coal fields to Midwestern industrial centers on the Great Lakes and to replace the aging "Simple Simon" 2-8-8-2 simple articulateds that climbed over the summit of the Alleghenies at (where else?) Alleghany, Virginia, on C&O's line from the coal fields to the ocean at Newport News. Instead, Trumbull designed a Super Power simple articulated that along with the N&W "A" (1936) and the Union Pacific "Jabelman" Big Boys (1941) would comprise the "Big

Three" of Super Power articulated design. Trumbull took the C&O T-1 2-10-4 design and proportionally enlarged it to an ultimate high horsepower machine—a 2-6-6-6.

To supplement C&O's 100 heavy Mikados of the 1920s (class K-3) at the start of the War, the AMC relied on an existing AMC design instead of going for a new design as with the class H-8 Alleghenies (2-6-6-6). Thus from 1943 to 1947 C&O purchased from Alco and Lima ninety Berkshires (called Kanawhas on C&O) that were essentially copies of the 2-8-4s the AMC had designed for the Nickel Plate (1934) and Pere Marquette (1937). This all-around heavy "level land" freight engine was then copied by the Virginian (1946), Wheeling and Lake Erie (1937), Louisville and Nashville (1942), and Richmond, Fredericksburg, and Potomac (1943). The C&O 2-8-4s, called "big Mikes" or "K-4's" by employees, were main line engines. True, they went into the heart of the Kentucky and West Virginia coal fields but they were on divisional runs, taking coal trains of up to 144 cars from assembly terminals to marshalling yards at Russell for westbound traffic and Handley for eastbound. The locomotives that went from the seven assembly terminals to the coal mine tipples were almost always 2-6-6-2s (though sometimes 2-8-2s and 2-8-0s were assigned) . The light Mallets were so suitable for mine-run service that C&O's last order for road locomotives was for 2-6-6-2s.

No new Super Power designs appeared on C&O after the K-4 2-8-4s of 1943. There were of course repeat orders of the 2-8-4s, 2-6-6-6s, the Baldwin 4-6-4s and Lima 4-8-4s until 1948. The 4-6-4s of 1948 did have a major change in steam distribution, from piston valve to poppet valve (Hudsons 310-314). The adoption of the "Franklin System of Steam Distribution" was probably the last major innovation in appliances for a C&O Super Power locomotive.

Three major locomotive projects came in the mid and late 1940's in addition to the repeat orders cited above. One of these was a major project even though it resulted in only three new locomotives—the collaboration of Baldwin and Westinghouse Electric in 1947 for three steam-turbo-electric locomotives to power a new "streamliner" that board Chairman Robert R. Young was trying to introduce at War's end. These three coal burning turbines (class M-1) were not AMC projects and were not "Super Power" because they were essentially electric locomotives, not reciprocating steamers. The second major project was conversion of five F-19 class heavy Pacifics (1926) to Hudsons (class L-1) in 1946-47 for use on "side" sections of the Washington to Cincinnati streamliner that Robert R. Young was championing. (The 490-494 numbering of the Pacifics was carried over to the five Hudsons). The conversion to Hudson wheel arrangement was completed at the well equipped Huntington Locomotive Shops for all five, but streamlining was applied only to the first four locomotives. It

became clear in 1947 that the streamliner (to be named "Chessie") would never be put in service, even though both the locomotives and Budd built cars had been delivered. These engines, like the Baldwin Hudsons of 1948, had the Franklin System of Steam Distribution. The third project involved placing in service the last steam locomotives to come from an American locomotive builder for domestic use.

Thus, in summer of 1949 Baldwin delivered to C&O ten new 2-6-6-2 Mallet compounds identical in principal dimensions with the class H-6 Mallets of 1920-23 (Nos. 1475-1519). Intended solely for coal field mine-run service, there were originally twenty-five on order, but strikes

in the coal fields cut into the budget for new steamers. They were the last domestic order for steamers turned out, as it developed, by Baldwin, Lima, and Alco. As to looks, engines 1300-1309 had lines that were quite functional and modern. The cab was roomy but sloped at a pleasing angle conforming to the slope of the boiler backhead, and the bulbous steam and sand domes protruding from the original H-6 boilers were replaced by covers with more pleasing contours. Having 57-inch drivers and lacking feedwater heaters, these were far from being Super Power, but as powerful "switchers" under mine tipples and for traversing narrow, winding hollows of Appalachia, they could not be beat. C&O's faith in steam

Beginning 1941 C&O's 60 H-8s would supplement the 40 T-1's on the Russell-Toledo haul just as the 50 H-7 2-8-8-2s had supplemented H-6 Mallets on the Russell-Toledo haul before the T-1s arrival in 1930. But the main job of the H-7s from the mid1920's until about 1944 had been as "mountain territory" freight haulers up the New River and across the Alleghenies. Around 1944 the H-8s made the H-7s superfluous. Some were reserved for hump service, as was 1572, seen in September 1951 ready to push a cut at Toledo's Walbridge yard. (R. J. Foster, collection COHS)

came to a halt early in 1949 with the road's first large diesel order. No better evidence of the loss of faith in steam is that shortly after getting on the property thirty brand new eight-wheel switchers from Baldwin late in 1948, C&O sold them to rival Norfolk and Western, who liked them so much they built more of their own!

C&O was completely dieselized by late August, 1956. Mainline passenger service was dieselized several years before mainline freight operations, and branchline operations were the last to go diesel. That helps explain why 2-8-0 No. 1041, a G-9 Consolidation of 1909, was still under steam at Thurmond, West Virginia, after countless Super Power mainline freight and passenger locomotives had bit the dust. For a summary of the retirement dates for modern C&O power, consult George H. Drury, *Guide to North American Steam Locomotives.*

"The Van Sweringen roads benefited from the engineering efforts of their Advisory Mechanical Committee, a clearing-house for development and design of everything from loco-motives and stations to signs and tools." – Kevin Holland in Mike Schafer's *More Classic American Railroads*, 2000

On C&O the Van Sweringen Berkshires (or Kanawhas) performed varied assignments, including pushing 140 loads of coal – with another 2-8-4 on head end – up the Kanawha past Mt. Carbon and up the New to Hinton, during export boom in 1955. C&O 2-8-4s had longer cabs than the other AMC Berkshires in order to give more room for fireman and head brakeman. (E. L. Huddleston, collection COHS)

Chapter 3

Designing C&O Super Power

Prior to 1929 C&O, headquartered in Richmond, made its own decisions about locomotive design and policy. Until 1927 American Locomotive Company, head-quartered in New York, had a major locomotive plant in Richmond, and C&O's presence was commanding. Studying locomotive orders from 1909 to 1929, one finds most of C&O's orders going to American, whether in Richmond or Schenectady. This close kinship suggests a "revolving door" relationship among the senior engineers in both organizations, though any records to substantiate this suggestion are long gone. Without warning to the C&O's Mechanical Department, the newly formed Advisory Mechanical Committee, in 1929 took control of

C&O's motive power designs and policy shifted to Cleveland. C&O still had lots of financial clout, but by hook or by crook, C&O had become part of the railroad empire controlled by O.P. and M.J. Van Sweringen. The Advisory Mechanical Committee, formed in early 1929 for the four major roads – under Van Sweringen control -- was charged with rationalizing and standardizing the mechanical procedures and designs of the four roads, which otherwise still operated independently of each other.

Since the AMC, from 1929 to 1949, was in complete charge of C&O's motive power destiny, the term "committee" is misleading. The AMC was far from being

In November 1944 officials from Lima, C&O, and the AMC celebrate completion of H-8 1630, first of 15 more Alleghenies, bringing the total to 45. A. G. Trumbull, CMO of the AMC, is fifth from left. On Trumbull's right, fourth from left, is Clyde B. Hitch of Richmond, C&O's Chief Mechanical Officer. Right of Hitch (third from left) is N. M. Trapnell, Supt. Of Motive Power of Richmond. To Trumbull's right (sixth from left) is A. H. glass, C&O's Chief Motive Power Inspector. Trumbull and Mike Donovan, an English mechanical engineer who went to Lima shortly after this, represent the AMC staff (so far as is known). At right Daniel Ellis, Vice-President of Manufacturing for Lima since leaving his AMC post in 1943, stands next to Bert Townsend, Lima's Chief Engineer. (COHS collection.)

Quite a change in front-end styling in just four years! All C&O K-3 Mikes, like 1241, had "flying pumps" on smokebox front. For engines he designed (until 1941), Trumbull's signature was, besides a flat front end with headlight in middle of smokebox front, a small platform between air pump shields. Trumbull was obeying an A.R.A. rule of 1915 stating "Locomotives having headlights which cannot be safely ... reached from the pilot beam ... shall be equipped with ... steps suitable for getting to and from such headlights." T-1 3002 is at builders, September 4, 1930. K-3 1241 is at Richmond, 1949. (both COHS collection.)

just a collection of distinguished senior engineers. Records reveal a "paper trail" from which one can infer a structure requiring a formal chain of command and an extensive body of employees to assure smooth flow of data. And what a collection of data it was! The "Standard Maintenance Equipment Instructions" (known as SMEI's) showed that the "Committee," between projects, was busy turning out detailed descriptions covering every aspect of car and locomotive upkeep, construction, and operation. What is more, the AMC's collection of drawings and printed matter, shows that the committee had practically complete control over construction of rolling stock and locomotives for C&O, Erie, NYC&StL (NKP), and Pere Marquette (the order presented on AMC plans and documents). Among the most notable of the locomotive designs were the 40 Texas and 60 Allegheny type locomotives for C&O, plus 80 Berkshires (2-8-4) for the Nickel Plate, built by Alco and Lima, that were copied so often and so successfully that in the words of English locomotive historian Philip Atkins, the Van Sweringen Berkshires came nearest to "a modern U. S. standard steam locomotive design, although individual batches varied considerably in detail."

Most historical accounts of locomotive development either fail to mention the committee or mention it without identifying its members. Because so little is known about the Advisory Mechanical Committee, the question arises as to the identity of the individual on that committee most responsible for its great design achievements. That person is Alonzo Trumbull, chief mechanical engineer of the Committee from its formation to 1947. But one would never know this from reading most accounts of the histories of locomotives turned out under the auspices of the AMC. Either the accounts fail to mention the AMC, thereby forcing an assumption that the road's own mechanical department was in charge of the design or — since its chief designs were in the Super Power category and built by Lima Locomotive Works — that the Super Power originator at Lima Locomotive Works, Will Woodard, was responsible. Or, some accounts, genuinely trying to give the AMC its due, look to William G. Black, because of releases from C&O's publicity department, that put him in the forefront. Alonzo G. Trumbull had the education and experience to stand out from other men on the Committee, whether college trained or self-educated. He was also the only member of the committee having the continuity of tenure to participate in the designs of all the Super Power locomotives that have the stamp of the AMC on them. Born in Hornell, New York, he attended Cornell University, where he was a member of Sigma Chi fraternity and where he met his future wife. He obtained his degree in mechanical engineering in 1899 and entered railroad service on the Erie. Cornell must have had a fine engineering program, for getting their degrees there in the same general period were Ralph Johnson, future chief engineer at Baldwin Locomotive Works and author of *The Steam Locomotive* (1944), and William G. Woodard, designer of the first Super Power steam locomotive. In 1903 Trumbull was promoted to Mechanical Engineer and in 1905 became assistant mechanical superintendent at the Meadville, Pa., shops. From there, beginning in 1907, he worked his way up in the motive power department to general mechanical superintendent. In 1922 he was named chief mechanical engineer, headquartered in New York. He kept the same title, when early in 1929 he moved to Cleveland, to serve on the AMC, headquartered in the Midland Building, until 1947. Railway Mechanical Engineer for December, 1929, documents Trumbull's authority: "Mr. Trumbull will have supervision over the mechanical engineering forces for the advisory mechanical committee, with headquarters at Cleveland, Ohio."

One might wonder why Trumbull did not participate in the fanfare accompanying completion of Lima's largest locomotive and one that proved in 1943 to have produced the highest horsepower in the field of any steam locomotive. The reason probably is that Trumbull was uncomfortably aware of the weight problem that had developed with the first ten 2-6-6-6s under construction. Certainly he was present for group pictures on completion of the second order of Pere Marquette Berkshires earlier in 1941. One must assume Trumbull had no part in the weight deception practiced by his boss D.S. Ellis, for C&O's assistant general attorney of law left Trumbull's name out of his lengthy official account of the scheme to falsify the weights at the Lima plant.

Fortifying the contention that Trumbull was the man behind the superior designs of the AMC requires clarifying the roles of two men on the Committee who might be construed as Trumbull's "boss." One is Daniel Ellis. For the years 1932 to 1943, Ellis's signature appears on AMC document approval pages right below Trumbull's. "Chief Mechanical Officer" would seem to be an administrative post, and Ellis's role in overseeing construction of the first 2-6-6-6s (as presented in *The Allegheny, Lima's Finest*) bears that out. Ellis, a self-made industrial executive, often gave papers at the same national engineering conventions that Trumbull attended. Ellis graduated from high school in Warwick, New York. From being a clerk on the Lehigh and Hudson river, he moved on to the New York Central as clerk in the office of auditor of freight accounts. Later he became a machinist, then "assistant engineer of motive power" for New York Central. In 1929 he was named sales manager of the Railroad Division of Worthington Pump and Machinery Co. According to his entry in *Who's Who in*

Railroading, in 1932 he became "engineer of motive power" (standard title for entry into AMC upper ranks) for AMC, and in 1936 (by his own account) "mechanical assistant to vice-president, C&O, NKP, and PM." (Since the Chief Mechanical Officer reported to a vice-president, he could presumably honestly use this title.) On April 30, 1943, Ellis left C&O (and AMC) and became Vice-President Manufacturing for Lima Locomotive Works, keeping his Cleveland address.

One can guess that Ellis's rise in locomotive manufacturing industry was predicated more on his function as an "efficiency expert" than on being a creative engineer. The same guess holds true for the only other man to hold a position superior to Trumbull's. William G. Black apparently held firmly to the coat tails of the famed "Doctor of Sick Railroads," John J. Bernet, for he went with Bernet to the Erie when Bernet (who had been President of the NKP since 1916) assumed its Presidency January 1, 1927. Black is important enough to the story of the AMC designers to require quoting background on him (from *Railway Mechanical Engineer*) prior to Bernet's naming him "mechanical assistant to the president" on assuming the Erie's Presidency: "His early education was received in the grammar schools and supplemented with a business education at Metropolitan Business College, Chicago. In 1893 Mr. Black entered the service of the Nickel Plate and served a machinist apprenticeship at its Stony Island shops, Chicago. After completing his apprenticeship he entered Armour Institute, Chicago, in 1897 for the purpose of taking a post graduate mechanical course. ...On February 10, 1893, Mr. Black reentered the service of the Nickel Plate as a machinist and was promoted to machine shop foreman July 1, 1903." In the next twenty years Black rose to be superintendent of motive power for the Nickel Plate. We know nothing objectively of Black's career from his going to the Erie with Bernet to his death. We do know something, but it is strongly colored by the "spin" given it by a well known Van Sweringen lines publicist. Black died in 1936 at age 59, following a two month illness. Writing a full page obituary in the C&O employees' magazine *The Rail* was L. C. Probert, brilliant public relations man (with title of a C&O Vice-President) who originated the "Chessie Cat" logo and the slogan "Sleep like a kitten." Probert put the best light possible on Black's career, perhaps as a kindness to Black's son and widow. For example, Probert wrote: "Black first came to the notice of the late John J. Bernet, when the latter, as president of the Nickel Plate Road, engaged in its rehabilitation, wanted some locomotives designed. The two men saw eye to eye for higher steam pressures, greater boiler capacity, greater coal and water capacity, higher speeds, and greater pulling power." This makes NKP's improvements in motive power in the 1920's more progressive than they really were. When in 1923 Black became head of NKP power, the road had already started buying copies of the

USRA light Mikado, which it had received as originals in 1918. According to George Drury, NKP bought 61 copies between 1920 and 1924. "The first five," he added, " carried minor improvements in the boiler and firebox, plus cast trailing trucks." The biggest improvements were on engines 616 – 671: booster engines on the trailing axle. These achievements in motive power hardly justify Probert's claims, neither about Black's tenure as head of

Nickel Plate power, nor his time on the Erie, nor on the AMC, where he supposedly "worked wonders on motive power and equipment", according to Probert.

The main reasons for ruling out Black as designer of AMC motive power is his being "kicked upstairs" to vice-president of C&O, NKP, and PM following his appointment to the AMC, the absence of his name on approval forms issued by the AMC, and the Erie influ-

C&O #600 at Charlottesville, VA (1939)

Pere Marquette #1215 at Detroit (1938)

ence in the styling of the locomotives designed by the AMC during the 1930's — from the C&O T-1 through the NKP and PM 2-8-4s, and first order of C&O 4-8-4s. Black is a puzzling figure. He was given official credit, and accepted it openly, as designer of the C&O's pace making 2-10-4 of 1930. From an interview before he died, for a "coffee table" book by Otto Kuhler and Robert S. Henry, the authors asserted that the T-1 was "designed by the late W. G. Black of the Chesapeake & Ohio. Mr. Black's father designed locomotives for the Rock Island more than 45 years ago; his grandfather designed locomotives for the old CH&D nearly 70 years ago" (*Portraits of the Iron Horse*, Rand McNally and Co., 1937). When Black went to the Erie with Burnet early in 1927, his title was "mechanical assistant" to Burnet. When Black went with Burnet to Cleveland in May, 1929, he kept the same title, with Burnet assuming Presidency of the C&O, NKP, and PM, a position he held until his death in 1936. The next change in Black's status, as reported in *Railway Mechanical Engineer* was in November 1931 with his appointment as "assistant vice president of the C&O and Pere Marquette [and later NKP] with jurisdiction over purchases and stores mat-

ters." Interestingly, in June 1931, both Trumbull and Black gave papers at the convention of the Mechanical Division of the ARA in Chicago. Black had signed himself as "Mechanical Assistant to President, C&O," and Trumbull as "Chief Mechanical Officer, C&O." Sometime, then, between June and November, Black had been "kicked upstairs." For a mechanical man, whose career focus had been on the workings of machinery, to be suddenly transferred to a chief bookkeeping job must have been disheartening.

That he was no longer "in the loop" regarding motive power is confirmed by the absence of his name on project approval forms from the AMC, either as a railroad representative or as an officer of the AMC. (From 1929 on, Trumbull signed for the AMC; beginning 1932 D. S. Ellis cosigned below Trumbull.) In tracing the interesting presence of Erie design details (and Erie class designations) in the first two jobs for the AMC — the C&O 2-10-4 of 1930 and the NKP 2-8-4 of 1934 -- we can see the hand of Trumbull, not Black. The Erie had been good to Trumbull. Regardless of his new salary as CME of the AMC, it must have been hard to take up roots and move to Cleveland. If Black had allegiance, it must have been

Three Trumbull designs featuring his "signature" front platforms are the Nickel Plate 2-8-4s of 1934, the C&O Greenbriers (4-8-4) of 1935, and Pere Marquette 2-8-4s of 1937 and later. These designs are represented by NKP 764 at Fort Wayne, Indiana (1957), by Pere Marquette 1215 at Detroit (1938), and by C&O 600 at Charlottesville, Va. (1939). Front end of the NKP 2-8-4 has been modified by a Mars safety light retrofit. (NKP 764, E. L. Huddleston; PM 1215, H. H. Harwood collection; C&O 600, Ted Gay, Joe Schmitz collection.)

to the NKP, where he had risen from machinist apprentice to superintendent of motive power. It is only speculation, but there could have been tension between Trumbull and Black over the direction of the AMC. Trumbull's temperament is unknown, but Probert's fulsome obituary speaks of Black's "brusque exterior and a great and tender heart."

Further supporting Trumbull as the "brains" behind the outstanding AMC designs is the similarity in appearance (and in class designation) of C&O's 2-10-4 of 1930 with the huge 2-8-4s he had designed for the Erie beginning in 1927, for that is where his loyalty was, probably until the bankruptcy of the Erie in 1938. The

fact, too, that Erie clearances (originally graded for 6 ft. gauge) permitted Trumbull to "think big" in designing steam engines is more evidence supporting Trumbull. An impressive item on Trumbull's resume that might be overlooked is his appointment in 1918 to a committee, representing fourteen railroads, to help design the twelve classes of steam locomotives for allotment to the nation's railroads during World War I under auspices of the United States Railroad Administration.

The only other competitor of Alonzo Trumbull for title of chief designer for the Advisory Mechanical Committee is Will Woodard of Lima Locomotive Works of Lima, Ohio. For many locomotive historians, Lima

Though both AMC designed locomotives are on the Kanawha Subdivision of the Huntington Division, they are on different missions. 1653 is taking a "Tidewater" coal train (originating in east Ky.) from Russell to Handley, where 1653 will serve on the New River Subdivision during engine shortage of 1955-56. K-4 2732 coasts toward Russell with westbound from one of seven coal field terminals. Location is NC Cabin, Ashland, Ky. (E. L. Huddleston)

Locomotive rises above its competitors, Baldwin of Philadelphia and American (Alco) of Schenectady, New York, by virtue of its inventing "Super Power" locomotives and in adhering to a Midwestern work ethic that prized quality over volume. To these historians, Lima must have had a big hand in the C&O, PM, and NKP designs because almost all Super Power steamers produced for these roads came from Lima. True, Lima engineers worked closely with AMC engineers. AMC staff could take turns riding a business car from a siding at Cleveland's Terminal Tower to a spur near Lima's office building reserved for office cars. Certainly it was a privileged way to travel. Eric Hirsimaki, in his history of Lima, gives another reason for AMC usually granting Lima its

The reason the ninety C&O AMC 2-8-4's lacked Trumbull's "signature" platform was that Trumbull found room there for the air after-cooler unit that Westinghouse Air Brake company had developed in 1941. K-4 2789 (now at North Judson, IN) leaves Russell with No . 92 for Hinton in 1947. (E. L. Huddleston, collection. COHS)

locomotive contracts: 'While the builder's bid was important," Eric noted, "It wasn't necessarily the deciding factor." Sometimes a builder would be on the railroad's lines, and thus be both a potential supplier and shipper. Such was the case with Lima. The fact that Will Woodard had originated the concept of Super Power at Lima in 1925 leads some historians to assume he had a hand in the specific designs of the AMC. (Of course, Lima had its own in-house designs that Woodard did have a hand in.) However, Woodard (who died in 1942) made a condition of his employment as Lima VicePresident that he work out of New York City. His assistant, J. Edgar Smith (*Railroad*, August 1974) told of productive days — mostly with poppet valves not with specific contracts — at their office at 17 East 42nd St. Woodard was a restless experimenter, having been awarded 92 patents on various mechanical features of steam and electric locomotive design.

It would be giving Alonzo Trumbull too much credit if one were to fail to recognize those men (there were no women so far as we know) who worked with and under Trumbull in designing AMC's "giants of the rails." It is hard to trace down the engineering staff of the AMC, but besides Black, Trumbull, and Ellis, there were at least the following serving at one time or another during the existence of the AMC: D. J. Sheehan, F. J. Herter, J. B. Blackburn, Mike Donovan, Richard Vinning, T. P. Irving, and E. R. Hauer (not necessarily in that order). Herter and Irving held the title of "engineer of rolling stock." later changed to "engineer car construction." The rest entered AMC service as "engineer [of] motive power." Probably the most impressive of these

lesser men was Ed Hauer, who took over Trumbull's job (for the short time it existed) after Trumbull's retirement. Hauer, graduate of the Mechanics Institute in Richmond, Va., worked for both Lima and C&O before joining the AMC. He took leave from the AMC to serve as Assistant and Associate Director of the Office of Defense Transportation from April 1942 to July 1944.

While credit is being given, one adds that there would have been no AMC without John J. Bernet. The Van Sweringen brothers of Cleveland, putting together their railroad empire, sensed that Bernet was the right man at the right time and made him president of the Nickel Plate. They knew nothing about railroad operations and management. Bernet did. Upon going to the Erie, he made motive power central to his rehabilitation of the road. Herb Harwood, in *Invisible Giants*, makes this dear: "From his earliest Nickel Plate days, Bernet was an emphatic believer in running heavier trains faster. In 1925, the Lima Locomotive Works ... had developed a new high-horsepower design, the 2-8-4 [Woodard designed] "Berkshire" type. Bernet immediately saw its possibilities and ordered fifty [of larger design] for the Erie in 1927 and fifty-five more in the following two years. ...Their effect on Erie operations was astonishing; ... compared to their predecessors, the new [Erie] Berkshires hauled 17 percent heavier trainloads using 32 percent less fuel — and improved running time by 34 percent." True, without the orders from Bernet there would have been no new designs. With the orders, as executed by Trumbull, there came into being the "Van Sweringen superpower" that occupied the first ranks of steam design until steam gave way to diesel power.

Paper Trail

by Eugene L. Huddleston

Testimonies by those who designed, built, and operated C&O Super Power are increasingly difficult to get, and the written word becomes the only means of mastering the mystique of these great machines. Though records kept by manufacturers of heavy American industrial machinery tend not to be archived, there is an exception for records of steam locomotive production. Although records from builders Baldwin and American are extant for C&O Super Power, the records at Lima Locomotive Works in Lima, Ohio, seem especially open to examination mainly because of efforts of the C&O Historical Society and the Allen County Museum in Lima. One should keep in mind that there is a "paper trail" for every class of C&O Super Power that, if traced down completely, would offer fascinating insights. Because most C&O Super Power came from Lima, the search most conveniently starts there.

Eric Hirsimaki, in his recently reprinted Lima: A History, has summed up the construction process at Lima from initial inquiry to formal contract and complete set of specifications. His emphasis is on industrial process. The emphasis herein is on the content and volume of the paper trail left by builder and customer in conforming to the process. Eric notes the importance of a few identifiable forms from Lima in systematically following the process. This study considers the whole mass of records still extant and tries to understand its content. But because this study is limited in scope, it cannot look at the most popular part of that record — the erection cards and drawings. They are popular because they present the locomotive in ideal form, and provide modelers with precise measurements. The sheer number of drawings for a single Super Power locomotive class, though it might overwhelm the casual observer, were essential for accuracy in construction and parts exchange in shopping.

C&O Historical Society owns "*Drawing List, C&O Class J-3, Engines 600-604, 22RC Tenders, Lima Order 1131.*" This 96-page loose-leaf booklet, produced in 1935, references, by count, 2,685 original drawings from the AMC and Lima. If new, redrawn, and duplicate drawings (as designated in the tally) are included, the total is over 4,000. The scope of this compilation is indicated by its taking fourteen drawings to cover the bell and its yoke, twenty-four for ash pan and dumpers, and 240 for pipe fittings (and clamps) on the engine. The manufacturer provided the drawings for specialties, some with familiar names like General

Steel Castings and New York Air Brake to less familiar Viloco Railway Equipment, Garlock Packing, or Huron Manufacturing.

The Advisory Mechanical Committee, though it designed all C&O Super Power, could not dictate to C&O management when it needed new power or what wheel arrangement that new power would be. Nevertheless, as a self-sufficient organization, it covered all bases in steam locomotive design, procurement, and maintenance for the Van Sweringen roads. Hence, the AMC kept voluminous records to document its decisions and to add authority to its many recommendations, queries, and pronouncements. However, the most impressive file of Super Power locomotive records in possession of the C&O Historical Society is one assembled by Lima, not the AMC, though this packet comprising "Lima Locomotive Works Engineering Dept. File on C&O J-A 4-8-4" would not have grown to approximately 600 pages without AMC and Lima Locomotive Works closely cooperating to produce the best possible locomotive in the circumstances. (Though the packet includes page after page of mathematical, double-checked computations made by Lima's Calculating Engineer, it includes no drawings whatsoever.)

Undoubtedly the basis of most of this cooperation was the fact the Chief Mechanical Engineer for Lima in 1947-48 was Mike Donovan, who had been employed as mechanical engineer by the AMC before going to Lima. Perry Percy, long time Estimating Engineer for Lima and the one responsible for the packet's donation to the C&O Historical Society, knew its historical value. Closely examining it reveals that major revisions to the weight and to the overall cost of the five Greenbrier type passenger locomotives, had to be made after AMC's initial submission of the specifications to Lima and Lima's making an estimate based on these specs. (One needs remember, too, that Lima was approaching a crisis, for after these five Greenbriers were delivered to C&O in June 1948, Lima's last steam locomotive would be delivered in April 1949!) What had seemed to this observer, before discovery of this packet, like ethically suspect decisions on "specialties" for these engines became sound from an economic and engineering standpoint after its discovery.

Perhaps the most telling evidence of the Advisory Mechanical Committee's determination to "cover all bases" in doing its job is its continuing issuance to the railroads involved of its "Standard Maintenance Equipment Instructions." Put together, these bulletins form a clear, concise but thorough maintenance manual for locomotives designed by the AMC. Such instruction manuals, widespread in industry, have often infamously illustrated the abuse of technical language, so that only a specialist could decipher the instructions. Aside from vocabulary terms common to all machine shops — e.g., broach, chamfer, grommet — there is little phrasing that the layman can call "gobbledygook." Put together, the total of SMEI's, as they were called, add up to hundreds of pages. (An index for the locomotive SMEI's covers some 353 topics.)

The AMC's printed output included general locomotive specifications, which, among other things, required of the builder "two copies of [a] material book, showing all information necessary for ordering parts for these [2-8-4?] locomotives and tenders." On top of that, the AMC's specs required the builder to keep copies of all correspondence "passing between the locomotive builder and specialty companies" and vice versa. Specs could also require the builder to conform to the SMEI's. For example, the specs for the C&O class L-2 4-6-4, in specifying certain bolt fastenings for the new engines, refers to SMEI instructions: "Double nuts, lock nuts, and castle nuts shall be applied in accordance with Railway Company's SMEI's." (Left unexplained here is the equivalence of "Railway Company" with the AMC, which was an accepted fact.)

There seems no end to the paper work in constructing and operating C&O Super Power. Left unexplored here are the many operating and maintenance manuals provided by specialty manufacturers like Franklin Railway Supply Company. Its 114 page illustrated instruction manual (1927 edition) is typical. Then there is the 142 page (8 x11 format) *Manual for Locomotive Firemen* prepared in 1947 by the C&O in Richmond, Va. Because its main illustrations are of C&O 2-8-4's and because so much detailed writing is involved covering so many topics, one suspects that the AMC in Cleveland, not C&O in Richmond, prepared this impressive tome to keep busy in the last days of steam! Another interesting publication of the AMC was the operating and maintenance manual issued by the Office of the Chief Mechanical Engineer in Cleveland and timed for the delivery of the first 2-6-6-6 to C&O. Because the Allegheny was a unique locomotive design, it required special attention, like noting (in italics) that "these locomotives should never be operated over a hump." A thorough handbook on locomotive welding was also an AMC contribution.

RIGHT — Huntington Division fireman Banks of Russell, on 2755, at Sproul, 1949. Compare with photo on page 122 chapter 9.

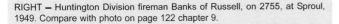

"Gone were the articulated trailing truck, limited cutoff, and outside dry pipe [of the Lima A-1 of 1925]. Instead, the T-1's followed conventional design practices. ... In many ways, these 2-10-4's were as important to the evolution of the modern reciprocating steam locomotive as the A-1."
— Eric Hirsimaki, *Lima, the History* (1986)

C&O T-1 Texas #3018 coming off Limeville bridge with empties. June 1948 — Photo by Eugene L. Huddleston

C&O Texas Type The T-1

"She's the sweetest little rosebud, that Texas ever knew,
Her eyes are bright as diamonds, they sparkle like the dew.
You may talk about your Clementine, and sing of Rosy Lee,
But the yellow rose of Texas is the only one for me."
"Yellow Rose of Texas" (1858)

No name was more appropriate for the 2-10-4 type than "Texas." Like the state, the most advanced developments of this type were big and brash, but these engines could back up this brashness by "hanging tough" on the road. The name for the new wheel arrangement came in 1925 when the Texas and Pacific took the Santa Fe type (2-10-2) into the Super Power arena with an order from Lima for a number of 2-10-4s very similar in design to the Will Woodard's famous A-1 (2-8-4) demonstrator, particularly in having 63" drivers. The evolution of the type had been inevitable, given the tendency in the U.S.A. to build ever bigger versions of a once adopted model. Putting ten-coupled driving wheels on a freight locomotive was a logical enlargement of the ever popular Consolidation (2-8-0) type. The 2-10-0 type, called the Decapod, was more popular outside North America than it was in. About 4,100 engines of this type were built in the United States, but only about 700 were for use in the U.S. The rest were exported to Russia and other European countries where low axle loadings were important. Five hundred ninety-eight heavy engines of one model of the 2-10-0 were built for and by the

Pennsylvania Railroad between 1916 and 1923! Besides their bulldog appearance and rough riding, a famous feature of the Pennsy T-1s Decapods was their flange-less drivers on numbers 2, 3, and 4 axles, a necessity because they lacked lateral control devices.

The 2-10-2 type, with its firebox completely behind the last driver, became popular when the invention of lateral motion devices permitted some flexibility in the sideways movement of driving wheels and side rods. The type had originated on the Atchison, Topeka, and Santa Fe in 1903 (hence the name Santa Fe). The type only became popular around 1915 with the development of lateral control devices, according to Alfred Bruce. The high point of the Santa Fe type was probably reached in 1918-1919 with the design for a "heavy" (293,000 lb. weight on drivers) 2-10-2 for allotment to those roads needing big power (but averse to having Mallets) by the United States Railroad Administration during World War I. What made this version a better performer than the "light" USRA version was 63-inch drivers, vs. 57-inch for the "light."

With the Super Power "revolution" introduced at Lima in 1925, it was inevitable that the 2-10-2 would evolve into a 2-10-4. However, Woodard and the other Lima engineers had not learned that 63-inch drivers on a 10-coupled engine were not tall enough. Alfred Bruce elucidated the problem in his 1952 history of the steam locomotive: "The cylinders on the 2-10-2 type were often

Because Russell's westbound coal classification yard was hidden from view between Raceland Car Shops and the Ohio River, few knew its great size. T-1 3038 on a summer eve in 1947 takes 160 loads from one long track in this yard without "doubling" one cut on the other.
(E.L. Huddleston, COHS collection.)

A man given to careful measurements, Joe Nelson "clocked them at 50 mph with 160 empty gons." These two T-1s (one of them "deadheading") might be at this speed in southern Ohio in 1950, for the eastbound, with 160 empties, has the "Big Mo" going for it, coming off a slight downgrade. (E. L. Huddleston, COHS collection.)

as large as 31 X 32 in. [USRA "heavy" was 30" X 32"], which, with 200 psi steam pressure, gave a piston thrust of about 151,000 lb. For such a piston thrust very heavy moving parts were required, but they could not be properly counterbalanced in the 63-in. main driving wheels, which were the maximum size used on the 2-10-2 type engine. As a result destructive effects were produced when the revolutions per minute exceeded perhaps 210, as required for a running speed of 40 miles per hour. Most damage is done, of course, at the higher drifting speeds or with spinning drivers suddenly released by slippage. Intermediate counterbalance 'bob weights' were sometimes applied ...as a corrective measure, but they ...were of little effect. The only solution was larger diameter driving wheels."

A significant aid in reducing the piston thrust from the big cylinders on the T-1 was the new (for that time) "Tandem Rod Drive," designed by Franklin Railway Supply Company. The company's advertisement in *Railway Age* for March 28, 1931, told how: "To transmit the tremendous piston thrust of the world's largest two cylinder locomotive, the Tandem Main Rod Drive was incorporated in the design. Thus the thrust is divided over two driving axles [Nos. 3 and 4] and four outside main crank pins, reducing the work of the main pin and keeping bearing pressures within reason."

Applying 69-inch drivers to a ten-coupled locomo-

tive took a leap of faith, for it would take a huge boiler and firebox to provide the steam and give the traction to make 69-inch drivers practicable. Luckily, at this time the right designer, the right topography, and the right occasion came together. The right designer was Alonzo Trumbull, Chief Mechanical Officer of the newly formed Van Sweringen roads' Advisory Mechanical Committee. The right topography was along a line through Ohio which either had no clearance problem (on the part of the line north of Columbus) or which had surmounted these problems (the line south of Columbus) by adhering to liberal clearances during construction, which had begun in 1917 and was completed in the late 1920s. The right occasion was the opening of the huge coal assembly yard at Russell capable of assembling Great Lake bound coal trains without "doubling" the 140 or 160 car trains from one track to another before leaving.

Elsewhere in this book the story of Alonzo Trumbull is told. His genius was leading the way into really great Super Power — "pushing the envelope" as they say. At the time Trumbull designed this engine, he had been working for the Erie for thirty years, getting one promotion after another. His loyalty to the Erie is seen in the styling and class designation of the 2-10-4 he designed for taking mile-long coal trains from C&O's classification yards at Russell to Walbridge yard at Toledo, where "pullers" would take the trains on to the Toledo Docks on

Lake Erie. Every new C&O road locomotive received between 1918 and 1930 — and there were over 300 of them — had the "flying air pumps" either applied new or retrofitted at the Huntington Shops. Yet the forty T-1s that showed up at Russell in 1930 had a smokebox front unadorned except for a headlight in middle of boiler. Furthermore, the Erie 2-8-4 's of 1927-29 that provided the model in terms of steaming capacity and driving wheel height for the T-1 had been assigned the "S" series. The next logical class series for big freight engines on the Erie would have been "T." Erie never got those engines, but C&O, part of the Van Sweringen group of roads, did. C&O's own series for the big 2-10-4 would have logically been "B" or "M," certainly not "T" for even "N" was not used until the Pere Marquette merger of 1947.

The newly formed Advisory Mechanical committee did not have much time to design a new Super Power engine after its formation in 1929. But, then, Trumbull already had a powerful, high-horsepower non-articulated engine on the Erie that might fill the bill. One wonders what Trumbull would have done if he had not had something to work with. His idea of Super Power at that time probably had not yet evolved beyond a two-cylinder engine. The only articulateds on the Erie had been flops. It would take development by the Union Pacific and Norfolk and Western in 1936 of articulateds with 69 and 70 inch drivers to awaken Trumbulls's interest in a Super Power simple articulated.

Meanwhile, Trumbull had an Erie S3 (Baldwin 1928) selected and sent to Huntington for some alterations. There No. 3377 had its boiler pressure raised from 225

to 240 psi. Weight was added to its drivers, because if the Erie 2-8-4's had a fault it was slipperiness caused by too low a factor of adhesion (ratio of weight on drivers to starting tractive effort.) "This done," as Tom Dixon wrote, "brand new C&O dynamometer car, DM-1 [on permanent display at B&O Museum] was coupled on, and the tests began in May, 1929. On May 21, a train of 155 loads was taken from Columbus to Toledo with surprisingly satisfactory results.... Overall, in comparison with an H-7a [2-8-8-2 simple articulated] the 3377 made the trip at about the same speed (20.65 mph, as opposed to 20.51 mph, for the H-7). The tests resulted in the positive conclusion that the locomotive required for through service would have to have much larger drivers than the 2-8-8-2's 57-inch wheels, and that the engine would have to have considerably more power than the Erie S3 in order to provide a safe operating margin in other than test conditions, but with approximately the same sized drivers. The committee [the AMC] also concluded that a tender large enough for operation between Russell and Columbus with only one stop would be needed. A study of the design of the two engines left only the H-7 as a candidate, but it was found to be impossible to provide sufficient boiler capacity to supply steam for a 16-coupled engine with so large a driving wheel diameter. After considerable additional study of various designs then in vogue, the 2-10-4 was settled upon for the new locomotive, because it would allow for the incorporation of larger drivers, have more power [supplied by trailer booster] than the H-7 (for starting heavy trains), and would allow for a larger tender without exceeding the length of an H-7 over the couplers [necessary to keep within 115'

K-3 #2345 and T-1 at HV Junction. in 1936

The T-1 2-10-4 single handedly took 160 loads from Russell to Toledo, except for two helper districts. One was a feature that civil engineers could not have eliminated; the other could have been avoided by a longer fill. Powell Moraine, a huge glacial swelling in the plains north of Columbus, required 14 miles assistance by a heavy Mike. In one view K-3 2345 and T-1 are at HV Jct. at the base of the hill in 1936; in other view, K-3 2348 assists 3033 on .4% to .5% segment of hill near Lane Avenue north of Columbus in 1951. (2345 by W. R. Osborne — 2348 by Wayne P. Ellis)

turntable clearance]."

"The boiler that Trumbull designed for the T-1 was the secret of its success. William Withuhn of the

Smithsonian Institution explained the principles involved in an issue of the *C&O Historical Society's Newsletter* of February 1977: "The primary determinants of locomotive boiler power are as follows: (1) grate area, (2) furnace volume, (3) gas area, (4) draft efficiency, and (5) evaporative surface. These five factors will largely determine the quantity of steam which can be produced in a given hour. Also, whatever improves the maximum boiler power also improves boiler efficiency; i.e., any pre-determined, less-than-maximum quantity of steam can be generated with less total fuel consumed than if that same quantity of steam were generated by a smaller boiler. That is, the more powerful boiler can also generate its steam with less fuel burned per pound of steam evaporated... Three of the primary determinants of cylinder power and efficiency are (1) high superheat, (2) high boiler pressure, and (3) easy steam flow through the [piston] valves. These factors are of critical importance in determining how much power at the drawbar the cylinder can extract from the quantity of steam delivered. "

"The C&O T-1 made influential progress in all these areas. Compared to the Erie 2-8-4, classes S3 and S4, the T-1's boiler jumped from 100 square feet to nearly 122 square feet of grate area, and from approximately 5700 square feet of evaporative [heating] surface to over 6600 square feet. In terms of furnace volume, while the Erie S-class lacked combustion chambers, the T-1 added a 66-inch long combustion chamber, and thereby jacked furnace volume to the huge value of 826 cubic feet. In terms of gas area, the . . . designers were concerned with providing the maximum possible free cross-sectional area through the tubes and flues. Of most importance in increasing gas area were larger boiler diameters. From the Erie S's 100" of maximum outside boiler diameter, the T-1 leaped to the enormous diameter of 108 in. This value was rarely exceeded to the end of steam, and it allowed the unprecedented free gas area in a two-cylinder engine of 12.75 square feet (this value was greater than for most articulateds). After 1930 ...the boiler diameter of 108" was not exceeded [on Super Power locomotives] until the C&O H-8's were built with 109-inch boilers."

"Both the Erie S-class and the C&O T-1 used the Type E superheater. But while the S's varied around 2500 sq. ft. of superheating surface, the T-1 jumped to over 3000 sq. ft. This additional superheating surface increased superheat temperature, and thereby increased cylinder efficiency. For boiler pressure, the S1 and S3 carried 225 psi; the Lima S2 and S4 carried 250. The T-1 moderately increased this to 260 psi, which was very high for the day."

" Easy steam flow through the valves was aided by keeping the large 14"-diameter valves and long, 9-inch valve travel of the Erie S in the T-1... Also in the smokebox, the T-1 used the American Multiple-Valve Front-End throttle, as did the Erie Berkshires. The front-

2-8-8-2 C&O #1584 pusher crew and laborers wait on siding at Limeville. (Engineer Clark Sandy is at right.)

end throttle materially improved the ease of steam flow to the cylinders and greatly aided the responsiveness of the locomotive." As for "draft efficiency," cited above, tests with dynamometer car DM-1 of newly completed T-1 No. 3000, under load, revealed that operating "back pressure" of steam exiting the cylinders was "somewhat higher" than what was considered "good practice." Test engineers measured back pressure by recording back-pressure gauge readings with changing percentages of valve gear cut-off as the engineer "hooked her up" or "hooked her down into the corner." Further tests (reported in *Railway Age*, January 17, 1931) to determine proper exhaust nozzle size resulted in a larger area in the nozzle and a larger smoke stack. Diameter of nozzle was increased from eight inches to ten inches, and "new stacks [on all forty engines] 24 in. in diameter were installed to replace the original 21-in. stacks." Around this time boiler pressure was increased five pounds to 265 psi, producing more calculated tractive effort.

As a result of these improvements, the T-1 turned in statistically impressive results. *Railway Age* reported fuel economy achieved with the T-1 in its July 2, 1932 issue: "In 1929, prior to the receipt of these locomotives, the fuel consumption per 1,000 gross ton-miles on the division [Russell to Columbus] over which these are now operating was 118 lb. In 1931, this fuel consumption was reduced to 79 lb, or 33 per cent."

Dixon explained that deliveries of the T-1 "started with No. 3000, which left Lima on August 29, 1930 (construction number 7516). The entire order was completed on November 24 with the shipment of #3039; it was

among the last orders completed before Lima closed as a result of the worsening Depression." The forty T-1s continued hauling 160 car trains through 1951. Car count rather than tonnage determined train length, and with the arrival of more and more 70-ton capacity coal cars after World War II, the T-1 was taking often more than 14,000 tons (counting caboose) from Russell to Toledo. The T-1 might have been around for a few more years if the grade to the Sciotoville bridge over the Ohio had been kept to 0.20% on the approach on the Kentucky side of the river. But to save construction costs the "hill" was shortened with the result that the grade reached 0.70% for about a mile and a quarter. Thus a helper engine was needed. Three-unit diesels did not need helpers.

But back to the achievement of the T-1's. Withuhn sums them up well: "It can be said that the C&O T-1's brought the Lima "Super Power" concept to its peak. As David P. Morgan has pointed out, the T-1's outperformed sixteen-drivered simple articulateds that were only four years old, and did so on 14% less coal. When delivered, the T-1's were the most powerful two-cylinder engines in the world. In later years there were more powerful 2-10-4s (notably the AT&SF 5011-class of 1944) . . . but none had the lasting influence on steam design that was exerted by the C&O T-1. And to outperform the T-1, the C&O had to build the most powerful steam locomotives ever constructed-the H-8 Alleghenies."

Braking Super Power Trains
by Terry G. Seaks

Super power locomotives like the T-1 and H-8 could move a heavy train at speed, but that was of little use if there were not a safe way of controlling the heavier trains. During the super power era, two important braking advances occurred. One was the Westinghouse AB freight car brake valve of 1933. The second was the Westinghouse 8-ET locomotive brake equipment introduced in 1934.

George Westinghouse had first manufactured the straight air brake in 1869. Three years later he developed the automatic brake that reduced train line pressure and worked through car-mounted triple valves to apply brakes using an air reservoir on each car. As train length grew, reductions in brake pipe pressure took longer to propagate through the train. In 1887 Westinghouse added an equalizing reservoir mounted on the locomotive. Brake pipe reductions made by the engineer showed up immediately on the equalizing reservoir gauge and the entire brake pipe of the train eventually equalized to this pressure, hence the name equalizing reservoir.

Four essential air pressures were read from two duplex gauges on the locomotive in a system still used today. One of the two-needle gauges showed main reservoir pressure and equalizing reservoir pressure. The other gauge showed brake pipe pressure and locomotive brake cylinder pressure.

In 1907 Westinghouse introduced the K Triple Valve whose quick service function provided for service reductions in the brake pipe to propagate at approximately 125 feet per second. The K Triple valve and the 6-ET locomotive brake equipment represented the industry standards in the early part of the 20th century on the eve of super power.

On a train of 100 cars with K valves and approximately 5000 feet of brake pipe, a service brake application would take about forty seconds to reach the end of the train. In the early 1930s the T-1s were beginning to haul 150-160 car trains from Russell to Toledo. The AB valves of 1933 quadrupled the service propagation rate of the K valve to about 500 feet per second. With the new AB valves, a service application would propagate through a 150 car train with roughly 7500 feet of brake pipe in about fifteen seconds.

In addition to faster application, faster recharge rates, and positive release, the AB valves brought two other major innovations that are still in use. One involved the double compartment air reservoir, with separate auxiliary (service) and emergency portions. Now an engineer could make an emergency application after a service application because there were separate reservoirs for each function. The other was the three-way division of the brake valve into an emergency portion, service portion and pipe bracket. A measure of the success of the AB valve was the fact that the next major refinement would not come until the ABD valve in the 1960s.

For locomotives, Westinghouse introduced the 8-ET automatic brake equipment in 1934. C&O's Alleghenies were equipped with the 8-ET brake and so were the Kanawhas. Westinghouse pictured the Alleghenies in ads for the 8-ET brake in Railway Age in the 1940s. While similar to the 6-ET in many ways, the 8-ET brake coordinated the application of locomotive and car braking and offered better control of the slack in the longer trains possible with super power locomotives and AB car valves. The 8-ET equipment controlled slack action by introducing a first service position on the engineer's automatic brake valve.

The notched quadrants on the No. 8 contained six positions: release, running, first service, lap, service, and emergency. C&O rules in the 1940s specified a brake pipe pressure of 90 pounds for freight trains on mountain grades where the H-8s ran, and the running position maintained this feedvalve setting in the brake pipe. The release position was used to recharge the brake system and obtain quick release on long trains by briefly feeding main reservoir air at 130 pounds into the brake pipe.

The new first service position provided a rapid reduction of equalizing reservoir of 6 pounds followed by a much more gradual reduction that would reduce equalizing reservoir by 20 pounds in about 2 minutes. This new feature was designed to let brakes apply gradually and uniformly throughout long heavy trains to better control slack action. On the earlier No. 6 brake, the quadrant notches were the same except that first service had been a holding position. Moving the brake handle to holding following a service application resulted in a release of train brakes but held locomotive brakes applied. The 6-ET brake equipment was installed on the T-1s of 1930 and also on Greenbriers #600-604 of 1935.

Service position provided for more rapid reductions in equalizing reservoir than did first service. A 20 pound reduction could be made to equalizing reservoir in as little as 10 seconds using service position. While the other positions on the quadrant were all single position notches, the service position was a wide notch that provided a range of service applications: moving the handle further into the service position provided more rapid rates of reduction. Whether the reductions were made using the first service or service position, the brake handle then had to be moved to lap to stop the reduction in equalizing reservoir and brake pipe pressure.

Thus, an engineer might begin a ten pound brake application by moving the handle to first service position. The No. 8 would quickly reduce the equalizing reservoir to approximately 84 pounds, and then much more gradually decrease the pressure. The engineer would move the handle to lap when the desired 80 pounds was obtained on the equalizing reservoir and the brake pipe would eventually equalize to 80 pounds also.

Despite its advances, the 8-ET lacked the pressure maintaining feature that would be an option with 24-RL brakes and standard on 26-L. The maintaining feature supplied just enough air into the brake pipe to offset brake pipe leakage and maintain exactly the reduction the engineer had made. This was important on mountain grades where leakage would cause brakes to apply harder over time, eventually bringing the train to a stop.

Releasing brakes on steep grades was dangerous because the train would quickly run away before the reservoirs on the cars had time to fully recharge. The solution was provided by "retainers" on cars. When manually turned up by a brakeman walking the train, they would retain car brake cylinder pressure even when the engineer moved his brake handle to release or running. This allowed for safely recharging car brake reservoirs during descent, albeit at the expense of lost time to stop and turn up retainers on each car at the top of a grade and then another stop to turn them down when safely down the mountain.

The 24-RL brake is almost synonymous with first generation diesels but its introduction in 1941 allowed its installation in some super power locomotives. It had the same handle positions as the 8-ET brake equipment but was designed to adapt to steam, diesel, or electric engines in freight or passenger service. The 24-RL included options that interacted with the electrical systems of the diesel and electric locomotives and allowed for automatic sanding and power cut-off during emergency brake applications and even an option for electro-pneumatic brakes. C&O installed the 24-RL on Greenbriers 610-614 built in 1948 because it planned to utilize this last-named feature.

Today 6-ET, 8-ET, and 24-RL brake equipment can be found on museum locomotives and some tourist railroads. Freight railroads and Amtrak almost universally employ the newer 26-L that provides the features of the 24-RL in a much smaller and lighter package. For further reading, Ed King provides a good treatment of braking on mountain grades in the April 2004 issue of *Trains*.

The mile and a half approach to Sciotoville bridge made for a .7% grade to the Ohio River bridge. As originally surveyed the fill would have extended east another mile or so reducing the grade to .2%, and not requiring pusher. The three shift pusher crew waited on siding at Limeville, as shown by 2-8-8-2 pusher and crew and laborers. (PAGE 38) (Engineer Clark Sandy is at right.) BELOW - In another view, a T-1 (without pusher) climbs the .7% grade in 1950. (E. L. Huddleston, COHS collection.)

The T-1's achievements are easy to dwell upon because there are so many testimonials to its excellence.

For example, in *Railroads at War* (1944) Long Island sportsman and author S. Kip Farrington could evaluate the performance of C&O's T-1 by virtue of riding the cab

About a year after its 1930 delivery, 3015 is at Parsons Yard, Columbus, giving view of original, smaller smoke stack and of multiple bearing crosshead guide anchored to same extension of frame as the Baker valve gear. (J. H. Dean, Ray Curl collection.)

of one for almost sixteen hours straight. On April 25, 1942, Farrington rode extra 3029 west from Russell to Toledo with about an hour's layover at Parsons Yard, Columbus; the train had 160 cars of Lake coal, 13,500 gross tons (not counting engine and caboose). He left Russell at 2:10 PM and arrived Walbridge Yard, Toledo, at 5:25AM! This was not Farrington's only good ride on a T-1: "this is the 7th run I have made [from Russell to Toledo] on these engines with their 160 loads and I have always considered it one of the top one-half dozen moves in the U. S..." And he added , "This was truly one of the greatest locomotives ever built..." Because of the boldness of the design and its success in service, one can keep coming back to the C&O T-1, like Farrington, without fear of exhausting what to say about it. Well

known writer Bert Pennypacker also cited the experience of a man in the cab, this one an engineer on the Toledo Subdivision, in Railroad, December 1964: "I was called for a Walbridge [Yard] coal job out of Columbus. When I got to the [Parsons] roundhouse, the new T-1 looked mighty impressive. She was the largest non-articulated hog I had ever seen, but when I looked at the train tonnage slip [prepared at Russell from precise scale weights], my pride in the new engine vanished and I wished for a dependable H-7 class 2-8-8-2. She'll never pull this train, I thought, but we had a road foreman aboard, so it'll be his responsibility when we stall. Well, we got out of town easily with a helper [a 2-8-2 up 14-mile long Powell Hill]. The road foreman lent an assist at the throttle because I didn't have the 'feel' of her and

Both 3007 and 3018 (shown on page 32) are coming down the Limeville fill on the same sweeping curve needed to approach the Sciotoville bridge from the Kentucky side at a right angle to the river. The same hill contours in Ohio show in both photos. (both, E. L. Huddleston)

This 1944 view at the north (west) end of Parsons yard is much the same view the engineer on a T-1 called for Walbridge would have had in 1930, referring to Bert Pennypacker's testimonial to the T-1's power in *Railroad*. From left to right are Buckeye Steel Castings buildings, the mainline coal dock, the engine terminal coal dock, and the general yard office building. (C&O Ry. Photo, collection COHS)

made the drivers spin frequently. As we rolled across the Ohio flatlands, the T-1 thundered defiant stack music. I was amazed to realize that she had increased her speed to double that of an H-7. Oh well, she's a fine puller, but just wait until we stop for water and can't get started. My T-1 took slack and actually walked away from the water tank [at Marion] with the booster cut in, and was I surprised! That trip sticks in my memory as the best I ever made. It changed my mind about articulateds being better than two-cylinder engines, at least as far as T-1s go."

Other highlights in the story of this famous Texas type include the T-1's riding qualities, some wrecks of note over the engines' twenty-one year career, comparisons with other notable 2-10-4s, and miscellaneous items, like the T-1's pioneering use of multiple-bearing type crosshead guide. Then there's the attempt by the Pennsylvania Railroad to "perfect perfection" by expanding its J-1 copy of the T-1 into a giant Duplex.

Whether it be a 2-10-0, a 2-10-2, or a 2-10-4, the coupling of five driving axles in tandem produces a tremendous force on the rails as the main and side rods revolve. Ralph Johnson defines this force, called "dynamic augment," as "the centrifugal force caused by

the over and under balance in the [driving] wheel. It tends to lift the wheel from the rail when in one position and enhance the static load in the opposite direction." On a 10-coupled locomotive the force is especially strong because of the massive main and side rods driving all ten wheels. The riding quality of the 2-10-4 type was greatly improved by the appearance of the C&O T-1, which was the first 10-coupled locomotive to have 69-inch drivers (63 being the maximum before the T-1). Larger drivers left more room on the surface of the wheel for counterweights to balance the forces, and increased diameter meant fewer revolutions per mile. Counterbalancing, however, was not as simple as it sounds. Bill Withuhn explained in *Trains* (1974): " . . . Suppose only the rotating mass of the rods was balanced by the counterweights. Then, in obedience to Newton's third law [of motion] the terrific oscillating horizontal motion of the pistons would cause the engine to react by trying to 'nose', or to yaw from side to side, doing much damage to the engine and to the track. . . The overbalance [of the reciprocating mass] compensates dynamically for the reciprocating inertial force on the main pins, which if it were not compensated would result in a twisting action about the engine's vertical axis -i.e., nosing. This leaves a new problem, however. The excess mass used for the overbalance results in the drive wheels being out of balance in rotation. If the speed of the engine is high enough, the drivers can lift themselves off the rails . . . ."

The C&O 2-10-4 had a problem with rough riding and damage to the track in later years. This was partly because of dynamic augment and partly because, in 1930, when the T-1s were built, the casting of solid frames (with cylinders included) had not been perfected yet. As a result, over the years the T-1's frames became somewhat "unglued," increasing the imbalance of the wheels. Evidence that the T-1s were hard on track comes from an extra track gang being assigned to take out the kinks that constantly developed on the long curve near the bottom of Gregg Hill, a .80% grade for a mile and a half against eastbound traffic. The long curve at the bottom (near Waverly, Ohio) has a maximum curvature of 6 degrees, 32 minutes. Even those unacquainted with the engineering principles involved can see why a monstrous T-1 coasting downgrade and being shoved along by the momentum of 160 loaded coal cars would cause havoc with the track alignment.

Ralph Johnson, in his *The Steam Locomotive* confirms that bad track on Gregg Hill was not an isolated condition. He cited how a 2-10-2 (Santa Fe type) placed in service in 1919 — on an unnamed railroad — continually gave trouble. Having only 63-inch drivers the 2-10-2 was "placed in service requiring higher speeds than the engine had been designed for. The railroad engineers found over 700 bent rails in a distance of 100 miles, occurring always at the foot of a descending grade." Excessive speed was, of course, the main factor in deter-

mining just how jolting would be the effects of dynamic augment. Joe Nelson, C&O supervisor with long first-hand acquaintance with the T-1, reported, "I have clocked them doing 50 m.p.h. with 160 empty 'gons'." Coal trains on the Northern Subdivision in steam days were supposed to be kept to 40 m.p.h., but since most freight engines had no speedometers, there wasn't much except his engine "jumping up and down" to hold the engineer back. And at 50 the jolting must have been pronounced.

Because competent engine crews generally ran T-1s on well-maintained double track from Russell to Toledo, there are few major accidents to report between their arrival in 1930 and their demise in 1952. Two notable wrecks occurred in the 1940's. On March 24, 1945, T-1 3017 "turned over on an embankment, killing its crew." This "derailment" (an ICC investigative term) resulted in the deaths of the engineer, fireman, and head brakeman. Location of the wreck was approximately at milepost 2 of the Toledo Subdivision north of the Olentangy River bridge at HV Jct., Columbus. Undoubtedly the train was headed east, descending Powell Hill, for if the train was headed west (north), it would not be going fast enough to plunge over an embankment. Derailment of the two-wheel leading truck led eventually to the locomotive turning over; the men in the cab could not immediately tell if the lead truck was "on the ground." A device known as the "Little Wright Watchman" functioned as a dead man control and would apply the brakes if the truck derailed. However, investigation disclosed that the device on this engine had been disconnected.

Much has been written about the explosion of T-1

Scene at Coal Branch, looking west, identifies spot where a T-1 overturned in 1943. The eastbound engine fell on its side where the highway and tracks are closest, at start of the "S" curve. H-8 1655, in "pool" service with T-1s on the Russell-Toledo route, will pick up 160 L&N loaded coal cars at Limeville and proceed through Ohio to Columbus and Toledo. (E. L. Huddleston, COHS collection.)

C&O 2-10-4s were never used over Allegheny Mountain, but they did run up New River into Hinton and back to Russell if the manifest was long enough (reportedly 70 cars or over). Otherwise, K-4 2-8-4s took the manifests up the Kanawha and New River Divisions. In January 1951, 3038 (with roller bearings on lead truck) starts up Scary Hill east of Milton-on-the-Mud with manifest no. 92. (E. L. Huddleston, collection. COHS)

no doubt thought their seats too far back from the boiler "backhead" to permit easy handling of the controls. According to *Railway Mechanical Engineer* the extra space was intended "to afford an unobstructed view of the water column and gauges."

Though the T-1 and the AMC designed 2-8-4s had the "standard" AMC Super Power 69-inch drivers, they had far different sized boilers, with the 2-8-4s at 98 inches, maximum outside diameter, and 108 inches on the T-1. This difference in size comes most clearly from examining the front of the T-1. (One needs remember that steam locomotive boilers were mostly conical in shape – or were "wagon topped" with conical top and flat

bottom — and that the maximum diameter of the boiler came just ahead of the firebox.) Though the oversized cab of the T-1 threw "off balance" the cab's relationship with the boiler, this imbalance of perception was not a problem with the PRR J-1, which had a relatively short cab. The J-1 had another perception problem, however. The air after-cooler unit (which the T-1 never had), mounted on the front end, covered the lower part of the smokebox door, its presence de-emphasizing the "big barrel" effect produced by the unadorned front of the T-1. For both types, the "big barrel" look was enhanced by photographs in which the camera was at stack or headlight level. The perspective in photos taken from

On six-mile tangent of the Cincinnati Division along the Ohio flood plain near Grays Branch, Ky., T-1 3010 has clear stack and 160 loads of coal bound for trip up the Northern Sub to Columbus in summer of 1948. As on most T-1's, homemade pilot has replaced the original. (E. L. Huddleston, collection. COHS)

ground level emphasized the mass of the pilot, pilot beam, and shields, and made the top of the boiler appear to be "leaning back" slightly. Thus it was hard from most camera angles to capture the "top heavy," or "big barrel," look that the T-1 had.

It might seem odd that a steam locomotive designed and engineered in 1930 should never be surpassed as a two-cylinder freight locomotive (with drivers 69-inches or higher) in tractive effort. (The C&O T-1 and PRR J-1 both exceeded the Santa Fe 2-10-4 in starting tractive effort,

not counting the tractive effort added by the booster.) Although steam engines in America continued to be constructed until 1952, yet by 1930 the formulas, tables, and graphs had been devised, that in the hands of an inventive mechanical engineer, would yield measurements that skilled draftsmen could give form to. That steam locomotive technology had climaxed at about the time the Depression started is evidenced by requirements for a college degree in mechanical engineering. For example, beginning in 1937, course offerings relevant to

steam engineering were reduced in the official catalogue of courses in the Department of Mechanical Engineering at what is now Michigan State University. In 1935-36 the "College" offered for the last time (aside from "power plant engineering") a course in steam power: "A study of the principles underlying the construction and operation of steam power equipment including fuels, combustion, theory of steam generation, boilers, stokers, steam engines, steam turbines, and the testing of steam power equipment."

The Pennsylvania Railroad's adopting a 1930 design in 1942 also demonstrates that steam power technology had climaxed on the eve of the Great Depression. The PRR did not order 125 of these engines because the federal government forced the purchase. (War Production Board mandates did not go into effect until after June 1942 and did not apply to such large orders.) The T-1 was the best engine tested, and minor improvements that could be incorporated by 1942 made them even better-like cast-steel frames and cylinders. (But only about 35 J-2a's had such frames; the rest were built up like the original T-1s.) Also, better lubricants enabled steam pressure to be raised ten pounds per square inch. The T-1 and the J-1 were the same height-16 ft., 5 1/2 inches. That was about as tall as a steamer could get and thus was another reason steam locomotive development stopped around 1930. Maximum heights, widths, and lengths had been reached as prescribed by "standard gauge" track.

The 125 J-1 2-10-4s were put in service from December, 1942, until 1944. In February 1943 PRR was going to order 25 more 2-10-4s. But something had happened within PRR's high command. The Pennsylvania, which prided itself on being "the standard railroad of the world" did not want more copies. It wanted to surpass the C&O design with its own product! One month after canceling the order for 25 more J-1s, the PRR management authorized construction of the first of a new class-the Q-2 duplex, with a novel 4-4-6-4 wheel arrangement.

The PRR motive power department could hardly hold up pride in its own company's R&D as the chief reason for not buying more imitations of the C&O machine. So it found other good reasons, the best being that a duplex (a two engine non-articulated) would eliminate pounding of the rails and poor riding that came with coupling ten driving wheels to one transmission. The dual drive of the Duplex would greatly reduce dynamic augment. Also, Ralph Johnson, chief engineer of Baldwin Locomotive Works, located in PRR's headquarters city, was pushing duplex development; hence the PRR's prior experiments with a 6-4-4-6 and a 4-6-4-4, plus production runs of the famous 4-4-4-4 passenger duplex.

Thus the Pennsylvania proceeded to build twenty-six heavy 4-4-6-4 freight locomotives in its Altoona shops that were, from the road's viewpoint, the C&O T-1 and PRR J-1 brought to perfection. The resulting class Q-2 looked good in its semi-streamlined cowling, and its engine weight of 621,100 lbs. was far above the C&O T-1, the PRR J-1, and the Santa Fe 5012 series 2-10-4s. From the view of test plant performance, it was a winner too. The Q-2, riding on huge rollers within the test building, was measured at 7987 indicated horsepower at a simulated 57.4 MPH. (I.H.P. is power developed at the cylinders.) It is said the PRR J-1 produced 7,000 I.H.P. under the same conditions. Thus, as Phil Atkins wrote, the Q-2 was "the largest and most powerful ten drivered engine ever built."

If the story ended here, the Q-2s would not have been stored on the "dead line" in 1952 while the J-1 class was still going strong with some even running in 1958. Working out on the "treadmill" for the Q-2 was not the same as working out on the road. In service, the engines slipped badly at running speeds. It was not hard to make a reciprocating steam locomotive slip its drivers in starting, particularly if the rails were wet or slick and if the person at the throttle "gunned" it carelessly or deliberately. But the Q-2 just could not convert all that horsepower produced at the cylinders into horsepower at the rails. There were two reasons for its slipping when it should not slip. First, the factor of adhesion (ratio of weight on drivers to tractive effort) was 3.58, whereas 4.0 or a fraction above was considered acceptable. The second reason was more subtle and harder for a layman to understand. Two engines on a rigid frame (as opposed to two on an articulated frame) set up harmonic vibrations caused by the two engines (with differing bores and strokes) getting in and out of synch.

The introduction in 1939 of the highly successful EMD (General Motors) FT model three-unit road diesel effectively ended steam locomotive development except for those railroads and locomotive manufacturers that had a vested interest in keeping coal as a fuel and in making use of otherwise idle manufacturing facilities.

"According to *Time* [April 1945] magazine [designer] Dorothy Draper demanded that no coal locomotive be allowed to stoke up within five miles of White Sulphur Springs lest their smoke mar her spotless white hotel, but the C&O was compelled to put its foot down on that request."
– Robert S. Conte, *The History of the Greenbrier* (1989)

Newly made fill eases curves near Goshen, Virginia, as J-3 606 powers "Sportsman" westbound in 1944. (C&OHS collection)

Chapter 5

C&O Greenbriers

When the Greenbrier resort hotel formally opened after World War II, Robert R. Young threw a huge party at which "arrived such personalities as the Duke and Duchess of Windsor, Bing Crosby, William Randolph Hearst, Jr., Mrs. Joseph P. Kennedy, . . . as well as son John, then a young Congressman." These were heady times for passenger travel in the mountains of West Virginia and the twelve C&O 4-8-4s, called Greenbriers, added their class to the grand reopening, held in April 1948. Guests arrived, "by 14 private railroad cars, and by limousine, and private plane." (The last five J-3 class Greenbriers, Nos. 610-614, actually did not arrive in West Virginia until early June that year) The pride in heading the "F.F.V.," the "Sportsman," and the "George Washington" during their stops at the Greenbrier resort was matched by their handling "specials" to the spa. (You'd often find the locomotives "laying over" behind the colonial white depot.) The Greenbriers also took pride in hauling long special trains up the Hot Springs branch to the Homestead resort at Hot Springs, Va. A local citizen of the Covington — Clifton Forge area told this writer , a youthful visitor, that he had once seen, while working in a field, two Greenbriers double heading a special train up the steep and scenic Hot Springs branch to the Homestead hotel. (As late as September 1960 C&O was running specials up the branch; a train of business executives out of New York stalled on the steep grade, with diesels pulling of course.)

"Greenbrier," denoting the West Virginia river, resort, and county, is an apt name for C&O's 4-8-4 type. The "official" name was "Northern," after the first 4-8-4s, built for the Northern Pacific in 1926. The type was widely popular. The thirty pages of photos of American and Canadian 4-8-4s in Walter Lucas' "*Pocket Guide to American Locomotives*" will convince the reader of their variety, far beyond other Super Power wheel arrangements. Other names besides the foregoing for the type included the Pocono, Niagara, Wyoming (for the valley in Pennsylvania), and Golden State, according to Lucas. Driver diameters for the 30 pictured engines varied from 69 inches to 80 inches. All C&O's 4-8-4s were 72 inches, though some sources give 74 inches. Nuckles and Dixon in their comprehensive 1994 book covering the C&O 4-8-4s have reviewed the problem: "For all three orders Lima Engineering Department records show 72-inch drivers. This is repeated by *Railway Mechanical Engineer* in a February 1936 article on the Greenbriers, and is shown in the erection drawing. C&O diagrams dated 1948 show 74-inch drivers on all three orders... We have used the 72-inch figure throughout. The difference could result from later application of thicker driver tires — new tires — one inch thicker than the original tires would increase the diameter by two inches." Official specifications for all three orders show drivers with 66-inch wheel centers; for 72-inch diameter this would mean tires measuring three inches from rim to flange.

What made the 4-8-4 the most popular type of Super Power steam locomotives on American railroads was their use by most in both freight and passenger service. But this dual service capability was achieved at the expense of traction needed for heavy freight service. An extra axle up front absorbed engine weight that otherwise would have given the engine more power. For steam locomotives the "factor of adhesion" was calculated by dividing the weight on drivers by the starting tractive effort. A ratio of 4.0 or above was necessary for good traction. For roads like Santa Fe, Union Pacific, C&O,

Terminals with roundhouses stabling Greenbriers were Hinton, Clifton Forge, and Charlottesville. That's where you'd find them! J-3 602 waits at Charlottesville's Main Street station to head No . 5, the "Sportsman" west. Train probably came from Washington behind a J-2 Mountain or an F-18 Pacific. (H. H. Harwood, Jr.)

C&O Greenbriers

In 1948 at Clifton Forge M-1 turbine # 500 waits to take No . 4, the "Sportsman," over Mountain Subdivision to Charlottesville. Ditto for Greenbrier #604, with Newport News section of "Sportsman." (E. L. Huddleston.)

and Norfolk and Western, who used 4-8-4s only in passenger service (a state not necessarily maintained in the years approaching the end of steam), the loss of starting power was not a problem since passenger trains weighed much less than freight trains. Further, these roads were known for designing extremely large machines for whatever wheel arrangement they adopted. So they compensated in introducing increased boiler size to make up for whatever power was lost from having the front end rest on four wheels rather than two.

This increased size generally meant that 4-8-4s had very big boilers. Maximum diameter for later Santa Fe and the Norfolk & Western Northerns was 102 inches and for the Union Pacific 4-8-4s, New York Central Niagaras, Milwaukee S-2, Wabash O-1, and C&O J-3, 100 inches. (The remaining North American 4-8-4s were mostly either 96" or 98.") The reason generally given for a four-wheel leading truck was that it was more stable in "tracking" than the two wheel, so that "nosing" and "hunting" of the front end could be controlled. However, the freight counterpart on C&O of the Greenbrier 4-8-4s -the 90 Kanawha 2-8-4 types (plus the PM 2-8-4s acquired in 1947) — had excellent adhesion (and boilers of 98 inches, maximum outside diameter) but could still operate at passenger train speeds (of around 70 mile after mile). Furthermore, the C&O 2-8-4s had 2,400 lbs. more starting tractive effort than the C&O Greenbriers, and that extra edge meant a lot for engines assigned to freight service. (Both types had trailer boosters to add more starting power.)

Horsepower more than tractive effort (which never was a problem because of the trailer boosters supplied all twelve Greenbriers) was the chief claim to fame of C&O's Super Power 4-8-4s. The boiler on a steam engine is only good insofar as it can generate steam, and the C&O 4-8-4's (of 1935 and 1942) 5,538 sq. ft of evaporative heating surface was, in the words of Englishman Brian Reed, "higher than that of any 4-8-4 bar none." It also had the largest combined heating surface of any 4-8-4. *Railway Mechanical Engineer* (February 1936) explained how heating surface was converted into horsepower: "The relatively high percentage of radiant heating surface is relied upon to produce a heat transfer which, combined with care throughout the design to effect high economy in the utilization of steam in the cylinders, is expected to provide a locomotive capable of developing not less than 5,000 cylinder horsepower."

A complication in evaluating the C&O 4-8-4s collectively for their "evaporative" capability is that the last five Greenbriers, while having such quality features as roller bearings for all axles and crank pins and rods, plus frames and cylinders all in one casting, should not have thermic syphons in the firebox, features that on engines 600-606 considerably added to the evaporative heating surface total. The use of four circulators in the firebox of 610-614 instead of two syphons and two arch tubes (in combination on engines 600-606) helped lower the heating surface figure to 4821 sq. ft. for 610-614. Another reason the figure went down is a shortening of tubes and flues due to an increase in the length of the combustion chamber.

As to appearance, the first C&O 4-8-4s, the J-3's of 1935, were a lot like the T-1 (2-10-4) of 1930 and the Nickel Plate 2-8-4's of 1934. This was to be expected, since the Advisory Mechanical Committee in Cleveland had designed all three types. All featured the Worthington open-type feedwater heaters, had their steam domes ahead of the sand boxes, and used the same smokebox door design, as well as the distinctive shields over the two air pumps and a platform raised off the pilot about a foot or so. One variation in the C&O J-3 design was use of the Walshaerts valve gear instead of the Baker, which had been on both the C&O 2-10-4 and NKP 2-8-4. Perhaps the less complex Walshaerts was adopted to save weight. In any event, around 1942, the Baker replaced the Walshaerts on 600-604, and the next two J-3's of 1942, had the Baker as original equipment.

Shortening the tubes and flues and substituting circulators for syphons might seem short sighted on the part of the AMC. The reason for this sacrifice in total heating surface was a rather peculiar one — peculiar in the sense that many observers would see the changes made to the specifications for the new engines as coming a little late — after bids had been sent out. Yet this is what happened, as a result of the need of the AMC to reduce the engine weight and to save money, at the behest of C&O management. (Both revisionist goals are "down on paper" among the hundreds of pages preserving the specifications of 610-614.) Saving weight would enable 610-614 to run straight through from Clifton Forge to Newport News and Phoebus at Tidewater. The sudden need to save money arose from a crisis over C&O's transportation ratio. The last-minute revisions to the specifications for J-3's 610-614 resulted in a sizeable "paper trail" covering the many alterations either actually made or considered for the engines while under construction.

The first four Greenbriers were named after Virginia statesmen of the early Republic. A name board mounted on the side of the sand dome featured four-inch letters cut from metal attached to a removable plaque. Because the letters were uniformly four-inches high, some names had to be shortened;. e.g., "TH. JEFFERSON" for No . 600. The two wartime Greenbriers (contemporaneous with the L-2 Hudsons from Baldwin) were ordered from Lima in 1941 and delivered in January 1942. As Phil Shuster wrote in *C&O Power*, they "were duplicates of the earlier engines [600-604] except that they were somewhat heavier, the steam dome was placed behind the sandbox, the drop coupler pilot was omitted, and the headlight was lowered to the pilot beam position with an oval number plate occupying the smokebox door location." No. 605 was named "Thomas Nelson, Jr." and No. 606 the "James Monroe." However, probably because it was wartime and skilled labor in short supply, the names were painted on the sandbox, not inscribed on metal. (Nos. 610-614 of 1948 were not named.) Grime and soot from tunnel roofs would soon make the names hard to see! All seven new Greenbriers went into mountain passenger service hauling named trains and mail-express trains between Hinton and Charlottesville and

4-8-4 C&O #610 accelerates east with mail-express train from Hinton depot in 1950. (E. L. Huddleston).

Charlottesville and Newport News. As Nuckles and Dixon point out, "The seven Greenbriers teamed up with the ancient Mountains... to haul the expanding traffic. In the peak year 1944 the C&O carried six times as many passengers as when the J-3s first arrived in 1935." Alleghany summit, the Blue Ridge, and Great North Mountain were the domain of these beautiful locomotives, and their powerful exhausts and melodious whistles added immeasurable glory to the beauty of the scenery.

In late 1946, when the AMC drew up plans for five new Greenbriers, it was again "nothing but the best" for C&O motive power. The future of passenger traffic on C&O looked good. Those who rode standing-room-only passenger trains so frequently in World War II were expected to continue their patronage, and Robert R. Young, C&O's Chairman of the Board, put so much of his company's money into passenger projects that he seemed reckless to many and a hero to a few. Also, the future of steam power seemed assured because C&O was a great coal hauling road.

Thus, when new power was in line after World War II to replace aging class J-2 4-8-2s in mountain territory and class F-19 4-6-2s on more level divisions, there was no doubt that for level service the L-2 class 4-6-4 of 1942, the world's heaviest Hudsons, would be duplicated, and for mountain service the J-3 Northerns (4-8-4s, called Greenbriers on C&O) of 1934-35 and

1942, the biggest — in terms of height, length, weight, and boiler diameter — two-cylinder engines ever to serve on C&O with the exception of the giant 2-10-4s of 1930. The Greenbriers were thus bigger than the famed Van Sweringen Berkshire (2-8-4) freight locomotives of the Nickel Plate, Pere Marquette, and C&O. In early 1947 C&O was still "on a roll" in spending for freight and passenger locomotives, and the real austerity program would not come until late 1948, when an order for 25 "mine run" Mallets was reduced to ten and 30 brand new 0-8-0 switchers were sold as second-hand and when wholesale cuts were made in local passenger service.

The C&O, working with the AMC, spared no expense in planning modern innovations for the five projected Greenbriers. But some drastic developments affected the order at about the time it was made. One development was the failure of the new "Chessie" streamliner to go into service, leaving some very expensive coaches and turbine locomotives unused. This was coupled with an enormous cost increase in providing local passenger train service to practically every hollow C&O served. Another was that work stoppages in the coal fields cut into revenue. Finally, there were huge line relocation projects in the mountains to pay for, that were principally intended to keep the "Chessie" streamliner on a tight Cincinnati to Washington schedule.

Obviously cost cutting was going to have to take place, and the new Greenbriers under construction were

Amtrak's "Cardinal" has followed for over thirty years the same route through Virginia and West Virginia that the twelve C&O 4-8-4's followed with the "George Washington," "F.F.V.," and "Sportsman. RIGHT - "East of Little Rock Tunnel Greenbrier 606 doubleheads "Sportsman" down slope of the Blue Ridge towards Charlottesville in 1949. BELOW - No. 601 on "Sportsman" westbound departs Waynesboro Union Station in 1948. N&W passes under C&O at right. (both, J. I. Kelly, COHS collection.) BOTTOM RIGHT - J-3 602 blasts "Sportsman" upgrade east of White Sulphur Springs, June 1951. (E. L. Huddleston, H. H. Harwood collection.)

likely targets. Although direct figures are not available, one can extrapolate their costs from the cost of each of five class L-2a Hudsons — with poppet valves — purchased at the same time. Lloyd Stagner provides the evidence: "Costing $353,346 each, these later L-2s were among the most expensive steam locomotives ever built, costing 80 percent more than the first eight L-2s bought in 1941." The assumption that the new J-3s would cost more is that they were bigger, but their lacking poppet valves (Franklin System of Steam Distribution) would reduce the overall cost. (No. 614 and sisters had the ever reliable Baker valve gear to control steam admission and exhaust to the cylinders.)

Ed Hauer and Alonzo Trumbull of the AMC started looking for ways to reduce costs. But they were also under pressure to reduce weight on these big boilered 4-8-4s. The Advisory Mechanical Committee wanted the best engine possible in order to reflect on the Committee. But sometimes the Committee failed to take into account considerations of the operating people about the restrictions that would have to be enforced on operating territory if the engine was too heavy. The operating departments wanted the new engines to operate all the way from Clifton Forge eastward, without change, across the Appalachians to Tidewater at Newport News, and that included some wooden trestles on the extension to Phoebus, Va. and the order for two J-3's turned out by Lima in 1942 had been too heavy. Engine weight had been 503,500 lbs. in contrast to 477,000 lbs. for J-3's 600-604. Preliminary estimates by Lima calculating engineer showed weight increases over what could be allowed in the operating areas intended. G. O. Beale, chief purchasing agent for C&O, had cautioned the Vice-President of Lima about the weight problem in his formal solicitation of a bid: 485,000 lbs. engine weight was, he stated, the "absolute maximum that will be permitted." Thus began careful calculations and weight comparisons of specialties by both Lima and the AMC to meet this requirement.

A decision against streamlining was one way to reduce weight and costs. Initially, the specifications for the new order (in December 1946) included "skylining, skirting, and nose." No pictures or drawings of these features exist, but the styling might be quite similar to the streamlining of rebuilt L-1 Hudsons Nos. 490-493 (No. 494 excepted) because specifications called for 610-614 to have "streamlined type headlight same as used on L-1 locomotive" and "cab arrangement similar to class L-1 with sloping front wall." Needless to say, streamlining was the first alteration made in the specs.

Another reduction was use of Baker valve gear instead of poppet valves. The consideration was weight, not cost, that made Hauer and Trumbull abandon poppet valves for the Greenbriers. (They retained them for the Hudsons that Baldwin was building at the same time.) Franklin Supply engineers calculated that for 610-614 to have the Franklin System of Steam Distribution (poppet valves) the boiler's maximum outside diameter would have to be reduced from 100 inches to 98 inches, a step the AMC was unwilling to take.

One feature that showed C&O had wanted nothing but the best was an advanced braking system; namely, a brake stand in the cab capable of electrically controlling the train's air brakes. Electro-pneumatic brake con-

I. C. C. Form No. 1.

MONTHLY LOCOMOTIVE INSPECTION AND REPAIR REPORT

Form L-135 CF 9-47
Made in U. S. A.

THE CHESAPEAKE AND OHIO RAILWAY COMPANY

Sometimes forgotten is that boilers — even those of Super Power — were washed out every month under federal inspection. This requirement put steam locomotives at a big disadvantage compared to diesels, because of time lost from service and expenses in the roundhouse. (After the fire was "dropped" at the ash pit, the hostler moved the engine to a roundhouse stall, where according to directive, for proper drainage, "all washout, arch, and water bar plugs must be removed" and "the spindles of all [three] gauge cocks and water glass cock shall be removed and cocks thoroughly cleaned of scale and sediment.") A monthly inspection form, 6 X 9 inches, "shall be placed under glass in a conspicuous place [above fireman's seat] . . . before the boiler inspected is put into service." Reproduced here is the last posted monthly inspection form, for C&O 2-6-6-6 No . 1604, completed at Hinton, W.Va., February 22, 1956. The government required the form to be notarized, as evidenced in the lower left corner.

trols on 610-614 were compatible with the order to Pullman-Standard late in 1946 for 284 light-weight cars to completely replace C&O's heavy-weight passenger equipment. For the feature to work, all cars in the train needed compatible wiring and piping. Each car would then be independent of the others in the train. Electricity permitted instantaneous brake application no matter how long the train, in contrast to the standard method of reducing air pressure in the "train line." Electrical control of the brakes made for smoother braking on fast passenger trains by safeguarding against wheel sliding and at the same time maintaining higher average retardation during brake applications. The electro-pneumatic feature would not be needed because the car order was eventu-

It took over ten years, from time of the T-1's in 1930, for the AMC to change the position of the steam dome on its engines from in front to behind the sand box. J-3a 610-614 had the steam dome inside the sand box! Greenbriers 605 and 606 as an economy move, probably, had the names of the Virginia statesmen painted on the sand box. On these two engines, built in 1942, there were six pipes that fed sand to the front of all drivers, the back of the rear driver, and to the rear axle of the trailing truck. (CSPR, COHS collection.)

Greenbrier 604 rests at Charlottesville engine terminal September 3, 1937, before alterations to headlight location and type of valve gear. Even though the Baker was heavier than the Walshaerts (seen here) it was more reliable. (Franklin Precision Reverse Gear actuated the valve gear.) Reasons for moving the headlight lower might be to save weight (no platform needed for cleaning) and to illuminate the rails more directly. (Ditch lights were unknown then.) (COHS collection.)

ally severely cut back due to delays in delivery and to needs to economize in passenger spending.

Controls on most locomotives were still the 8-ET type (engines 600-606 had the even earlier 6-ET). The 24-RL, which would become standard for diesel locomotive cabs later, was planned because its stand had the fittings built in for the optional transmitter necessary for operating the electro-pneumatic brakes. (The record on what actually developed with equipping 610-614 with the 24-RL vs. the 8-ET is unclear. Correspondence at Lima during early construction first indicated that the 8-ET supplied by New York Air Brake would replace the 24-RL. But later data suggests that the 24-RL was used, minus the electro-pneumatic feature.)

Simply amazing was the plan to spend so much money to produce a "state of the art" locomotive in the waning days of steam. Nothing, or so it seemed, was going to be sacrificed to equip the new Greenbriers with the latest features and best specialties. Enthusiasm was still the word in early 1947, as this writer recalls from being told about the latest order for Greenbriers from Lima Locomotive Works by locomotive engineer Vince Hiltz (later promoted to traveling fireman). Invited into the cab of a big T-1 2-10-4 waiting to leave the Russell yard, I learned these "super" engines would be delivered in June 1948. Among the innovations Mr. Hiltz described to the young steam fan (that I can recall today) were an aluminum cab and boiler jacket, a boiler of nickel steel, and, of course, electro-pneumatic brakes. If he mentioned a streamlined jacket (which had been planned initially for the five new 4-8-4s and 4-6-4s), I don't recall it; neither do I recall his mentioning Franklin poppet valves for the new Greenbriers in keeping with the poppet valves that had been applied to the Pacifics rebuilt to Hudsons in 1946-47 and that would be applied to the five new Hudsons coming from Baldwin Locomotive Works in

1948.

Mr. Hiltz did not bring up the fact that 610-614 would have General Steel Castings cast steel frames, probably because all ninety C&O 2-8-4s were equipped with them. But for passenger locomotives, these and the class L-1 rebuilt Hudsons plus the five new Hudsons building at Baldwin would be the first so equipped. Neither did Mr. Hiltz discuss the major dimensions of the Greenbriers, of course, for they were mostly identical in all three orders. There was, however, one significant change in dimensions, as Robert LeMassena pointed out, in his appraisal of the later Greenbriers as "superb." On 610-614 the combustion chamber ahead of the smokebox was made a foot longer; the tubes and flues, thus reduced a foot in length, were, at 20 ft. long, precisely the length needed for best absorption of heat. And enlarging the combustion chamber, in the words of Ralph Johnson, "increases the length of the path the gases must travel before entering the flues and thereby allows more time for combination of the combustibles and air."

However beneficial these alterations might have been over the long run, they were done in the short run to reduce weight, as official correspondence at Lima over specifications for the new engines make clear. The point was that the expanded space for the combustion chamber was "empty." The space thereby reduced was formerly occupied by the tubes and flues, which were heavy pipes. Furthermore, the flues were fitted inside with superheater tubes that permitted reheating of the "saturated" steam by feeding the steam back into, and out of, the larger flues. To reduce the area occupied by flues filled with superheater tubes, the diameter of the flues was increased from 3 1/2 to 4 inches, without an attendant increase in the size of the superheater tubing.

All twelve C&O 4-8-4s had tandem main rods, as described by author Brian Reed: "To transmit adequate-

At Russell's engine terminal in June 1955, J-3a's 610 and 614 have been coaled and are awaiting calls to service doing the same jobs as the K-4 Kanawhas. Idea of streamlining these five engines was given up, but some records still survive that suggest a look similar to streamlined L-1 Hudsons 490-493; e. g., specifications for "streamlined type headlight same as used on L-1 locomotives" and "cab arrangement to be similar to class L-1 with sloping front wall" and "skylining, skirting, and nose." (E. L. Huddleston, collection. COHS)

ly the 148,000-lb. piston thrust, tandem or articulated main and side rods were fitted to the main and third pair of drivers, and this reduced main crankpin loading by 50%." The Advisory Mechanical Committee had specified tandem main rods for all its two-cylinder designs since 1930. The fitting of the main rod to the side rods required a clevis joint on the main rod. Such a fitting had the advantage of making the brasses on the main rod wear more evenly. However, on engines 610-614 there was no need to worry about worn and hot brasses, because there were not any. Timken roller bearings were supplied to main and side rods and crank pins. (Other C&O Super Power had come equipped with roller bearings on the driving wheel axles, but none before had them fitted to the rods and eccentric crank.) There were more roller bearing surfaces on the 610-614 than on any other C&O Super Power locomotives.

As these construction details confirm, one reason C&O 614 (the one Greenbrier restored to excursion service) lasted so long and performed so well is its durability, achieved at an expenditure of so much money that clearly someone high up in C&O management had a real commitment to steam. That person, according to author Doug Nuckles, was Ed Hauer, the last remaining member of the Advisory Mechanical Committee, which — under the leadership of A. G. Trumbull — had originally designed the C&O 4-8-4s. Hauer served on the AMC as engineer of motive power, 1936-42; in 1942 he left to become assistant and then associate director of the Office of Defense Transportation in Washington. In July 1944 he returned to AMC as engineer of motive power and in 1947 he was named to succeed Alonzo Trumbull as CME of the AMC. The original design of the Greenbriers in 1935 and 1936 had been by Alonzo

Trumbull of the Erie dominated Advisory Mechanical committee. Trumbull shared with Hauer decisions about this order well into 1947.

It would be helpful if the men on the Advisory Mechanical Committee in 1936 were still around so we could ask them about an appliance that came as original equipment on all the C&O 4-8-4s, and practically all other AMC designed locomotives. These were over-fire air jets, otherwise known as "smoke consumers." Four of them could be seen on each side of the firebox running parallel with the fire bed a couple of feet or so above it. They had come in use on American railroads in response to the smoke abatement movement, characterized in most large American cities by ordinances that fined those responsible for emissions of black smoke from coal-fired boilers, whether stationary or moving. About all known of them specifically on C&O is that the Fireman's Manual of 1947 instructed in their use. The application of smoke consumers was taken for granted in the specs for engine 610-614, and they were never considered for abolishing even during the period when every feature, seemingly, of the new J-3's was under scrutiny for its weight or cost. It is difficult to find articles about smoke consumers in the trade press, and anecdotal evidence suggests that enginemen objected to their use principally because they were quite noisy. (They used steam jets to force air into the firebox above the fire. The forced air had to be heated; otherwise the advantage of more oxygen for combustion would be lost to the low temperature of the air from the atmosphere.) Eventually, dampening material was applied at the jet openings, in order to insulate the high-pitched sound. None of the 12 Greenbriers had these mufflers (which usually looked like tin soup cans), although 610-614 did have the four openings on each side staggered so that the air eddies would circulate more freely above the firebed.

Members of the Advisory Mechanical Committee might not be around to ask about the efficacy of over-fire air jets, but there is interesting evidence available about whether the devices actually improved heat transfer in the firebox, in addition to clearing up black smoke. Apparently they did not, if results from the Pennsylvania's Altoona stationary test plant are reliable. According to an article by E. C. Poultney in *Railway Gazette* (July 1948) and reported on in Chapelon's *La Locomotive a Vapeur*, PRR Duplex 4-4-4-4 No. 6175 was fired up and tested at speed in the plant : "The boiler [6175] was tested with and without secondary air admission through hollow stays in the firebox sides — a practice often used in the U.S.A. to minimize smoke emission — although the excess air introduced with the latter arrangement did not seem to have improved the combustion efficiency."

Aside from the apparently unproven smoke consumers, one's examination of a list of appliances for the new locomotives reveals a consistency that conforms with past selections of practical and proven specialties, such as Franklin high-speed trailer truck booster, Alco reverse gear (with long notched quadrant for ease in using lever to set valve cutoff), and Box-Pok driving wheels. Because many other locomotives on many other railroads used Alco reverse gear and Baker valve gear, there was little to set them apart. However, American railroads only selectively applied boosters and Box-Pok drivers.

Franklin Railway Supply Company's advertising in the 1947 *Locomotive Cyclopedia* is a good source of information on boosters. "The locomotive booster provides increased drawbar pull at starting... by applying power to otherwise idle trailing wheels. The increase can be effective to 30 or 35 mph and can be as much as 15,000 pounds at starting. The booster is a simple reciprocating double-acting steam engine which is self contained and is attached to the frame of the [trailer] truck through a 3-point suspension. It transmits its power to the [rear] axle through an idler gear which can be engaged or disengaged at will. It uses an air-operated control which is semi-automatic."

Box-Pok drivers were so special they call for some commentary. The ad for the Box-Pok in the 1944 *Locomotive Cyclopedia*, by its manufacturer General Steel Castings, tries to explain it: "As the name implies, it has box-section spokes instead of the usual solid type, is stronger ... and is also arranged for proper counter-balance [and cross-balance], reducing dynamic augment at rail..., thus permitting higher speeds with less wear and tear on the locomotive and track. "Ralph Johnson, chief engineer at Baldwin Locomotive Works, explained the advantages of the disc-type driving wheel with more precision: "A difficulty encountered in balancing driving

Official photo at Lima, Ohio, of tender of 610. Of interest are the electrical conduits, the "Tight-Lock" coupler, and what appear to be four separate hoses held in place by three chains and a spring loaded support for the steam heat line. Apparently the three hoses are the air-brake hose, the air communicating hose, and a conduit for the electro-pneumatic brakes which presumably 610-614 had. (CSPR, collection COHS)

wheels is the fact that there is often not sufficient room in the wheel to take the amount of lead required for proper balancing. ...There are now on the market several types of disc or box section wheels which not only are stronger than the spoke type but make it possible to reduce the diameter of the axle and crank pin hubs, hence lightening the upper part of the wheel and affording more space in the lower half for the lead in the counterbalance. This type of wheel also eliminates the trouble experienced from shrinkage cracks in spokes and provides equal pressure of the rim on the tire."

An exception, however, to the use of practical and proven specialties was selection of the Hancock exhaust-steam injector, which was an anomaly not only on the new Greenbriers but in C&O motive power practice generally. On road engines of the modern steam era there were, as required by law, two methods of getting water into the boiler, one by the "non-lifting" live-steam injector, a fairly simple device usually mounted under the cab on the engineer's side of the locomotive. (Evidence of such an injector seen from inside the cab was the big priming lever located on the floor of the cab below the engineer's seat box.) The second method could be another injector, installed on the left side. But usually a

ABOVE - J-3a 610, in heavy freight service, blasts into Russell yard (after stopping) in June 1955 with coal train off Coal River, Guyan Valley, or Big Sandy.
BELOW - Sister engine 614, twenty-five years later, gets ready for first run, from Baltimore, after rebuilding at Hagerstown Shops. Major difference in looks of the two engines is absence of Hancock exhaust-steam injector ("poor man's feedwater heater") on rebuilt 614. As seen on 610, the Hancock injector consisted of pump mounted on extension of frame in front of trailing truck, and connected to it, two large pipes curving upward under the running board. (610, E. L. Huddleston, collection COHS; 614, Thomas W. Dixon, Jr.)

feedwater heater was installed, more complicated and thus more expensive than an injector but guaranteed to be more efficient — at least when the engine was running — because it used exhaust steam from the cylinders to heat cold water from the tender before it was pumped into the boiler.

If one considers the "late steam" period beginning with the T-1 2-10-4 of 1930, he will find unbroken, on new C&O road and passenger locomotives, the use of the Worthington "open" type feedwater heater ("open" in that the exhaust steam mixes directly with the feedwater from the tender). Even on the C&O F-19 Pacifics rebuilt into Hudsons in 1946 and 47 the Worthington open type replaced the Elesco "closed" type supplied to the Pacifics new in 1926; likewise, the M-1 steam-turbo-electrics of 1947-48, Nos. 500-502, had Worthington open types hidden under the cowling. Needless to say, all preceding Greenbriers were so equipped. An exhaust-steam injector — whether a Sellers, an Elesco, or a Hancock — had never been applied to a prior C&O steam locomotive.

By some accounts, the exhaust-steam injector was a second-rate appliance, whether the Hancock, Elesco, or Sellers brand. They simply were not as efficient as a feedwater heater. Alfred W. Bruce, in his authoritative history of the steam locomotive, called the exhaust-steam injector the "poor man's feedwater heater," meaning that it tried to combine, not always dependably, the simple function of the live-steam injector with the more complicated exhaust-steam feedwater heater. (The Hancock started with live steam and switched over to exhaust steam while the engine was working.) Bruce's epithet suggests that the chief intent of selecting the appliance was to have the benefits of a feedwater heater without the expense of purchasing one.

Bruce not only labeled the exhaust-steam injector a "poor man's" heater, he tended to put it down while explaining its function: "In this device the required energy to enter the boiler was imparted to the feedwater in two stages: the first by the use of exhaust steam and the second by the use of live steam. It started as a relatively simple device, but soon became more and more complicated and is in little use today [1952]. " There's no "luxury" here! The three manufacturers of exhaust-steam injectors in the late-steam era were: William D. Sellers Co. (Sellers), the Superheater Co. (Elesco), and Locomotive Equipment Division of Manning, Maxwell, Moore, Inc. (Hancock). Interestingly, Bruce, a high official at American Locomotive Works, denigrated exhaust steam injectors, even while his own company supplied to Union Pacific's last Challengers and to all "Big Boys" Elesco exhaust-steam injectors. Union Pacific's reason for not using the Worthington open-type (model SA) on its big articulateds was the difficulty of finding space under the smoke box for the hot-water pump and its piping.

Whatever the reason for UP's using it, the Elesco gave some problems according to Union Pacific locomotive authority William Kratville: "The operation of the Elesco exhaust steam injector required a two-phase starting sequence, the first being priming the line, the second the admission valve. If the injector failed to pick up, which occurred frequently, the engineer's non-lifting injector [the Nathan] had to be cut in. It was often necessary to 'double gun' (using both injectors) if the Elesco was not doing the proper job. An operational situation affecting the exhaust-steam injector was that when the throttle position was changed it often broke the circula-

tion and the injector cut out forcing the 'double gunning'."

It is not known whether the Hancock exhaust-steam injector gave trouble on engines 610-614. Presumably it did not, for the appliances remained in use during the years 610-614 were in regular passenger service, plus the year or so all five were in freight service on the James River line and the additional year 610 and 614 worked on freights eastward out of Russell, Kentucky. Though not as efficient as a feedwater heater, they were competitive in cost, as Ralph Johnson pointed out in *The Steam Locomotive* (1944): "The maximum feed water heating ... obtained with pump [type] feed water heaters cannot be secured with exhaust steam injectors... but considering their lesser first cost and maintenance, they compete on all-over economic grounds."

Steam locomotive historian Phil Shuster warns not to jump to conclusions about the Hancock's performance on 610-614. There is nothing in the "files" to indicate they were ever troublesome or that employees did not know how to use them effectively. When all five Greenbriers went in storage in 1953, they were equipped with Hancocks, and when in 1955 610 and 614 were pulled off the storage line and returned to heavy freight service for over a year, they retained the Hancocks. (During this time they, of course, also retained their Nathan live-steam injectors, located under the cab on the right side. The only appliance that appeared removed before the 1955-56 firing up was the second turbo-generator, located on a bracket on right side above (Nos. 3 and 4 drivers.) Around the time in 1956 that 614 (numbered 611 to avoid renumbering of leased RF&P Northern 614) was put in storage outdoors at Russell, Kentucky, it lost its Hancock; this is known because photos of 611 (614) in storage at Russell show it removed. A major part of its equipment — including the turbo pump - was located on the fireman's side just ahead of the trailing truck on a large flat bracket which was an extension of the locomotive's cast steel underframe connections.

Luckily, No. 614, saved from scrapping, was stored until 1975, when it was cosmetically restored at C&O's Huntington Shops and put on display at the B&O Museum in Baltimore. Finally, in 1979 614 was taken to the Hagerstown (Western Maryland) shops and after restoration, costing a million and a half dollars, was "fired up" again. From the time in 1980 614 returned to "service" hauling the Chessie Safety Express and the Family Lines Express, through its tests as 614T on the ACE 3000 Project in 1985, to its last excursions in New Jersey, 614 has been equipped with a second Nathan live-steam, non-lifting injector, the redundant injector fulfilling federal requirements that there be a back-up means of supplying water to the boiler. Such injectors, being less complex in construction and operation than the exhaust-steam type, would presumably have a longer life in storage. No longer occupied by the Hancock apparatus, the small frame connected platform ahead of the trailing truck (left side) has since 1980 been occupied by a hose and reel assembly. A retrofit little affecting the original appearance of 614 is the Union Switch and Signal cab signal and speed control system installed by NJ Transit in 1998. The inductive pickup device is mounted just behind the leading truck.

A question remains: why did the Advisory Mechanical Committee (formed in the Van Sweringen heyday) choose the Hancock live-steam injector when customary practice, as revealed here, would have been to select a Worthington type SA feedwater heater, the best feedwater heater available? Saving money does not seem to be the reason, since C&O Hudsons 310-314, under construction at the same time, had the latest Worthington BL type open feedwater heater. The answer clearly is weight control. Tables of weight comparison in the specifications packet and letters of inquiry from the AMC to the Superheater Company (for the Elesco) and to Manning, Maxwell, and Moore in Cleveland (for the Hancock) bear out this conclusion. The dates of these inquiries indicate the decision as to type was made early-on in the ordering process. The AMC judged the Hancock the winner both for its much lighter weight than the Worthington and for its reliability over the Elesco.

This need for Lima and the AMC to take a second look at the costs and weights of the new order for J-3's could have come at a time when certain decisions about construction of the locomotives had already been made and could not be reversed. The boilers of nickel-steel would have already been fabricated and the aluminum cab already assembled, and roller bearing side and main rods already custom made for this order. But it would not have been too late to cancel the streamlined jacket that was planned for 610-614, nor would it have been too late to cancel appliances like feedwater heaters.

One other major alteration in the order was made as a result of the crisis over company revenues and over the desire of the C&O operating people to control where the locomotives could and could not be used. This was the use of circulators rather than syphons, Three kinds of support for the firebrick arch were used on a modern steam locomotive: arch tubes, Security Circulators, or Nicholson Thermic Syphons. Syphons generated more steam than circulators and circulators more than arch tubes. (Arch tubes and syphons could be used in combination.) The AMC's preference for syphons is apparent from the T-1 2-10-4 design of 1930 right through the orders for the NKP, PM, and C&O Berkshires. The original L-2 4-6-4s (300-307) had syphons; engines 310-314 (BLW 1948) had circulators, though provision had been made on the official diagrams for insertion of syphon data. The same procedure had been followed on engines 610-614. The "syphon" line on the diagram had been inked out. This suggests a last minute change, motivated by the demand from the

C&O's chief purchasing officer that 485,000 lbs, was "the absolute maximum that will be permitted" for 610-614. (The fact that 310-314 did not seem to have an equivalent weight problem suggests perhaps another reason for circulators on the new Hudsons.)

It seems certain that 614 will eventually end up in a museum — hopefully displayed indoors. When it does, observers will be able to peer between the driving wheels and see something they don't often see on steam engines; the single big cylindrical air reservoir, cast into the frame, sitting above the axles and the two rear-most driving boxes and filling practically all that hidden space, this tank replacing the multiple smaller reservoirs mounted below the running board on older locomotives. They will not be able to see the piping and pumps and condenser of the Hancock injector, but they will see the Box-Pok drivers, the 24-RL or 8-ET brake stand (if access to cab is provided) , and the Nathan injector (or injectors). In a word, the 610-614 class was "superb," an evaluation made by no other than Robert A. LeMassena.

Above all, they will not be able to see 614's stubborn traction, unless it is on one of those video tapes available of 614's passage with a long excursion up the Blue Ridge on the C&O in Virginia or up the Allegheny Front on the B&O in northern West Virginia in the early 1980's. On those steep grades 614 proved its mettle by seldom if ever slipping. A ratio calculated for every steam locomotive was its factor of adhesion. According to Ralph Johnson, Baldwin's CME, "a ratio of adhesion of 4 is generally used or 25 per cent of the adhesive weight. For electric and Diesel-electric locomotives, a ratio of 3.33 or 30 per cent is allowable as the torque on the wheels with a motor drive is more uniform than with a reciprocating steam engine." A steam locomotive with a factor of 4 or above should not slip on clean, dry rail. Any number below 4 (calculations are usually carried to the hundredth) increases the chances of slipping with a load, either in starting or at speed. The C&O J-3 4-8-4s had adhesion factors well over 4: for 600-604 it was 4.11; 605-606, 4.41; and 610-614, 4.29. For comparison, the F.A. on the RF&P Virginia statesmen 4-8-4s (613-622) of 1946, used for a time in freight service out of Russell in 1955-1956, was 4.24. The ex-Reading T-1 of 1945, 2101, in Chessie Safety Express excursion service on C&O in 1977-78, had 4.09, and the famous NYC Niagaras of 1946, 4.47. The most well known streamlined 4-8-4s, the N&W Class J, had F.A.s below 4 even before steam pressure was increased on all in the fall of 1945 to 300 psi. At 275 psi, the F. A. was 3.93 and from 1945 on, with 300 psi, it was 3.6. (Raising steam pressure of course increases the tractive effort; on the Class J there was no corresponding increase in adhesive weight, that is, weight on drivers.)

Pinpointing details of C&O Greenbriers 610-614 might seem insignificant in the larger scheme of things but not to those who recognize what a mechanical mar-

Greenbrier 614, which had been in storage at Russell for years, was rebuilt to serve as excursion replacement for ex-RDG 2101, which burned in accident in round-house at Stevens, Ky., in 1978. Now, 614 runs past Whitcomb Boulder east of Fayette Station in the New River Gorge with fall foliage excursion sponsored by the Huntington Chapter, NRHS, in 1980. In regular service, 614 and her sisters never ran over the New River Subdivision between Hinton and Handley. (Wayne W. Carman, COHS collection.)

vel the steam locomotive really was. They find delight in a prime mover that has its power and functions clearly in view, unlike those of a jet aircraft engine or a space rocket engine where the operator punches in a code for starting the action rather than releasing a lever or opening a valve or reading a gauge and where observers have to view the take-off or lift-off from a considerable distance. Following several years of successful excursions based

in New Jersey, Ross Rowland, owner of 614, sold it to Andrew J. Muller of the Reading and Northern Railroad in northeastern Pennsylvania. No. 614 joined there ex-Reading T-1 Northern No. 2102 and ex-Gulf, Mobile, and Ohio 4-6-2 No. 425 on the R&N's steam roster.

LOCOMOTIVE EQUIPMENT.
CHESAPEAKE DISTRICT.

Class	TYPE	Symbol	Series	Owned
A-16	Atlantic	4-4-2	275-293	13
B-1	Santa Fe	2-10-2	2950-2959	10
B-2	Santa Fe	2-10-2	2000-2005	5
B-3	Santa Fe	2-10-2	4000-4001	2
C-3	6-Wheel Switch	0-6-0	15	1
C-6	6-Wheel Switch	0-6-0	125-129	3
C-7	6-Wheel Switch	0-6-0	25-33	7
C-8	6-Wheel Switch—Fireless	0-6-0	35-37	3
C-12	10-Wheel Switch	0-10-0	130-144	15
C-14	8-Wheel Switch	0-8-0	60-79	20
C-15	8-Wheel Switch	0-8-0	110-124	15
C-16	8-Wheel Switch	0-8-0	175-284	110
F-11	10-Wheel Passenger	4-6-0	377-378	2
F-12	10-Wheel Passenger	4-6-0	405-409	4
F-13	10-Wheel Passenger	4-6-0	89-91	2
F-15	Pacific	4-6-2	430-456	25
F-16	Pacific	4-6-2	460-467	8
F-17	Pacific	4-6-2	470-475	6
F-18	Pacific	4-6-2	480-485	6
F-20	Pacific	4-6-2	486-489	4
G-3	Consolidation	2-8-0	150-159	8
G-4	Consolidation	2-8-0	161-169	4
G-5	Consolidation	2-8-0	700-708	8
G-7	Consolidation	2-8-0	790-947	18
G-7-S	Consolidation	2-8-0	960-1001	37
G-8	Consolidation	2-8-0	710-711	2
G-9	Consolidation	2-8-0	1010-1059	48
G-15	Consolidation	2-8-0	1085	1
H-3	Mallet	2-6-6-2	1275-1297	15
H-4	Mallet	2-6-6-2	1376-1473	73
H-5	Mallet	2-6-6-2	1520-1539	20
H-6	Mallet	2-6-6-2	1300-1324 / 1475-1519	70
H-7	Chesapeake	2-8-8-2	1540-1589	11
H-8	Alleghany	2-6-6-6	1600-1659	60
J-1	Mountain	4-8-2	540-542	3
J-2	Mountain	4-8-2	543-549	7
J-3	Greenbrier	4-8-4	600-606 / 610-614	7 / 5
K-1	Mikado	2-8-2	1089-1155	64
K-2	Mikado	2-8-2	1160-1209	50
K-3	Mikado	2-8-2	1210-1259 / 2300-2349	50 / 50
K-4	Kanawha	2-8-4	2700-2789	90
L-1	Hudson	4-6-4	490-494	5
L-2	Hudson	4-6-4	300-307 / 310-314	8 / 5
M-1	Turbo-Electric	4-8-4-8-4	500-502	3
T-1	Texas	2-10-4	3000-3039	40
	Grand Total			1023

LOCOMOTIVE EQUIPMENT—OCTOBER 1947
PERE MARQUETTE DISTRICT

DESCRIPTION		Wheel Arrangements	Series of Numbers	Total No. in Service
FREIGHT TYPE				
C-2	Consolidation	2-8-0	276-375	6
C-2	Consolidation	2-8-0	501-509	5
C	Consolidation	2-8-0	601-625	25
SC	Consolidation	2-8-0	901-925	23
MK	Mikado	2-8-2	1004-1008	3
MK-1	Mikado	2-8-2	1011-1040	30
MK-2	Mikado	2-8-2	1041-1050	10
MK-6	Mikado	2-8-2	1095-1099	5
SF	Santa Fe	2-10-2	1101-1115	15
SF-6	Santa Fe	2-10-2	1198-1199	2
N	Berkshire	2-8-4	1201-1215	15
N-1	Berkshire	2-8-4	1216-1227	12
N-2	Berkshire	2-8-4	1228-1239	12
	Total Freight			163
PASSENGER TYPE				
SP	Pacific	4-6-2	707	1
SP-3	Pacific	4-6-2	711-722	12
SP-2	Pacific	4-6-2	725-729	5
DEP-1	Diesel Electric	A1A-A1A	101-102	2
DEP-2	Diesel Electric	A1A-A1A	103-108	6
	Total Passenger			26
SWITCHING TYPE				
C-16	8-Wheel	0-8-0	240-254	15
S-2	6-Wheel	0-6-0	467-483	5
S-1	8-Wheel	0-8-0	1300-1339	40
S-	8-Wheel	0-8-0	1401-1410	10
DES-1	Diesel Electric	B-B	10	1
DES-1A	Diesel Electric	B-B	11	1
DES-2	Diesel Electric	B-B	51-54	4
DES-3	Diesel Electric	B-B	55-64	10
DES-4	Diesel Electric	B-B	20-22	3
	Total Switching			89
	Total All Classes			278

Reprinting this roster from the 1948 official C&O "station book" (on sale by the C&O Historical Society) discloses the place of Super power in the "family" of C&O and Pere Marquette locomotives at the end of new steam locomotive acquisitions by C&O. Little did the employee who prepared and double-checked this roster know that it was the "last hurrah" for Super Power steam or indeed for any steam on the C&O. Another surprise for him would be that Pere Marquette would run no locomotives under steam after December, 1951. Yet another surprise would involve H-6 Mallets 1300-1324. Here he was given the wrong figure. The original H-2 Mallets of 1911 (Nos. 1302-1324) had gone off the roster entirely by 1935. The twenty-five H-5 Mallets ordered from Baldwin in 1948 were given this empty numbering slot, a classification reserved for Mallets and simple articulateds . The problem was that an economic crisis on the combined C&O and PM was coming to a head. Though 1948 had been the best year for total operating revenue in the company's history, a crisis was in the making because of declining passenger revenue, overspending on Chairman Robert R. Young's various programs, and strikes and protracted short work weeks by the United Mine Workers of America, led by firebrand John L. Lewis. Thus, the purchase of twenty-five brand new Mallets for coal field service could be put off, and so only engines 1300-1309 went into service at Peach Creek starting July 1949.

Another oddity about the roster is that though the PM-C&O merger had been completed by the publication date of the "station book" the classification system by which the PM locomotives diesel and steam — would be absorbed into the C&O roster had not been worked out. Thus, there is duplication of engine numbering. The only confusing case of this arises from the purchase in 1930 of fifteen 0-8-0 switchers for PM. T.W. Dixon and Art Million in their *Pere Marquette Power* give the particulars: by 1930 the Advisory Mechanical Committee of the Van Sweringen roads had "prepared a new standard design 0-8-0, which — except for the addition of a few modern appliances — followed very closely the USRA concept. Eighty engines were ordered to this standard from Alco in 1930 — the C&O received 65 and the PM got the other 15. They were given class C-16 on both railroads (in the C&O's classification series). The PM's engines received road numbers 240 through 254 (following the C&O's, which were numbered 175-239), completely outside the normal assignment of road numbers on the PM." These were the last new switchers that PM ever received. Then in 1942-43 the AMC, adhering to the same design, authorized construction of 15 new C-16's for C&O, giving them the same numbers as the PM C-16's, 240-255. To top this off, C&O sold its 15 C-16's in this number slot to the Virginian Railway in 1950, which itself retained the same numbers! The PM C-16's were finally renumbered for the C&O roster (380-394) before being scrapped in 1953-54.

There are other anomalies in the last roster, like the appearance that C&O liked the Santa Fe (2-10-4) type. It might seem C&O had this preference because C&O had received 40 2-10-4's in 1930, and the 2-10-4 type evolved from the 2-10-2 (and in turn from the 2-10-0 type). But C&O's 2-10-2's were all second hand and were never used in mountain territory service. Ten 2-10-2's (classed B-1) came to the C&O with Hocking Valley Ry. merger of 1930 (2950-2959, used mostly on freights into Potomac Yard). These were originally built for the Lehigh Valley in 1917. In 1945, a big increase in westbound coal traffic following the end of the War, prompted C&O to lease seven 2-10-2's to supplement C&O's heavy 2-8-2's and 2-8-4's, mostly on Huntington and Big Sandy Division coal drags. The five engines of the B-2 class were built for the Chicago and Eastern Illinois in 1918. The two B-3's (4000-4001) originally had been built for the Wabash Railroad in 1917 and had gone to the C&EI in 1942 and to the C&O in 1945. Further, C&O inherited 15 Santa Fe's (class B-4, 1918) from the PM merger. These Santa Fe's were scrapped in January, 1952, a month after the PM's complete dieselization.

Chapter 6

Super Power Hudsons

'Within the narrow Kanawha Valley, where trains come and go at all hours, Charleston is unusually train conscious. Particular attention is paid those on the Chesapeake and Ohio road on the south side of the river... People check the trains in and out almost automatically, identifying them by name or number — "The George Washington's four minutes late tonight.' or `Number Three [the F.F.V] is right on the dot."
— West Virginia: *A Guide to the Mountain State* (1941)

Looking across the river from downtown Charleston to the stately C&O station, practically on the river bank, one could see a fine display of big passenger power, especially on those running in the daytime – Nos. 3 and 6 and the morning mail-express 104. (Locals too had interesting power, but just not as big.) First, for the mainliners were the classic "Georgian" styled heavy Pacifics of the 1920s and 1930s with "Flying Pumps" and star studded cylinder heads and emblem adorned feed-water heaters. Then, shortly after entry of the United States into World War II, the world's heaviest Hudsons nos.300-307– were out shopped by Baldwin Locomotive Works (designated class L-2) Then came five Hudsons (class L-1) rebuilt from heavy Pacifics in 1946-47 (all but one streamlined), and finally in 1948 came five more L-2 series Hudsons from Baldwin equipped with the Franklin System of Steam Distribution (poppet valves.). Almost

without warning early in 1952 these modern steam engines were replaced on the main line by thirty General Motors E8 twin-motored passenger diesels.

Despite its not being widely popular as a type, the Hudson, named for the river that the 4-6-4 type was initially most closely associated with, became probably the most well known type of steam locomotive among the general public because of the publicity given 4-6-4s built by American Locomotive company between 1927 and 1938 for the New York Central Railroad. The source of this publicity was the "tinplate" models produced by Lionel and American Flyer during the 1930s and 1940s. The streamlined version was especially popular, matching well the Art Deco tastes of the time. Henry Dreyfuss had completely redesigned the "Twentieth Century Limited" from streamlined Hudson to observation car, and its sixteen hour schedule from New York to Chicago gave the train world-wide fame. New York Central eventually owned (including subsidiary B&A) 275 Hudsons! Due to very restrictive clearances they were far from the being the biggest of the total of 418 Hudsons built in America. S. Kip Farrington, opinionated railfan author, believed the NYC Hudsons were overrated. He claimed that "they [the NYC] had many more troubles with them than were ever made public." (Farrington rode on many of them, including one run – maximum speed of 80 – across New York in 1935 with 13 cars.)

Across the Kanawha River from downtown Charleston, April 25, 1948, no3, the "F.F.V.", pauses as fireman takes water, engineer inspects stoker, and passengers board at the two-story station. (August A. Thieme, Jr.)

ABOVE - At South Portsmouth, across river from Portsmouth, Ohio, No. 6 drifts into station in 1948. In the picture is a "cut-in-two" school bus operated under license for passengers from Ohio boarding the train. Two tone paint and logo on bus door suggests blue and yellow paint scheme, but that scheme would not be adopted for at least another year! (Thomas D. Dressler collection.)

BELOW - A seldom pictured locale was the passenger line through Ashland. L-2 302, on No. 3, saving departed Ashland depot, crosses former tracks of the Ashland Coal and Iron Ry. at Ashland Jct., February 1948. Former AC&I shops are at left. (E. L. Huddleston, collection. COHS).

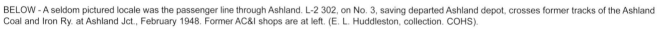

Tom Dixon, of C&O Historical Society, reports that C&O, with a total of 18 Hudsons, was the fourth largest owner of Hudsons. Thus, not many Hudsons were built overall. Probably railroads wanted bigger engines able to haul both freight and passenger trains. The Hudson was usually viewed as lacking high enough tractive effort for mainline freight service. Hence the proliferation of 4-8-4s from 1926 on, which many railroads assigned to both freight and passenger trains. Naturally, these roads had "level land" type of topography; for a 4-8-4 would have been out of place in mountain area freight service.

C & O – with both mountain and level topography – believed in separating freight and passenger pullers, even though many freight engines were equipped with the steam heat valves and air communicating lines necessary for passenger train operation. C&O's rationale against dual freight-passenger locomotives was based on C&O's attempt to match type of locomotive with demands of service. The weight of a passenger train was far less than the weight of a freight train. And far more power was needed to haul a train whether passenger or freight – up a grade than over level track. The differentiation between mountain and level-land service made some sense. Passenger trains demanded speed more than power. Sixteen cars was usually the maximum (because of passenger platform length). Freights were seldom run on major railroads unless car count (loads and empties) exceeded 50 cars. Jim Boyd in *American Freight Train* notes train length of between 80 to 120 cars (varying daily) on a 1970's Illinois Central scheduled freight, and a Nickel Plate yard clerk at Bellevue, Ohio, recalled that in 1956 a fast freight from Buffalo arrived with "60 cars, a maximum of 3600 tons, so the Berkshires could get it over the road at top speed." Thus freights required more power for the "long haul." As for mountain service, C&O around 1911 started differentiating between level land hauled by Consolidation type and mountain (Mallet type) freight service. Prior to 1911 Consolidations (2-8-0) had held sway system wide for

both level land and mountain freight service. Passenger power up until 1911 had no differentiation, for Ten-Wheelers and Pacifics held sway system wide. But in 1911 C&O originated a new passenger type for mountain service, by taking a Mikado freight engine design and putting a 4-wheel leading truck under it to create a 4-8-2, aptly named the "Mountain" type. From 1911 on C&O did differentiate motive power by type of service and topography.

The first Hudsons on C&O were designed for C&O's passenger routes – from Cincinnati to Hinton and from Hinton to Detroit – that saw the fastest running over the whole system and the longest runs. These were the routes of the "George Washington," the "F. F. V.," and the "Sportsman." The relatively low grade passenger routes for the same trains from Charlottesville to Washington and from Charlottesville to Newport News – Norfolk were out of the new class L-2's range because of clearance and weight restrictions. C&O waited until 1941 to buy its Hudsons because from 1914 onward it had been buying heavy Pacifics that were on a par of performance with the PRR's famed K-4 Pacifics (which oddly enough lacked stokers). The C&O heavy Pacifics were classics of their kind, especially the F-19 series of five built 1926. Their performance over the Cincinnati Division, C&O's "race track," proved their reliability and their ability to perform at speeds well over 70 mph for long distances. The AMC designed the L-2s (built by Baldwin) to haul 15 cars "at 90 miles an hour on straight level track." (The speedometer for these engines went to 100 mph.)

Five more Hudsons arrived in 1948, classed L-2a and identical to the L-2's except for poppet valves. The "Franklin System of Steam Distribution" enabled the Hudsons to make even higher speeds. Poppet valves, utilizing automotive-type valves instead of a single "back and forth sliding valve, considerably reduced back pressure within the main cylinders. The power within the power stroke was thereby considerably enhanced. So it is no surprise that the L-2a could go faster than the original L-2 class with its conventional Baker-type valve gear

No. 6 parallels U.S. 23 west of Greenup, Ky., with throttle halfway open, 1951. Vertical piping under cab includes injector feed and booster exhaust pipe. (E. L. Huddleston, collection COHS)

working on a single sliding spool valve. Tom Dixon, as President of the C&O Historical Society, interviewed Homer Fuller, retired Locomotive Inspector, at his Ironton, Ohio, home in the late 1970s. Mr. Fuller, one of two men on the entire system holding this job, stated that he could well remember riding the L-2a's on the Cincinnati Division at over a hundred miles per hour hauling the "George Washington." Mr. Fuller had a calm and analytical mind set. He was not prone to bragging. Thus we can be sure the L2's and L-2a's (300-307 and 310-314) were both powerful and fast.

Critical to maintaining high speeds over comparatively long distances was the application to the Hudsons of the most up-to-date engineering principles to stabilize the running gear, especially lateral motion of the locomotive. To prevent "nosing" or "hunting" of the front end, special attention was given to the leading and trailing trucks. The "initial and constant lateral resistance of the engine truck is thirty percent and ten percent for the trailing truck", the latter stabilized by the "usual" rockers on rear of the truck casting and by a Timken three-roller lateral motion device placed over the journal boxes of the front trailer wheels.

High drivers, highest on any C&O locomotive, also made possible high speeds. The Advisory Mechanical Committee was apparently convinced that high drivers were necessary for high speeds (although on some roads 84 inches rather than 78 were considered high.) By 1941 it was clear that increased speed was not dependent on increased driver diameter if the designers were willing to accept increased piston speeds, which more stable lubricating oils were permitting. The AMC,

however, did not want faster piston speeds. The 78-inch drivers on the L-2 and L-2a, and the relatively short piston stroke (30"), reduced piston speed considerably under the 32-inch stroke and 70" diameter of the N&W Class J 4-8-4, its fastest passenger engine. The Committee probably picked higher drivers and shorter strokes in order to reduce cylinder back pressure (always a problem at high speeds) and dynamic augment, a pounding on the rails that increased in severity with the length of stroke. (For comparison, C&O's mountain passenger engines, class J-3 4-8-4, stroke was also 30"; for the class K-4 2-8-4 "low land" freight engine, stroke was 34 inches. Although shorter strokes on modem passenger power could be found — e.g., the NYC Hudson's 29" — 30" was about standard.)

High speed was also made easier by all axles of engine and tender having double roller type bearings supplied by Timken of Canton, Ohio. Though at their best speeding along on "straight, level track," no one could say the C&O class L-2 Hudsons lacked starting power-that is, rapid acceleration from standing. "Chessie's" class L-2 and L-2a 4-6-4s, all built by Baldwin, were the heaviest of all in total engine weight and weight on drivers, and they exerted the highest total starting tractive effort of any ever built. (The C&NW streamlined Class E-4 and DL&W Class 1151-1155, built respectively by American in 1938 and 1937, exerted slightly more tractive effort, but neither was equipped with a booster.) Giving these big Hudsons their great power was a boiler and firebox very similar to the combinations used on the "Van Sweringen" Berkshires of the Nickel Plate, Pere Marquette, W&LE and Virginian. As Phil Shuster wrote in

Though this official photo of No. 6 at Catlettsburg is undated, it can be no later than 1943, the year C&O steamers were equipped with large illuminated number plates up front. It can be no earlier than 1942, for defense plant across the Ohio was a wartime project. (CSPR, collection. COHS)

Having gone less than a mile from a stop at the Russell depot, Hudson 304 accelerates No. 6 east along the banks of the Ohio in summer, 1948. (E. L. Huddleston, collection. COHS).

C&O Power: "In designing these 4-6-4s, the railway had used the same size firebox as on the NKP and PM 2-8-4s (and later in their own K-4s) and a boiler nearly the same size (except shortened by one foot over the tube sheets. The smokebox was lengthened by some eight inches, resulting in an overall boiler length only four inches shorter than the 2-8-4 boiler." If one gauges the size of the boiler based on its maximum outside diameter, the L-2 Hudsons were two inches less than the 2-8-4 Van Sweringen Berkshires all of which were 98 inches. (The Hudsons were thus 96", the K-4 2-8-4 98", and the C&O J-3 4-8-4 100".)

On the NKP, PM, and C&O 2-8-4's Nicholson Thermic Syphons,

aided by arch tubes, supported the brick arch in the firebox. It was logical for the C&O L-2 Hudsons to have syphons also because the grate area was identical to the 2-8-4's, all having syphons. It was also the policy of the AMC to supply all its road engines with syphons. And this policy was consistently applied to C&O Hudsons 300-307. However, in a last minute change in specifications, the AMC called for Security Circulators for Nos. 310-314. This caused a slight lowering in total heating surface for the 1948 L-2's. (Circulators, unlike arch tubes and Syphons, were four in number and mounted sideways in the firebox.) The last minute change might have been due to a personal preference of Ed Hauer, who succeeded Alonzo Trumbull as the AMC's CME upon Trumbull's retirement in 1947.

Their almost identical dimensions provided an overall length of engine and tender (from pulling face of front coupler to the rear) that was close, 104'-8" for the Hudson and 105'-2" for the Berkshire (or Kanawha, as known on C&O). Accounting for the half foot difference was the shorter cab on the Hudsons, which normally had no one riding on the seatbox behind the fireman. Because of the identical grate area under the firebox, the Delta trailing trucks were essentially same size and design, although the diameter of the wheels on the rear trailing axle of the L-2 and K-4 differed. Both trailing trucks of the two types were equipped with Franklin boosters powering (when cut in) the rear trailing axle, up to 35 mph on the L-2 and 13 mph on the K-4.

Except for roller bearings on all axles of the L-2 Hudsons and the K-4 Kanawhas, the tenders were practically identical. In adopting a tender for the L-2 in 1941, the designers for the Advisory Mechanical Committee chose one of sufficient capacity (thirty tons and 21,000 gallons) for both passenger and freight service. Less than two years after Baldwin built the L-2s, the first of forty K-4s arrived from American with essentially the same tenders. They were alike in having the engine for the Standard "MB" stoker mounted behind a panel in the front of the tender on left side, and the almost uniform distance from rail to cab deck level on both permitted easy interchange between the two types. With the L-2 and K-4 being nearly equal in length and height (from rail to stack and from rail to centerline of boiler) it's hardly surprising the two types could be confused when viewed in profile. The confusion could occur only between the K-4 and 1942 L-2's, not between the K-4 and L-2a of 1948, for the L-2a (310-314) had a single housing for the

steam dome and sandbox, instead of two distinct domes, as on the L-2 and K-4. The L-2, L-2a, and K-4 had the same design for the turret cover ahead of the cab, for the safety valves, Nathan low-water alarm device, Wilson centrifugal blow-off muffler, Pyle-National turbo generator, and bell (though newer models of both classes had bells mounted in fixed position without yokes).

C&O Super Power designs all had big sand domes, with squared off corners. The Advisory Mechanical Committee wanted sand at the front of every driver, plus sand for backing up at the rear of main driver, plus sand for the booster. This made for five pipes on each side for the 4-6-4s and six for the 2-8-4s. (The class L-2a of 1948 had sand and steam domes on one long casting.) Both L-2 and L-2a had sand domes cut down in size from the freight designs on the T-1 and K-4, apparently because of clearance problems posed by umbrella type station platform sheds. Once, a big T-1 2-10-4 was pressed into passenger service by an emergency near Russell, Kentucky. The T-1 was dispatched to bring the train, the "George Washington," into Ashland. Pulling into the station, the T-1's sand domes severely damaged two umbrella sheds before the engine could be stopped.

Breakdowns of passenger power on the road could not be tolerated because delays annoyed the traveling public. At the heart of mechanical dependability was lubrication. And a modern passenger locomotive, with numerous points of friction and fast moving parts,

Cincinnati Union Terminal, from about 1945 to 1955, was one of the chief railroad centers in the U.S. for engine picture collectors like R. J. Foster (who took most of these Hudson photos. One can study each photo for variants in detail, like an apparent substitution of a K-4 (2-8-4) tender for 303's original roller bearing equipped tender. (They were interchangeable.) Or we can note that only 301 (right side directly below second main air reservoir)) has been retrofitted with a small auxiliary air reservoir, required by ICC, to reverse locomotive (and thus stop it) in event of emergency. As distractions, we can also note that behind 303 is a NYC Hudson, and behind 311 is C&O list Pacific F-15 No. 431. (all, Joe Schmitz collection.)

C&O # 303

C&O # 301

C&O # 300

C&O # 311

C&O # 312

Inside cab of a poppet valve L-2a, No. 313 shows stoker, which feeds onto distribution table inside butterfly type fire door, and on either side, grate shaker attachments. On fireman's side are globe valves for distributing coal from stoker. Highest gauge in front of fireman is steam seat gauge. On engineer's side lever for reversing locomotive is in front of window, and lever for priming injector is next to cab seat. The turret panel, at top, controls saturated steam to appliances, including handles for steam seat access, stoker engine, main turret control, dynamo, water glass opening, and injector. (Official BLW photo, COHS collection.)

needed mechanical lubricators, one on each side, driven by the movement of the combination lever. The Nathan lubricator on the right side fed valve oil mainly to the cylinders, cylinder guides, feedwater heater hot water pump, air pumps, and stoker engine. Oiling the main cylinders and the steam chest was critical. Oil could not be fed by simple pumping action inside the chest and cylinders because of high pressures inside. Thus a steam atomizer, getting its steam supply from the line to the air pumps, sprayed oil inside. The lubricator on the left side fed engine oil to such touching surfaces as the radial buffer, the driving box pedestals, front and back furnace bearers, and "trailing truck radius bar fulcrum." These are by no means all the routes for oil lines emanating from the force-feed lubricators. But the ones listed do impress one with the complexity of lubricating the moving machine. Fittings designed for Alemite soft and hard grease as lubrication required air powered "grease

guns." These fittings on the class L-2 were located on the running gear: the main rods, side rods (back end), crank pins, crosshead wrist pin, and eccentric rods (back end).

The Baker valve gear assembly was equipped with needle bearings and needed lubrication only every few thousand miles with light grease. Thorough lubrication of a big steam locomotive is a subject taken for granted. Not taken for granted is the operation of the booster with which all L-2 and L-2as were equipped. Most people observing a steam locomotive have to search to find the booster. Just a small part of the two-cylinder engine driving the rear trailing axle shows behind the Delta truck casting. The only other sure indicator of a booster engine is a rather thick pipe extending from the front end of the locomotive to the space under the cab (on both sides) where ball joint connection is made to a vertical, hinged extension attached at the bottom to the booster engine. The exhaust pipe and extension on the right side is uninsulated, while the live steam pipe on the left is wrapped with insulation. At the front end the pipes on both sides disappear into the smokebox. The booster exhaust is vented through a slot in the smoke stack. The booster engine utilizes the 128,500 pounds of weight carried by the trailer truck as adhesion to add 12,600 pounds (L-2) and 14,000 pounds (L-2a) to the starting tractive effort when in operation, up to 35 mph. This extra burst of power enabled the Hudsons to resume "passenger train speeds in the shortest possible time."

To see a booster actually "cut in" on a big L-2 or L-2a was a sight not to be forgotten. At Ashland, Ky., one could regularly see this happen. At the same time he could witness Alemite lubrication of the locomotive while the train was at the station. (Ten minutes could be allotted for this activity while a switcher was adding cars to the rear of the train.) The lubrication and other support activity was necessary to enable one locomotive to take the train over three main line sub-divisions totaling 310 miles between Cincinnati and Hinton (A similar scene was enacted at Parsons Yard on the mainline for the L-2 hauling the "Sportsman" between Hinton and Detroit, which comprised the longest run for any passenger engine on the C&O.). Through notes while witnessing the servicing, the writer can take the reader down memory lane to 1948 at Ashland to observe servicing of the eastbound `George Washington': "Up the station platform from where the family car was parked, we could see a gang of men awaiting No.2's arrival. When the L-2

stopped, its three open pops drowning out all other noise, one of the men would climb to the cab and, with a long steel bar stored in the tender for that purpose, would start rocking the grate levers. One could see the redhot coals falling from the grates in the space between the firebox and the ash pan. Another man would have climbed onto the tender, opened the cover with a loud slam, and pulled the stand pipe chute over with a long hook. It would take several minutes to fill the tank with water. Another man, using a steam hose with a long nozzle and wearing goggles, would spray steam on the sloping surface of the ash pan to force the ashes out the bottom of the opened ash pan. The most interesting and noisy operation involved a man (one on each side) with a polished hand grease gun operated by air. The big gun, attached to an air hose, was heavy, and he would attach it carefully to the fittings, including the crank pins, crosshead wrist pins, both main rod connections, and back ends of the eccentric rods. Finally, one could hear from the cab the two weak but distinct whistles that indicated highball. (The conductor would give a hand signal to the baggage man who in turn pulled the air communicating cord , which sounded the whistle in the cab.) The engineer would turn on the booster, and it would idle with a rapid but rather indistinct exhaust (which vented through a slot in the stack). Then he pulled the throttle out as far it would go and quickly pushed it back in about half way. There was no immediate response, but finally the big wheels slowly started revolving. Soon there was was a sharp bark from the exhaust followed by another,

Prominent on this poppet valve L-2a Hudson at Huntington in 1949 are (1) long pipe from feedwater heater to hot water pump; (2) double steam admission to the horizontally mounted poppet valves; (3) drive shaft (with two universal joints) for actuating rotary cam shafts; (4) support (attached to frame) for drive shaft, reverser, and for mechanical lubricator and dynamo-at rear. (COHS collection.)

Nine heavy-weight cars were about standard for No. 6 out of Cincinnati. Thus in leaving Russell in April 1948 L-2 307 could apparently keep on the "time card" without cutting in the booster. (There is no photographic evidence of booster exhaust.) The 4-6-4 has accelerated about 800 ft. from its station stop and has seven minutes to cover the 4.7 miles to its stop in Ashland. (E. L. Huddleston, COHS collection.)

and then by another, each in more rapid succession, and the great bulk of the engine slowly moved forward. The slow, loud, sharp exhaust from the stack was counterpointed by the low, steady but rapid staccato exhaust from the booster. The deep resonant whistle blew a short, even blast for each crossing through the city, and the "George" would be on its way eastward into the night."

SUPER POWER LUBRICATION
Eugene L. Huddleston

People associate oil and grease with mess and with stubborn permanence. (Oil does not dry up). Lubricatus, the Latin root, means "smooth and slippery," a phrase with negative connotations. The unfavorable connotations of the word might explain why a more dignified term was coined in 1966 in London. Tribology — meaning "the science and technology of friction, wear, and lubrication — deals with the "phenomena occurring between interacting surfaces in relative motion." These citations from the *Encyclopedia of Tribology* (1990) add dignity to the concept, and the existence of a lengthy history of tribology, sanctioned by the ASME and published in 1979, attests to the importance of lubrication in keeping a steam locomotive running.

Friction is the resistance to motion of two moving surfaces that touch. Lubrication reduces friction between rubbing surfaces and reduces the heat that friction produces. (True, not every rubbing surface on a steam locomotive needed lubrication-brake shoes rubbing tire surfaces did not. Otherwise, even the expansion shoes connecting firebox with frame and the buffer plates between locomotive and tender did.) Lubrication alone will not eliminate wear. Wear being so heavy and so constant on a steamer, adjustment was an integral and regular part of locomotive operation. For an idea how C&O Super Power locomotives were lubricated, read the introduction to "Lubrication" in either the 1944 or 1947 *Locomotive Cyclopedia*. There one learns that grease (in hard and soft form) and oil-differentiated by viscosity into engine oil and valve oil-lubricated some 200 points on large locomotives. (Designer Andre Chapelon says up to 300 points.)

For most Super Power one can discount the hydrostatic mode as old fashioned. Hydrostatic lubricators, usually located on the boiler backhead in the cab, used steam pressure from the turret just ahead of the cab to supply oil to valves, etc., under pressure. One disadvantage was the device's being so far from the front of the locomotive, where most lubrication was needed. True, hydrostatic lubricators could be used on Super Power for special jobs. For example, on C&O's first order of class J-3 4-8-4s, a three-pint hydrostatic lubricator fed oil to the booster and stoker engines. Both these specialties, powered by double-acting miniature steam engines, used "splash" lubrication (like automobiles) for the enclosed drive rods, cranks, etc., but had to have oil for operation (or in idling).

The only disadvantage to the automatic lubricators, found on all C&O Super Power, was an inability to pump oil while the locomotive was immobile. These lubricators, plainly in sight, were mounted right above the combination lever, usually on both sides. Some engines — e.g. the T-1's initially — had a lubricator on only the right side; however, there could be two mechanical lubricators on the right side and one on the left. (Usually these were on passenger engines.) In every case, the lubricator was driven by an arm extending upward from the combination lever (or in the case of two, two arms in tandem). The arm converted reciprocating motion to rotary motion in one direction, operating a valveless pump on the lubricator. The reservoir and pump were built as one compact unit and made quite a pleasing addition to the detail on the locomotive. However, one must confess that a scale modeler would find it possible only in "O" gauge or larger to model it as a detail of the running gear. Mechanical lubricators had varying capacities; the C&O class J-3 of 1936 held 24 pints. The ninety C&O K-4 class (2-8-4) held 32 and 36 pints of valve oil and engine oil respectively. K-4's numbered from 2740 through 2789 (and J-3 class 610-614 of 1948) carried two auxiliary reservoirs, each containing ten gallons of oil. These reservoirs, looking like shallow "pans," were mounted in line with top of each lubricator and immediately behind it. This added detail made the lubricators even more impressive as appliances on the locomotive.

For its Super Power locomotives the C&O's Mechanical Department (one could more accurately say the Advisory Mechanical Committee) spread its business between the two major manufacturers of mechanical lubricators: Nathan Manufacturing company and Detroit Lubricator Company, the Detroit model mounted usually on the right side and the Nathan on the left. These lubricators fed lines that ran all over the frame of the locomotive and lower sides of the boiler. Valve oil, which was heavier than engine oil, had to be atomized before spraying inside the cylinders, piston valves, and steam chests (or as on some AMC freight designs, inside the steam pipes). Lubrication inside the cylinders was critical because of the high temperatures, high pressures, and fast piston speeds. The effects of these forces were vividly brought home to this writer at Alleghany, Virginia, in 1949. A 2-6-6-6 pusher engine, cutting off from its train after the long shove from Hinton, exhibited bright blue pistons. Whether this coloration came from heat of the metal or chemical changes in the lubricant, I am not qualified to say. Obviously, the strange color was connected with the H-8's high rate of steam production at full throttle up Allegheny Mountain. Engine oil went to driving box pedestals, engine and trailing truck pedestals and pins, and to most sliding surfaces.

Light and heavy grease under pressure was handled by the Prime-Alemite system, making use of hard and soft grease cakes or inserts. The grease was usually forced into cavities by heavy grease guns, a process railroaders called "Alemiting." Lube oil would simply break down under the enormous twisting pressures at the crosshead wrist pins, the connections of the main rods with the side rods, and at the crank pins. Hard grease was the answer to this friction. Softer grease inserts went to the valve motion, the power reverse gear, stoker gear case, etc.

Obviously, driving wheel axles, set in driving boxes which absorbed a great deal of stress, were the hardest rotating parts to keep "cool" in service because of the great weight resting on them. "Solid," or friction, bearings, depending on surface tension of oil to coat the large surface of soft metal against harder metal, were the rule. The "brasses" were kept separated from the smooth axle surfaces by a coating of oil picked up by a grease block making contact with the bottom of the axle. Such a primitive system consumed a lot of grease. Tapered roller bearings were the answer, but because they were very expensive, they did not get much use until after the Great Depression. One company, Timken of Canton, Ohio, championed them for steam locomotives, though SKF also made them for steam locomotives. Timken pushed railroads for their adoption, beginning in 1930. In the aftermath of the Stock Market Crash of 1929, it is easy to see why railroads generally, and C&O, NKP, and PM in particular failed to equip their early Super Power locomotives with roller bearings. Not until the early 1940's did C&O Super Power get roller bearings. The giant T-1 2-10-4's of 1930 would certainly have benefited from roller bearings on the driving wheel axles, for these engines were among the highest in axle load of any steam engines built to this time. However, Lima Locomotive Works had no interest in 1930 in pushing roller bearings. The company's ad in the 1930 *Locomotive Cyclopedia* failed to mention improved lubrication as a requirement for Super Power. Rather, the ad brought out what one would expect-the trailer booster, four wheel trailing truck, large grate area, tandem main rod drive, etc.

Eventually roller bearings, on at least the driving wheels, would be an accepted requirement for Super Power locomotives. And Timken advertising shows why that is so. For example, "Special oil is not required to lubricate Timken bearings. Regular valve oil may be used, and a relatively small amount is consumed. A test on engine trucks showed that Timken bearings operated for 300 days on the same amount of oil required by friction bearings for a single day's operation." All ninety C&O 2-8-4s-the famous Kanawhas-

had Timken roller bearings on all engine, driving, and trailer axles; the J-3 4-8-4's of 1948, beginning with 610, and all L-2 Hudsons (300-307 and 310-314) had them on all axles, including the tender. (J-3's 610-614 additionally had roller bearings on main and side rods and crank pins.) The L-1 Hudsons, rebuilt at Huntington from Pacifics with solid bearings, had roller bearings on all axles. All sixty of the mighty Allegheny H-8 2-6-6-6's had Timken bearings fitted on the six driving axles secured in twelve driving boxes resting in the frame.

For figures illustrating just how much lubricant a Super Power locomotive could consume in service, we go to records kept by a retired mechanical engineer (preferring to go unnamed) who was responsible for the successful run of Pere Marquette No. 1225 (Lima 1941) to the NRHS convention in Huntington, W.Va. — and on runs beyond — in 1991. In setting a budget for consumables that year, he estimated a mileage of 2,250 miles and for the quantity of lubricants needed to cover that mileage: valve oil, 60 gals., engine oil, 70 gals., journal oil, 40 gals. (for engine, trailer, and tender truck journals), air compressor oil, 5 gals., 80 tubes of soft grease, and 100 lbs. of crankpin grease. And No. 1225 didn't even have a booster!

Because C&O Hudsons were built for speed, one needs compare them for speed with other outstanding Super Power Hudsons in the United States. What Don Leach calls the "Big Three" of the Hudsons were the Santa Fe's 3460 class (3460-3465) of 1937-38, the Chicago and North Western E-4 (4001-4009) of 1938, and the Milwaukee Road's F-7 (100-105) also of 1938. Owned by roads with a big stake in pre-War passenger service, these three types were obviously built in competition for establishing the fastest steam run. The Milwaukee and the North Western Hudsons featured essentially the same streamlined jacket. (On only one of the Santa Fe Hudsons was there an attempt at streamlining.) All three had 300 psi boiler pressure and drivers measuring 84 inches, the only Hudsons to go so high in both critical dimensions. The "Big Three" were thus designed to be fast runners, and the speed surveys compiled yearly in Railroad during their ascendancy confirm this. If they had a down side, it would be in traction, for the extremely high boiler pressure combined with extremely high drivers increased the danger of wheel slippage. (Compare these figures with the C&O L-2's conservative 255 psi boiler pressure and its 78-inch drivers.)

In fact, the Santa Fe had, according to Lloyd Stagner, a real problem with the adhesion of the drivers of its 3460 class at high speeds. To remedy this condition, the Company was forced to lower, in effect, the tractive effort on an apparently over powered locomotive by moving the maximum cut-off from full "forward gear" of 80% to 74%, thus adhering to the principle of "limited cut-off." Doing this apparently solved the problem. One suspects the C&NW and MILW "Big Three" Hudsons also had to contend with similar problems in high speed running since in weights the three types were quite dose to each other.

The Santa Fe got great service out of its Hudsons over the Great Plains west of Chicago. According to Lloyd Stagner, "The 3460s were allowed a timetable maximum speed of 100 m.p.h." The Milwaukee Road, using its F-7 class on the "Hiawathas" between Chicago and Minneapolis, averaged 81 m.p.h., for exam-

Two light-weight new coaches from Pullman Standard, with their plush "Sleepy Hollow" seats are on No. 6 this day in 1951 east of Russell with an apparent reduced consist. Train is still impressive, for the powerful Hudsons have a most efficient system of distributing steam to the cylinders-valves that open and close like automotive valves. For over sixty years the F.F.V. has been making this run, and let's get its proud Virginia name straight-"First Families of Virginia." (Eugene L. Huddleston, COHS collection.)

ple, between Sparta and Portage, Wisconsin (Stagner). The C&NW E-4 class, running on the Chicago to Omaha UP transcontinental route, was limited to 80 m.p.h., according to Stagner. It is unclear whether the locomotive or the route determined this speed "limit." Since the Santa Fe engines were so similar to the Milwaukee and the C&NW in major dimensions, one assumes that they were capable of the same speed, but that C&NW and Milwaukee Road operating policy kept the speed down. This was certainly true in the case of the C&O's Hudsons, both 300-307 of 1942 and 310-314 of 1948. In

my *Appalachian Conquest* (2002), I point out that the best speeds on C&O in the early 1940s — regardless whether Pacific or Hudson — were made on the "race track" in the Ohio River Valley between Ashland, Ky., and the suburban approach to Cincinnati, Ohio. What I did not point out clearly was that higher speeds than those posted were possible except for one big reason — local speed limits that kept the big steamers from building up and maintaining high speeds over long distances. The only transportation route on the south side of the river was held by the C&O. There were no through highways.

Engines 300-307 and 310-314 were the queens of long runs. Impressively, on the "F.F.V." and "George Washington," they ran straight through from Hinton to Cincinnati, a distance of 309 miles. Even more impressive in distance and contrasts in scenery was the "Sportsman's" run from Hinton to Detroit on No. 47 and back on No. 46, approximately 475 miles. LEFT - Few people ever saw the roundhouse at Hinton because it was tucked under a cliff on the banks of the New River and offered no ready access. Truly artistic is the photo of 307 on Hinton's 115 ft. turntable, March 1946. (COHS collection.) ABOVE - West of Hinton the Hudsons twisted along the New for over fifty miles. Because the "Sportsman" ran in both directions along the New too early or too late at night to get pictures, we rely on other trains, like mailexpress No. 104, headed by 305 past Hawks Nest bridge, to exemplify running in the New River gorge. (E. L. Huddleston, COHS collection.)
BELOW -Power for "Sportsman, " No. 304 takes coal and water in Detroit engine terminal at 21st St., which PM shared jointly with the PRR and Wabash. (Joe Schmitz collection.)

The confined flood plain of the Ohio valley and the monopoly of the railroad in transportation forced little communities into close contact with the main line, and as a result first-class trains like the "George Washington " had to slow down to 30 mph or less through five small communities at which the "George" did not stop between Russell yard and Stevens yard near Cincinnati, a distance of 125 miles. One can be sure the situation was not like this on the trackage over which the Santa Fe, Milwaukee, and Northwestern Hudsons established their speed records in Railroad's Annual Survey! (It should be noted that in the 1940s, timetable speed over C&O's Cincinnati Division was 70 MPH maximum. In the year 2003 the CSX timetable speed over the same line has been raised to 79 mph, but there are still two communities (Vanceburg and Augusta in Ky.) where the Amtrak "Cardinals" do not stop that enforce speed limits below 30 mph for both freight and passenger trains.

The eight Hudsons delivered by Baldwin in 1942 had conventional Baker valve gear coupled to a Franklin Precision reverse gear, which they kept until scrapped. (This arrangement would be the choice on C&O's first 40

L-1 No. 494 at Russell, Ky., late 1946. Streamlined jacket and skirting not applied because plan for "Chessie" streamliner had fallen through. 490-494, as rebuilt to Hudsons, had Franklin System of Steam Distribution, Type A. A lever, similar in size and location to the combination lever for ordinary valve gear, actuated a gear box that converted reciprocating motion to oscillating motion of a cam shaft that opened and closed the multiple "poppet" valves. E. L. Huddleston, COHS collection.)

poppet valves, can now be brought up to date by adding five more locomotives of the 4-6-4 type for the C&O [class L-2a, 310-314]. This increases the number of poppet-valve-equipped locomotives ... to a total of 70. The [AMC inspired] specification of additional poppet-valve equipments for the new C&O locomotives is a result of the excellent performance of earlier applications, one of which [class L-1, No. 490] has completed nearly 18 months of trouble-free service." The Vice President concluded (without identifying the new system as the Type B) with a pleasing announcement: "A full size running exhibit of this type of the poppet valve system which will be applied to the C&O locomotives is exhibited in the Convention Hall. This type [Type B] is extremely simple in design, easy to maintain, adds very little weight to the locomotive, and as far as economy is concerned, gives the same results as the original type [Type A]. True, the Type B was "simple in design" but it looked more complicated than the Type A, which used a lever similar to a combination lever to activate a gear box out of sight behind the cylinder saddle (behind it, at least on the C&O L-1 class). The Type B involved a crank off the main drive-rod pin that, in revolving on the axle-line of No. 2 driver, drove a helix gear connected to a revolving rod, coupled by universal joints, to a worm gear transmitting the action of the revolving rod to a rotating cam shaft. (According to Parker Lamb, this power transmission is analogous to the "timing chain" in an auto engine.) "A full size running exhibit" of the Type B in action must have been something to see, especially if displayed inside a building! Esthetically the gear was not pleasing because the revolving rod and its connections had to be anchored to a awkwardly designed frame that also kept the reversing mechanism in alignment. Unfortunately for Franklin, the display made few if any converts.

2-8-4s in 1943.) By the time C&O management gave the AMC the go-ahead to add more level-land passenger engines to the roster in 1947, the AMC had come to realize the value of poppet valves, known as the Franklin System of Steam Distribution. The AMC had had nearly two years of experience with poppet valves, for they had been installed on C&O's "home made" Hudsons converted in 1946 from five heavy F-19 Pacifics of 1926. And certainly the AMC knew the value of the world's heaviest Hudsons of 1942, which needed no special improvements in design except for poppet valves replacing piston valves on the new order. Poppet valves were especially valuable on passenger engines, for "back pressure" went up considerably as speed increased. Use of poppet valves would reduce back pressure, for, like automotive valves, they opened and closed almost instantaneously.

A significant discussion of the Franklin poppet valves took place at the national convention of the Mechanical Division of the Association of American Railroads. As reported on in *Railway Age* (June 26, 1947), under "Steam Locomotive Development," there were at that time (February 1947) 65 locomotives in the United States equipped with poppet valves, most of those since 1939 having the Franklin Type A valve system and only one (a PRR K-4 Pacific) having the Type B. This tabulation is important because the C&O L-1 Hudson is part of the total of 65. A Vice-President of Franklin Railway Supply pointed out to the conferees that new C&O 4-6-4s on order would add five more to the list: "I would also like to mention that the list of locomotives in the United States, equipped with mechanically operated

One would never know this from discussions at the Convention, for the report on "The Further Development of the Steam Locomotive" noted how a "great deal of engineering thought" had been given to poppet valves. Among points offered were its advantages: (1) reduction of thermal losses by separating admission and exhaust valves; (2) improvement in the ease of steam flow through the cylinders; (3) reduction in inertia forces; (4) independence of valve events. In June 1948 C&O received its five new Hudsons, and apparent-

ABOVE - As rebuilt, No. 490 remained in revenue service from 1946 to 1953 (After 1952, on eastern end of road only). In spring of 1947 No. 490 heads the "F.F.V." westbound at Huntington, West Virginia. Light Pacific (F-15) in right background will take local No. 7 to Cincinnati in the afternoon. (E. L. Huddleston, COHS collection.)

BELOW - On this winter day steam vents at various openings as the engineer opens the throttle to accelerate No. 6 eastward following stop at Russell depot. From the stack, on the near side, steam exhausts after use in two cylinders of the booster engine. (E. L. Huddleston, COHS collection.)

ly much engineering thought had been given to the new Type B poppet valves (which differed mainly from the Type A in that the former had a revolving cam and the latter an oscillating cam for operating the valve lifters). By virtue of their performance over some four years, the class L-2a 310-314 merits Brian Hollingsworth's praise in his *Illustrated Encyclopedia of North American Locomotives*: "Technically the engines represented the final degree of sophistication of the American steam locomotive that came from nearly 120 years of steady development of practice and details upon original principles." (According to William Withuhn, two of the L-2a's of 1948 did give trouble until it was determined that Baldwin, in building the 4-6-4's, had not correctly lined up the quarter lead in the side rods; they were one-fourth inch out of alignment.)

One could say that the F-19 Pacifics rebuilt to Hudsons in 1946 were equally sophisticated, for the AMC and the workers at the C&O's Huntington Shops made sure these streamlined engines had practically all the modern appliances and proved innovations that the L-2 and L-2a Hudsons had. The sole intention of their rebuilding, though, was to make them suitable motive power for the "branch line" sections of the daylight streamliner "The Chessie" that was to be handled between Washington and Cincinnati by the three steam-turbo-electrics produced by a collaboration of Westinghouse Electric and Baldwin in 1947. Construction and features of the class L-1 Hudson (490-494) are examined in some detail in the chapter "Repair, Upkeep, and Improvement of C&O Super Power." One interesting set of statistics about the big Pacifics (4-6-2) rebuilt into Hudsons (4-6-4) was the increase in boiler pressure on the Hudsons without apparently any real changes in the strength of the boiler. The five boilers for the five F-19 class Pacifics of 1929 were reused for the five new Hudsons. Boiler pressure, originally 200 psi, was increased on the Hudsons to 210 psi. (This still kept the safety factor of the boiler well within the federal limit of 4.0) A good guess is that permitting the increase were improved lubricating oils that withstood high temperatures without breaking down inside the cylinders. Also, anecdotal evidence from a C&O locomotive engineer reveals that they could attain speeds of ninety-five mph with no problems arising from high speed (this taking place on C&O's "racetrack" along the Ohio east of Cincinnati).

BELOW - L-1 and an L-2 are side by side at the Ashland depot with two sections of the "F.F.V." in 1948. Maximum height of 306 is 15 ft., 9 inches. That of 491 is 15 ft. even. (It is difficult to compare heights in this photo because L-2 306 has not pulled up even with No. 491.) (E. L. Huddleston, COHS collection)

Here No. 302, with the "Sportsman" westbound, has crossed the River Rouge in June 1951, on Wabash tracks. Ford's huge Rouge plant is nearby. (Elmer Treloar. COHS collection.)

"On level, tangent track a single 2-6-6-6 moved a 160 car, 14,083 ton coal train to 19 miles per hour in one mile ...
– David P. Morgan, *Steam's Finest Hour*

It's only two miles from Handley to Montgomery, but little Handley lacks connection with much larger Montgomery because those West Virginia hills come right down to the Kanawha River between the two communities. An eastbound coming through Montgomery like extra 1616 made beautiful double beat stack music, but was held back in speed by the campus of West Virginia Tech (out of sight at left) and downtown business district at right. Wooden freight house is at left and brick depot out of sight at right. Train will enter New River Gorge in eleven miles. (Ben F. Cutler, collection. COHS)

Chapter 7

C&O'S 2-6-6-6 Alleghenies

"It was here [in Ohio north of Columbus] that the Alleghenies got their chance to roll and roll they did indeed. Ask any central Ohio railfan about the picture the H-8's painted as they stormed up Powell Hill every afternoon with No. 195 or No. 97, their double-cadence exhaust ...[lifting high] into the air."
— Phil Shuster in Shuster, Huddleston, and Staufer, 'C&O Power'

The Allegheny type was the largest and most powerful steam locomotive ever to operate on Chesapeake & Ohio, a road known for impressive locomotives. The tendency to bigness was natural, given that C&O was one of the foremost carriers of solid coal trains, weighing thousands of tons, from the rich West Virginia and Kentucky bituminous fields, bound for overseas and domestic industries. The name Allegheny might lead one to assume that their range of service was limited to the Allegheny Mountains. However, they also ran from Russell, Ky., on the "beautiful Ohio" River, up the length of Ohio to Toledo. This was the same route that in 1930 had led AMC designer Alonzo Trumbull to pull all the stops in design and come up with the most powerful two-cylinder locomotive in the world at that time — the C&O's 2-10-4, class T-1.

Even though the name "Allegheny" does not fully represent the regions the locomotive served, it does clearly identify this type, for the Allegheny's power and stateliness remind one of the old saying, "Give me men to match my mountains." The American Name Society recognizes the power of names, both their connotative richness and denotative identification, as with "2-6-6-6" and "H-8" and "1600." For practical information, one goes to the numerical designation of these locomotives. The naming is very systematic, for the so-called Whyte system of locomotive classification recognized engines by the number of their leading wheels, driving wheels, and trailing wheels. (For a locomotive with two sets of driving wheels, there were two numerals separating the leading wheels from the trailing wheels.) Designated this way, the C&O locomotive in question was a 2-6-6-6. Making it distinctive was its six-wheel trailing truck. Only two other locomotive types had six trailing wheels and they were both experimental (on the Pennsylvania Railroad). There was nothing experimental about the trailing truck of the sixty 2-6-6-6s C&O owned nor of the eight copies the Virginian Ry. bought. Their six wheels supported the weight of an enormous fire box, within whose interior burned a fire with a draft so fierce that the flames reached upward of 200 mph and which possessed heating surfaces to evaporate an unprecedented amount of water to steam — a gas with enormous expansive powers.

The development of a six-wheel truck to support even more grate area than the four wheel was logical, given the development of the first 2-10-4 type in 1925. In *Railway Age* for June 11, 1927, W. H. Winterrowd, Vice-President of Lima Locomotive Works wrote: "When the limits of the four wheel truck, firebox, and grate area are eventually reached, as they will be, by ever increasing demands of operation... the next step may be a still larger firebox and grate area, the weight of which may be carried by a six wheel trailer truck." Because of the Depression, this did not happen until C&O's order in 1941.

Naming this locomotive a 2-6-6-6 told that it was a distinctive wheel arrangement, but the Company's designation for it told a lot, too. C&O's designation, H-8, derived from "H" being assigned all C&O articulateds (two engines under one boiler) and "8" being the eighth such order or "class" of articulateds on the road. C&O employees who worked on or with them called them "H-8s" or "1600s." Determining their numbering as 1600s was that articulated classes — 2-6-6-2s and 2-8-8-2s — already were numbered in the 1200 through 1500 slots and 1600-1699 was open, as were 1700 through 2200, for that matter. (The 2000 slot was filled in 1946, with second-hand 2-10-2s...)

"Allegheny" is its most important name since it invites so many associations. The name applies to both the 2-6-6-6s owned by the C&O and to the eight owned by the Virginian Railway. In the beginning, individual steam locomotives were given names, but this proved impractical as more and more steamers were built. Most of those named had been 4-4-0s. When wheel arrangements started diversifying from 4-4-0 into 4-6-0 or 4-4-2 or 2-6-0, names were attached to differentiate them. Not every arrangement had a name, but most did. Some names were quite appropriate, like "Decapod" for the 2-10-0. Others like "Mastodon" for the 4-8-0 were not. "Allegheny" was quite appropriate, for the first ten C&O purchased in 1941 were intended primarily for service over the Allegheny Mountains. The summit of C&O's tracks across the Atlantic-Mississippi watershed was at Alleghany, Virginia. (Because Virginian's summit over the same watershed was near Merrimac, Virginia, in electrified territory, "Allegheny" would not work for the Virginian.

Hence the Virginian's claim to the "Blue Ridge" type. (The Virginian crossed the Blue Ridge via the Roanoke River — a water gap east of Roanoke.) The localized spelling "Alleghany" was not lost on the Cleveland financiers acting to make the C&O the principal road in a new Van Sweringen holding company

formed in the 1920s.

These investors and executives needed an apt name and "Alleghany Corporation" was it, according to Herb Harwood in his book *Invisible Giants*: "Alleghany, Virginia, is just barely on the road maps, a classic off-the-beaten-path spot nestled high in a mountain notch across the ridge from the West Virginia border. In 1929, it was less a town than a small collection of gray railroad buildings, sidings, and signals. But the name showed up in large print on the working timetables of the Chesapeake & Ohio train crews; when they passed the austere frame station, they knew their hardest work was over. For Alleghany marks the summit of the C & O's main line between the West Virginia coal fields and the tidewater docks at Newport News. Sitting 2,072 feet [sic] above sea level, it is the end of the grueling grind eastward up the Allegheny slope... The heavy coal trains would pause there to uncouple their ponderous [2-8-8-2 or 2-6-6-6] pusher locomotives and set their brakes

before dropping down the eastern slope to the yards at Clifton Forge. The mountain air at Alleghany was perennially filled with the sound of slogging steam engines and tinged with the sharp smell of coal smoke and hot oil."

It would seem from Harwood's account that the C&O 2-6-6-6's should have been "Alleghany spelled with an a" However, railroad employees seldom called them Alleghenies; they lumped articulateds under one heading – Mallets – pronounced Malleys, with accent on first syllable for the inventor of articulateds, more particularly compound articulateds, though seasoned railroaders made no distinction between compound and simple articulateds, the latter feeding steam directly to both sets of cylinders from the throttle valve, and the former using it first in the back set of cylinders and again in the front set in low-pressure mode. Obviously, only "Mallets" feeding high pressure steam equally to both sets of cylinders could generate sufficient steam to be called Super

Nothing goes better with the Alleghany type locomotive than Alleghany, Virginia. It's the place where pushers turned after the fifty mile shove from Hinton, as illustrated by 1614, (BELOW) which in June 1947, having backed off its train to release its caboose, is heading past the summit sign to the Alleghany turntable (Joseph E. Eppenstein). Or it's the place where you'd see a faster train overtaking a slower one, as illustrated by 1601 (ABOVE) passing empties at the summit. Interestingly, the company photographer had chased in his car, from Smith Creek Yard at Clifton Forge, 1601, (LEFT) heading a westbound time freight, to Moss Run, where he could drive up a side road to trackside. (CSPR, COHS collection.) He continued his chase by car to Alleghany station, having plenty of time to get ahead of the train, which was blasting up the 1.14% grade without a pusher. There he shot 1601 passing A Cabin, with a twin 2-6-6-6 waiting on the westbound main to proceed downgrade to Hinton. (both: CSPR, COHS collection.)

Power.

The late John A. Rehor has given a clear description of the dual frame and driver arrangement of the Mallet type. "The Mallet had a very large boiler and furnace supported by two independent engines each with its own frame, cylinders, drivers, and machinery. The rear engine was carried in a frame rigidly attached to the boiler in the usual manner, whereas the forward engine was secured only to the rear frame by a hinged connection... Although not actually connected to the boiler, the forward engine helped support it with sliding bearings. Thus, while traversing curves, the lead engine could move out of alignment with the rear engine."

For those who want to see the 2-6-6-6 type in as wide

Was there something magic about 1653? Yes, it was miraculously fired up after a year and half storage, and along with nine other H-8's was sent east from Russell to haul freights between Handley and Hinton on the New River Subdivision. All of these pictures were made in July and August 1955. ABOVE - 1653, with water over-flowing from priming injector under the cab, takes a train of Tidewater coal east from Russell on its "maiden" trip right after Russell roundhouse workers got it up and running in July 1955. Next in sequence (RIGHT) is 1653 about five minutes later, stopped by main line congestion at Bellefonte, west of Ashland. Engineer proudly poses for what he knows is a historic moment. Another photo, (BELOW) a month or two later, shows 1653 at the east end of Handley yard taking water prefatory to taking a train east. (All, E.L. Huddleston)

"The Allegheny type's great weight prevented use over Huntington Division (Russell to Handley) until new bridge was built at Catlettsburg, Ky., in 1947. By late 1951 dynamometer tests with DM-1 showed, too late, 2-6-6-6's could pull full tonnage trains over Scary Hill without pusher."

perspective as possible, one can cite the distribution of "Mallets" built for use in the United States. The list does not include all "Mallets," for the original American articulated was Baltimore and Ohio's 0-6-6-0, and there were 2-8-8-0's on several roads as well as 190 4-8-8-2 "cab forwards" on the Southern Pacific. Neither do the figures distinguish between compound and simple articulateds: (1) 2-6-6-2 — 42.7%; (2) 2-6-6-4 — 2.0%; (3) 2-6-6-6 — 2.2%; (4) 4-6-6-4 — 7%; (5) 2-8-8-2 — 22.5%; (6) 2-8-8-4 — 7.0%; 4-8-8-4 — 0.8%.

Nobody called the C&O simple articulateds "Limas," but "Lima" is a brand name of significance, because all 68 2-6-6-6s were manufactured by Lima (pronounced with long i) Locomotive Works of Lima, Ohio. In fact, the manufacturer's diamond shaped logo was applied as a metal stamping on both sides of the smoke box under the smoke stack. Each of the Big Three U. S. locomotive manufacturers applied its name plate (and serial number of the engine) to each new locomotive, and these builders' plates have become quite valuable to collectors.

Positive identification of a particular locomotive was its builder's serial number-which would never

change and would never be duplicated, unlike the number painted under the cab window. Also painted on the cab, in lower right corner on each side, were the calculated tractive effort of the engine (all in one class would be the same) and the company's class designation. The tractive effort figure was useful, in that tonnage ratings were calculated using that figure, which itself was a calculation from a formula. Thus was lettered on the 1600's: "H-8 " and "110,200 lbs" (one figure atop the other).

In naming and identifying locomotives, one thinks of the tender as part of the locomotive, since they seem mated when one looks at them together. Tenders held a supply of coal and water to feed to the locomotive, and in its recesses behind the cab were stored tools like grate shaker and fire raking bars. Locomotive and tender require a match of buffers and coupling bars (as seen on p. 131 of *The Allegheny, Lima's Finest*) plus mating of stoker screw, hose connections, and deck levels. Uncoupling of tender from locomotive is time consuming and labor intensive. However, as Phil Shuster has written, "It was discovered long ago that tenders could be switched from engine to engine to meet different operating situations. As engine rosters grew, memories could

H-8's regularly supplemented the T-1 (2-10-4) types between Russell and Toledo. They did not regularly operate between Russell and Handley — that was 2-8-4 territory. 1650, coaled and filled with 25,000 gallons of water, awaits calling at Russell's engine terminal in August 1950. After engine crew boards 1650, about an hour after this photo, it will proceed light about two miles to the west end of the "New Yard" and couple onto 160 loaded and weighed coal cars. (E. L. Huddleston, COHS collection.)

Headed from Columbus to Russell in December 1949, 1648 passes Limeville water tank on banks of the Ohio. Thirteen cars back in the train is a "high and wide" load requiring special handling. (E. L. Huddleston, collection. COHS)

H-8 1637 in 1949 starts to open up on the main line after its caboose has cleared the yard track it was on in Russell's "New Yard"-- the westbound coal classification yard. Train should be in Columbus in about four hours. (E. L. Huddleston. COHS collection.)

Manifest No . 190 has crossed the Sciotoville bridge to the Kentucky side in September 1950. It should be entering Russell's eastbound yard in half an hour. (H. W. Pontin, collection. COHS)

not always be trusted to keep track of which tender came with what engine in what year ... Thus some sort of classification system is necessary..."

Shuster continues, explaining how individual tenders were classified. This classification applied not only to the Allegheny locomotive tenders but to all tenders designed by the Advisory Mechanical Committee. " The tender classification system used by the C&O came into being in the early Thirties. It was an Advisory Mechanical Committee system devised for all the Van Sweringen roads — C&O, NKP, PM, and Erie. Under this system a number indicated water capacity in thousands of gallons (rounded to the nearest thousand); then, a letter indicated tender shape (R for rectangular, V for Vanderbilt, and S for slope-back), and another letter indicated the series or grouping within the specific category." Following the above classification was a tender number which denoted a specific tender. Thus, in 1948, the 25,000- gallon rectangular tender delivered with H-8 #1659 became #25-RB-1924. Shuster concluded, "Each tender carried its own number on a plate either bolted or welded to the frame on the right side."

Numerals are important not only in naming but in measuring the achievements of a particular locomotive or type. Statistics — numerical facts and data — are essential in measuring this achievement.. However, one must use these figures with caution, for while it is true that "figures don't lie" there is some truth to Mark Twain's famous apothegm, that there are three kinds of lies — lies, damned lies, and statistics. This is especially true in making comparisons. Some statistics about the 2-6-6-6s are impressive even without comparisons. True, the starting tractive effort of 110,200 lbs., while the highest ever calculated for a C&O engine, does not stand out for an engine of such magnificent dimensions. The tractive effort would stand out more if taken from measurements, not from formula. Twice in endurance tests the actual drawbar pull at starting, as measured on the drawbar behind the dynamometer car, was over 119,000 lbs. The highest reading, 119,350 lbs., was obtained when 1657 stopped and started 153 loads of coal westbound on the steepest part of Scary Hill west of St. Albans, West Virginia. Statistically, the Allegheny's great weight stands out, if only because

In November 1950, 1607 has uncoupled from its 160 loads of coal, as instructed, and takes coal and water at GB coaling station, 34 miles north of Limeville Jct. Nearest town is Omego, Ohio, across the Scioto and on the main line of the paralleling N&W. (E. L. Huddleston, collection. COHS)

the scale weights were manipulated unethically — to give a lower reading — during the initial weighing process at Lima Locomotive Works. Its proudest statistic is its horsepower as measured at the tender coupler — 7498 H. P. at 46 mph with 14,032 tons in tow across the Pickaway Plains of south central Ohio never being exceeded.

Sometimes, a scale drawing can do at a glance what trying to comprehend, through dimensions set up in a statistical table, would take lengthy pondering. Robert L. Hundman, trained as an engineer, has shown as a model railroad publisher a mastery of numerical details and a mastery of draftsmanship. Bob, in his *Locomotive Cyclopedia*, put in words about the Union Pacific "Big Boy" (4-8-8-4), often regarded as the world's largest conventional steamer, what he had demonstrated with a scale drawing in *The Allegheny, Lima's Finest*: "When the boiler of the Allegheny is drawn over the boiler of the Big Boy the difference in size becomes a bit more obvious. The Big Boy boiler would fit within that of the Allegheny."

Other statistics about the Allegheny made its builder and owners proud. Its performance as measured by a then state-of-the-art dynamometer car gave an Englishman studying these tests lots of figures to evaluate. O. S. Nock, a Westinghouse Air Brake executive who lived in Bath, wrote prolifically of American and European locomotives. One can presumably trust his statistics because he gives their sources (test reports examined at C&O's Huntington Shops) and because of his objectivity in evaluating them as a British, not an American, citizen: "During the tests on the Northern subdivision the `H8' locomotive performed some of its most spectacular work. On only one out of five test runs from Russell to Columbus was it necessary to take a pusher over Limeville Bridge. Why this should have been necessary is not apparent from the test reports. On the fastest of the northbound test runs the 109 3/4 miles from Russell (Kentucky) to Columbus (Ohio) were covered in 4 hrs 11 min. inclusive of a delay amounting to 27 min. The running time of 3 hrs 44 min. showed an average speed of 29.4 m.p.h. and of this time the engine was coasting for no more than 26 min. During the `working time' the regulator [throttle] was full open throughout and steam was being cut off [by the piston valve] on an average at 59 percent of the piston stroke. The actual working varied between 44 and 82 percent — the latter being `all-out' [i.e., maximum-cut-off]. Although this would be considered exceptionally severe driving on a British steam locomotive, the performance showed high economy in fuel. On all these runs from Russell to Columbus the coal consumed per hour for each horsepower exerted on the drawbar [coupler] was a little over 2.9 lbs. In Great Britain a figure of 3 lbs was considered the hallmark of a well designed locomotive working such train as the `Flying Scotsman' or the `Cornish Riviera Express', and to achieve comparable figures in such `all-out' conditions of working bespeaks an outstandingly good design."

There is another set of statistics that has been largely ignored, possibly because the figures mean little unless presented comparatively. The calculated maximum boiler evaporation predicts a steam engine's potential power, as these words by A. W. Bruce demonstrate: "The most vital characteristic of the steam locomotive is the evaporation that takes place in its boiler, without which there would be no steam locomotive." In his treatise on the steam locomotive, Ralph Johnson set up the factors determining the rate of evaporation, the first two being the most important: (1) the amount of direct heating surface contained in the firebox, combustion chamber, and arch tubes, syphons, or circulators (depending

on whichever of the last three the locomotive features); (2) the amount of indirect heating surface in the flues and tubes; (3) the length of the flues and tubes; (4) whether the locomotive is equipped with a feedwater heater, or exhaust steam injector. The quite complex calculations for evaporation also involve, indirectly, firing rate, gas area, superheater surface, plus grate area and percent of air opening through the grates. Ralph Johnson, Baldwin Locomotive Works chief engineer, calculated maximum evaporation using formulae he explained in a chapter on evaporation in The Steam Locomotive and in an article on the locomotive in Encyclopedia Americana (1944). In a table in his book, Johnson gives the maximum evaporation for 15 outstanding modern American steam locomotives, constructed between 1929 and 1942 and based on calculations of 80 lbs. of water evaporated per square feet of direct heating surface.

The C&O (and later Virginian) 2-6-6-6 rank first in calculated maximum evaporation (measured in pounds of water turned to steam) among the Super Power simple articulateds (Super Power being defined as having a 4-wheel trailer) that Johnson rather arbitrarily includes among the sixteen, his criterion for inclusion being that they are "typical." Of chief interest are these articulateds and their maximum evaporation: (1) C&O 2-6-6-6 — 124,596; (2) Duluth Missabe and Iron Range 2-8-8-4 — 123,105; (3) Western Maryland 4-6-6-4 — 113,899; (4) Union Pacific 4-8-8-4 — 109,156. In 1989 Ed King, in *The A: Norfolk & Western's Mercedes of Steam* takes Johnson to task for not listing N&W's Super Power simple articulated of 1936, the class A 2-6-6-4, of which 43 were built between 1936 and 1950. King complained, "The N&W and its works [the 2-6-6-4, 4-8-4, and 2-8-8-2] might as well have not existed upon the face of the earth." True, Johnson did not include the triumvirate of great Roanoke-made steam locomotives that have since received so many accolades. But had King remembered, his own book gave the maximum evaporation for the N&W class A: "The 1200 proved capable of evaporating 116,055 pounds of water — about 14,000 gallons — in an hour."

For maximum utilization of the evaporation taking place on simple articulateds, the path to the cylinders should be as direct as possible. With two engines under one boiler and with one engine hinged to the frame, achieving a direct path was a challenge to designers. On the Allegheny the path was a long one to both front and rear engine, but it was direct, with no sharp turns. On some articulateds, notably the N&W class A (2-6-6-4), a sharp turn at the flexible "sleeve" on the front engine above the cylinders required a pressure relief valve (mounted under the sleeve), which opened to the atmosphere if pressure in the sleeve got too great. The Allegheny type required no such "safety" valve.

Super Power originated in 1925 with Lima Locomotive Works' A-1 2-8-4, the first road locomotive

NEW RIVER SUBDIVISION — Scenic New River Sub-Handley to Hinton — actually began in the upper Kanawha Valley. "Level land" power ran west of Handley; "mountain" power to the east. (Passenger engines did not change at Handley.) Four photos represent activity in Handley engine terminal — 1648 on turntable; with Johnnie, the engine herder about to dismount, 1647 reaches end of yard track; 1647, having cut off train, backs to engine terminal, all August 1955. On another day, 1648 leaves Handley for Hinton, while 2711 readies for run on Huntington Division's Kanawha Subdivision. (all, E. L. Huddleston, collection. COHS)

ABOVE - Everyone knows about Hawks Nest overlook and dam and the famous bridge over the New River. Nowadays it is easy to get to the bridge, either by tram from the state park above or by car over one lane road. In 1950, I walked in from Cotton Hill, where I got off local No. 14. 1624, westbound out of Hinton, is taking the sharpest curve on C&O's mainline at about 15 mph. Macdougal depot is across the river. (E.L. Huddleston, collection. COHS)

BELOW - An H-8 near Cotton Hill fights upriver after stopping. H-8's had no pushers up the New River Subdivision. (C&O Ry. official photo)

equipped with a four wheel trailing truck — the additional axle supporting a large firebox that would generate enough steam so that when the locomotive reached its maximum power, it could sustain that power over long distances at a higher speed than the older "drag era" locomotives. Most C&O Super Power came from Lima: 2-8-4s, 4-8-4s, 2-10-4s, and 2-6-6-6-s (some C&O 2-8-4s and all 4-6-4s being the exception). The officials at Lima and the engineers of the Advisory Mechanical Committee worked well together, and AMC officers spent lots of rewarding time traveling to Lima on their private business cars from Terminal Tower at Cleveland.

While Lima had earlier proposed a 2-6-6-6 design (for the Monon Railroad in Indiana) the Allegheny was an AMC design and this organization was in complete control of the project, as a study of the drawings and textual instructions (that still exist) attest. Not a lot is known about the Advisory Mechanical Committee, since its personnel were independent of the four roads sharing the "advice" of the Committee, those roads being the C&O, NKP, Erie, and Pere Marquette. The AMC offered far more than advice to the particular road ordering a steam locomotive. It had complete engineering control of the project. In the case of the C&O Allegheny type, the man who actually designed this Behemoth was Alonzo Trumbull, Chief Mechanical Engineer for the AMC, who, as a graduate of Cornell University's Mechanical

H-8 1637 climbs .57% grade east of White Sulphur Springs. At end of "S" curve behind locomotive is White Sulphur Tunnel and below it (at right) is the town itself. (collection C&O Historical Society)

Engineering Department, had started his career with the Erie Railroad and had risen to be its chief mechanical engineer.

As for styling of the 2-6-6-6s , they merited the tag in *Railroad* by Henry Comstock "compact, handsome, powerful, fast." In truth, their compactness made them handsome: namely, 67-inch drivers, considerable height ("from tire to smoke stack rim") and width giving them bulk lacking in all but a handful of articulateds, skillful placement of huge steam delivery pipes and air tanks, enormous sand boxes, and space saving elevated front platform.

Henry Comstock came through again in his *Railroad* accolades for the H-8 by choosing just the right words for when, on a field trip, he saw them in action in southern West Virginia: "We've seen them battling past Hawk's Nest with half the state of West Virginia anchored to their tails and we've heard the soft whoosh of their double talk [from twin smoke stacks] as they eased a mile of hoppers past the point at Hinton [where New River and Alleghany Sub-divisions joined]." The service

for which they were first designed, beginning in 1941, was between Clifton Forge, Virginia, east to Hinton and Handley, replacing the aging 2-8-8-2 simple articulateds of the 1920s. A wartime influenced increase in business expanded their operating territory to that previously covered by the Super Power 2-10-4s of 1930. This embraced the heavy tonnage line from Russell, Ky., to Toledo, Ohio. "Heavy tonnage" meant 160 loaded coal cars over grades as steep as .70% (at Limeville, approaching Ohio River bridge) and .40% (up the 14-mile-long end moraine north of Columbus, Ohio, known as Powell Hill).

One big gap in assembling meaningful references to the 2-6-6-6 is a lack of audio recordings of the big engines in full throttled action. None that one could call "full throttled" exist as far as this writer knows. In light of this shortcoming one can attempt to do in words what otherwise would be heard. From notes preserved over the years, the author has tried to reproduce verbally the quality of the sound of the great articulateds in heavy action at Hilldale, West Virginia. In this area west of Big

About a mile up the valley from photo of 1637 struggling east is 1621 (with pusher) doing perhaps 15-20 mph. On top of ridge at right is West Virginia — Virginia state line, marking Gulf-Atlantic watershed. It's a hard pull up Dry Creek (below) to tunnel under this ridge. (E. L. Huddleston, collection. COHS)

Hostler, tending new H-8, 1626, in 1944, faces oil house and coaling station at Clifton Forge engine terminal. Prominent under cab is vertically positioned extension of frame which transfers weight to rear of locomotive, through rocker assemblies, to the truck casting below. (CSPR, collection COHS)

Bend Tunnel, the grade is .40% all the way from Avis Yard, Hinton. In this five mile stretch, the two 2-6-6-6s had to accelerate from standstill, one on the head end and the other on the rear end — 140 cars away — just ahead of the caboose. Thus they did not pick up much speed until they got to the flood plain of the Greenbrier east of Big Bend Tunnel. Let's turn back time: "Standing just above the west portals of Big Bend, I could sense the tranquility of the scene — mainly induced by the lack of autos and trucks. Below me was a broad cut leading to the twin tunnels, and beyond was MW Cabin. Minutes pass, and then I think I pick up a faint chant, or rhythm, reverberating from hillside to hillside in the narrow valley of the Greenbrier about a mile or so west of Little Bend Tunnel (since daylighted)."

"The sound, gradually taking shape and increasing in intensity, has a pulsating regularity. There is rhythmic counterpoint in the stack tempo. While the main beat is steady and distinct, accompanying its accented staccato is a slightly less forceful beat. (The more forcefully direct explosion from the front stack is accounted for by the direct exhaust of the front engine, and the less quickly timed blast from the rear stack by exhaust from the rear engine traveling farther to the exhaust stand in the smoke box.) At a speed of about 18 mph a discernible pause separates each double beat from the next. The sound suddenly is muffled as the lead engine enters Little Bend Tunnel (some 500 ft long) about a half mile from where I stand. After several seconds the "march" time resumes with steadily increasing intensity. Now the impact of reality exceeds the power of the imagination. You know the black monster with the single white eye will come into view soon, and there it is! The force and volume of the exhaust (caused by low back pressure, large exhaust passages, and the boiler's ability to make record amount of steam) produce a great towering cloud from the twin stacks of 1624. The mixture of steam and burnt fuel shoots straight up, maybe fifty feet, before billowing out into clouds of condensation. The huge machine's exhibition of raw power annihilates awareness of anything other than its consummate passage. You experience the ecstasy of a grand creation, like, say, when concentrating on the finale of Mahler's First Symphony."

There are many places to read in more detail about the design, performance, and service history of these locomotives (including the Virginian copies of 1945). Still in print is Huddleston's and Dixon's *The Allegheny. Lima's Finest* (Hundman Publishing) and Huddleston's *World's Greatest Steam Locomotives* (TLC Publishers). Those so motivated might sit at their computer screen and type in on their favorite search engine some of the key "names" discussed in this reprise on the Alleghenies. He or she will be astonished with what will come up. Web pages advertising models of the H-8 in various scales will be the most prominent. (Particularly pleasing is modelrailroadnews.com labeling the 2-6-6-6

"a plumber's dream.") Other sites, such as Trainweb, offer informative comparative accounts. Most sites offer capsule histories of these engines. Practically all sites give prototype information, of varying degrees of accuracy, but always fun to read. The best place to see an actual Allegheny close-up is the 1601, on permanent display inside the Henry Ford Museum at Dearborn, Michigan. No. 1604 is on display outdoors at the B&O Museum in Baltimore. By the time it was given cosmetic restoration at C&O's Huntington Shops, 1604 had been stored unattended for so long that some of the jacketing covering the main steam pipes had deteriorated past the possibility of restoration.

From Clifton Forge, Virginia, to the Atlantic Coast, the grade is mild because the main freight line follows the gentle valleys of the Jackson and James rivers. In this photo are several Allegheny 2-6-6-6's for the climb to Alleghany summit and several K-3 Mikados (2-8-2) for the long haul down the James. (CSPR, collection COHS)

Time freight #2712 on a crisp fall morning in 1951 accelerates eastward out of Russell over the Kanawha Subdivision.
(E. L. Huddleston, collection. COHS)

Chapter 8

C&O K-4 (2-8-4)

*"There'll be bluebirds over the white cliffs of Dover,
Someday, just you wait and see.
There'll be bluebirds over the white cliffs of Dover,
Tomorrow, when the world is free."*
  – "White Cliffs of Dover" (words, Nat Burton, 1941)

"Don't you know there's a war going on?" This cautionary question was often necessary on the home front in World War II because in the heartland of America there was no direct evidence of combat and conflict and death and destruction half a world away in both directions.

It was thus mostly business as usual when in 1943 (and into 1944) the first thirty of what would eventually be ninety 2-8-4s showed up at the busy freight terminal at Russell, Kentucky, from the Alco plant at Schenectady, New York. War impacted on their construction to the extent of requiring a steel bell (going "clank,, clank") instead of the customary brass bell, and shortages led to other substitutions for copper and copper alloys. (After the War, "real" bells were retrofitted.) The last ten of the first order of forty, supplied with steam heat, air communications lines and automatic train con-

trols, went into service at Clifton Forge, Virginia, hauling passenger trains and time freights over the Mountain Subdivision. The men at Russell (I don't know about Clifton Forge) called them "Big Mikes." Officially they were classed by C&O motive power department as class K-4, the "K" slot reserved for all Mikados (but they were not really Mikados) and the "4" for the fourth variation in design among orders for new Mikados and their Super Power cousins . The name given to the new 2-8-4 wheel arrangements in the 1920s had been `Berkshires', for the Appalachian range in western Massachusetts, where the first 2-8-4s had gone in service. Naturally, C&O could not call them Berkshires. What else but "Kanawhas," for the river in West Virginia that with its tributaries, cut through the very heart of the southern West Virginia coal fields. Eventually, C&O would receive a total of ninety 2-8-4s from Alco (rectangular name plate) and Lima (diamond plate). Built by Alco in 1925-26, the last Mikes C&O had received, before the Great Depression, were numbered 2300-2349, class K-3. Perhaps like Boeing Aircraft in its selecting a "7" as part of its numerical model identification, C&O thought the number "7" was lucky, for it skipped openings in the 2400, 2500, 2600, and 2800

"POWER AND VERSATILITY" — K-4 Kanawhas were regularly assigned fast time freights, long coal trains, and passenger trains. They also could keep their footing on grades or run fast on the level. With estimated tonnage of 11,500 tons-up to 144 cars - 2728 gets away from Peach Creek yard on the Logan Sub at Chapmanville. If the train is an "E.B.", it will follow the Guyandotte River to Barboursville and then head east over the Kanawha Sub. If a "CD", it will go west from Barboursville to Russell, April 1954. (E. L. Huddleston)

After taking water at Sproul , 2734 starts 11,500 tons down the Coal River to St. Albans, where it will head on the wye either to Russell or Handley, October 1949. As instructed, engineer has cut in the booster to aid acceleration of the long train strung out through two tunnels back to Blue Tom. Jet of steam at left of stack is evidence that booster is on. (E. L. Huddleston, collection COHS)

series for 2700-2789.

C&O Mechanical Department officials in Richmond knew they could trust the designs of the Advisory Mechanical Committee, for by 1943 the road had already been rewarded by superb performances of the big Texas type 2-10-4s of 1930, the J-3 4-8-4s of 1935, the Allegheny 2-6-6-6s of 1941, and the class L-2 4-6-4s of 1942 – all AMC designs. Such trust was necessary because of the geographical separation of the AMC headquarters in Cleveland from the C&O's in Richmond. If any more trust was needed in the design of the "big Mikes" it was that this same design had been proven in service on the two other roads – the Nickel Plate and Pere Marquette – that remained in the holding company controlling the C&O; namely, the Alleghany Corporation. (The Van Sweringen holding empire dissolved with the death of the brothers from Cleveland in 1936, but C&O's control of Pere Marquette and Nickel Plate continued, for NKP until 1942 and for PM until PM was merged into C&O in 1947.) Until 1936 the Erie had been an important component of the Van Sweringen empire.

The influence of the AMC on C&O motive power decisions lasted from 1929 to 1948. Alonzo Trumbull, chief of motive power for the Erie, first supervised design, in 1927, of a very large 2-8-4, the first with drivers higher than 63 inches. (The Erie's were 69, and later 70 inches.) Such a large engine was possible because of the Erie's liberal vertical and horizontal clearances on its right-of-way; the Erie had been originally laid out for six-foot gauge. The big boiler made possible great power for a 2-8-4, but the cost of increased power capacity was a low factor of adhesion. AMC, founded early in 1929, took the Erie design and, working out its flaws, applied it to an enormous 2-10-4 for C&O in 1930. This locomotive shows its Erie influence in its external styling and in its class designation "T-1."

In 1934, the AMC down scaled the very successful 2-10-4 to a 2-8-4 with 70% of the T-1 's tractive effort and weight. American Locomotive Company (Alco) made the low bid and constructed the first 15 of an eventual order for 80 Nickel Plate Berkshires (Engines 715-779 would all come from Lima Locomotive Works.) The AMC even made parts of the 2-10-4 interchangeable with the 2-8-4. The reason nine years elapsed before the AMC considered the 2-8-4 design for C&O was that C&O had in service throughout the Depression 150 heavy Mikados classed as K-2 and K-3. The K-3s could, and did, haul 160 loaded coal cars down the James River line from the base of the Alleghenies to Richmond and came back, unassisted, with that many empties.

C&O K-4 No. 2716 on Big Sandy Subdivision near Paintsville, Ky with northbound coal train in 1950

"CHANGES IN APPEARANCE" — AMC's design for 2-8-4's for the NKP, PM, and C&O was the same in principal dimensions but there were some changes in external details. Lima builders photo of 2744 in 1945 exhibits perfect balance among elements . Placement of running board, relative to engineer's sight line, adds greatly to this balance, as does the step downward to ladder at front. Running boards were federally mandated in 1915, but nothing was said about ladders or access to cab from running board. (Ray S. Curl collection.)

"CHANGES IN APPEARANCE" — C&O 2-8-4 2697, former Pere Marquette 1213, rolls down James River through Eagle Rock, Virginia, September 1952, with 160 cars. Most PM 2-8-4's kept the two features that distinguished the NKP and PM 2-8-4's from the C&O's 2-8-4's — namely, the location of headlight and shield over air pumps and the placement of steam dome ahead of the sand dome. (E. L. Huddleston, COHS collection.)

The NKP had gotten along in the 1920's and early 1930's with light Mikados, mainly because its manifest freight trains were lighter in tonnage than C&O's solid coal trains. NKP's Mikes, which were built in the early twenties, were essentially the standardized USRA light Mikado type, getting a heft in starting power with trailer boosters. They could move tonnage along but at "drag era" speeds. The problem was that the NKP ran practically parallel with the main line of New York Central. While the NYC thought it could haul its trains at "drag era" speeds, NKP knew that to keep the competitive edge (which it did under capable presidents like Bernet and Davin later) it needed to haul freight faster than its huge but bumbling neighbor. Here the AMC came to the rescue, in its first design job since the T-1 of 1930. It knew clearances would not permit an engine as big as the T-1 and it also knew the tonnage and grade requirements were less than with the T-1s. Hence it scaled down theT-1, and kept the same general appearance of the T-1 (especially the "face" of the locomotive) for the NKP Berkshires. (With the classification letters "S" and "T" the AMC was demonstrating the Erie's dominance in that Committee, for neither C&O nor NKP had a logical place for "S" in its system of class identifications). And

the front ends and steam and sand dome placement of the C&O 2-10-4s and the NKP 2-8-4s (and for that matter the Pere Marquette's as ordered later) were practically identical.

The story of the success of the "700s" — no "luck" involved here in numerical selection, for the 700 slot followed logically from the 600 series Mikes — has been told so often and so well there is no need to review how they kept in regular service to 1958. The Pere Marquette Railway, occupying mostly Michigan's lower peninsula, hauled about the same commodities as the NKP and ran across the same land forms-the glaciated Central Lowlands. It too had had no new power since it received ten modified light USRA Mikados in the late 1920s. As soon as it became apparent what a "winner" NKP had in the AMC designed 2-8-4s, the PM, under, joint management with C&O, placed an order for twins of the NKP
2-8-4s, with one fairly important dimensional change 26-inch cylinder bores instead of 25 inch for all NKP's. (A proportional increase in weight on drivers kept adhesion on both engines the same.) Front end styling on both models was almost identical, with the form of the pilot being the only significant difference (until NKP alone

"CHANGES IN APPEARANCE" — C&O 2699, former Pere Marquette 1215, built by Lima in 1937, ready to leave Detroit with fast freight September 1948. This Berkshire is unusual in appearance for two reasons —the C&O logo on the tender (not regulation, by the way) and the booster (note vertical pipe under cab), a feature on only ten PM 2-8-4's. Engineer Sam Chiddester of Grand Rapids thought the booster equipped 2-8-4s superior to those without. (Joe Schmitz collection.)

KANAWHA SUBDIVISION" The Kanawha Sub comprised the main line from Russell east to Handley. — Extra 2718 approaching Russell in 1948 over the Kanawha Sub could have originated at Handley, Cane Fork, Elk Run, Danville, Peach Creek, Shelby, or Martin — all divisional runs made each day of the working week. (E. L. Huddleston, COHS collection.)

"KANAWHA SUBDIVISION" Extra 2732 approaches Russell over three-track main in 1955. Bellefonte blast furnace towers in background. (E. L. Huddleston, H. H. Harwood collection.)

"KANAWHA SUBDIVISION" - Taken within an hour of each other, these photos of Kanawha type 2-8-4's indicate how busy was the Kanawha Sub a fall day in 1948. Photographer faces west in all views. On right is B&O branch from Huntington and at left is connection with N&W. Behind K-4 2787 is crossing of N&W main over C&O at the Kenova depot. (All, E. L. Huddleston, collection COHS)

"KANAWHA SUBDIVISION" — On Thanksgiving Day 1951, 2731 leaves Huntington eastbound, crossing the Guyan River near its confluence with the Ohio River. At right is flood wall and beyond, high Ohio hills. (E. L. Huddleston, collection COHS)

where they served for a while in a pool at Russell consisting mostly of C&O's 90 class K-4 2-8-4s. In a Clifton Forge pool they undoubtedly replaced whatever K-3 Mikes were still in service. Evidence of this is that in September 1952, this writer observed 2697 (former PM 1213) on a 160 car coal train heading down the James River from Clifton Forge to Richmond. No class K-4 2-8-4s were then being used on the James River line. But there were still several big K-3 Mikados and J-3s 610 and 614 also hauling 160 car trains to Richmond.

Recounting how the Pere Marquette got its first Super Power Berkshires from the AMC is as good a place as any to deal with the placement of the steam dome on the boiler top on the NKP S class, the PM N class and the C&O K class of 2-8-4s. It is as much an aesthetic as a practical consideration. The Chief Mechanical Engineer of the AMC, Alonzo Trumbull, placed the steam dome near the front of the boiler on the huge 2-10-4 that he designed for the C&O in 1930. Presumably this made for more space in the boiler for generating steam, for the big pipe (called the "dry pipe") leading from the dome to the throttle valves could be made shorter than if it ran from a dome located farther back on the boiler. Yet placing the dome well forward on a conical-shaped boiler meant that to insure the dry pipe would remain free of foaming water overflowing into it, the dome would have to be built up higher than it would if the dome were placed near the highest point of the conical boiler, which was a point just forward of the end of the combustion chamber. Trumbull evidently discovered, with the T-1, there were no overflow problems with dome placed well forward, so he carried the proportional placement and size over into the design of the NKP 2-8-4s. As it turned out all 80 NKP 2-8-4s adhered to this placement. Just three years after

added Mars oscillating headlights above the standard headlights.) All NKP and most PM 2-8-4s had "bar" frames instead of solid cast frames and lacked roller bearings — economy moves probably.

Because Pere Marquette became C&O in 1947, all 39 PM 2-8-4s were absorbed into C&O's steam roster. However, the Pere Marquette District had embarked on a rush to dieselization starting in 1949 — with EMD Geeps — that made most PM Berkshires superfluous by late 1950. Early in 1951, according to Art Million, eleven of the PM 2-8-4s were sent to the Chesapeake District,

designing the NKP 2-8-4s, Trumbull adhered to the same location and same dimensions for the first order of Pere Marquette 2-8-4s. Ditto for the second PM order in 1941. However, in 1944 PM's 1228-1239 featured the steam dome just forward of the section of the boiler marking its maximum outside diameter of 98 inches. The year 1942 seemed to be the pivotal year in this design dilemma. For in 1942, C&O's second order of 4-8-4s from the AMC (unlike the first in 1936) had the steam dome behind the sand box, as did C&O's L-2 class Hudsons from Baldwin and C&O's 2-8-4s which started arriving on the property in 1943.

By December 7, 1941, when President Roosevelt spoke of the "day that would live in infamy," C&O had received the first of its magnificent new Allegheny articulateds, plus new eight-wheel switchers, two new 4-8-4s and seven new 4-6-4s – all Super Power except the switchers. The 150 heavy Mikes still were rugged performers, but they were not Super Power. And C&O needed engines that were less in need of maintenance than the older engines with their "built-up" frames and solid bearings. The new C&O engines would have roller bearings on

KANAWHA SUBDIVISION" – An eastbound off Guyan Valley climbs the .30% grade of Scary Hill; 2-8-2 pushes 140 cars back. Though the Teays Valley provides a pre-glacial era dry river bed for the mainline, it nevertheless required pushers on coal trains east and west because "level land' power was used on this route.' (collection Eugene L. Huddleston)

all engine axles and solid engine beds with cylinders in one big casting. (In later orders for the C&O 2-8-4s, the main air reservoir was made part of this casting, set in the frame above the two rear driving axles.)

Rated starting tractive effort of the C&O 2-8-4s was 69,350 lbs. This is 5,250 lbs. more than that of NKP's 2-8-4s, mainly because of increased weight on drivers of the C&O (and Pere Marquette) engines, plus the inch larger cylinder bore. All ninety C&O 2-8-4s, plus ten of the 39 PM 2-8-4s were equipped with booster engines on the rear axle of the trailing truck, which added tractive power at starting or near stalling speed when moving. Because all C&O Super Power locomotives had

boosters (with exception of the 2-6-6-6, which nevertheless had provision for one) one gets curious about them. Trailing trucks had adhesive weight which made it practical (unlike tender axles with varying adhesive weights) for power to be supplied to the wheels.

Topography and tonnage had a lot to do with whether a road outside the Van Sweringen fold – that had nevertheless adopted the "Van Sweringen Berkshire" design – decided to equip its 2-8-4s with boosters. The Virginian Ry., the Wheeling and Lake Erie, the Richmond, Fredericksburg, and Potomac did not adopt them; all 42 of the Louisville and Nashville's 2-8-4s, nicknamed "Big Emma's," did. Both the Virginian

"KANAWHA SUBDIVISION" – Farther up the Kanawha Sub, an eastbound crosses Coal River at St. Albans in October 1947. VF Cabin, interesting 24-hour telegraph office, would soon be torn down after CTC installed. (E. L. Huddleston, collection COHS)

and L&N hauled long coal trains, but the Virginian had bigger engines than 2-8-4s (which were intended for manifests) to haul its coal – the eight 2-6-6-6s of 1945. The L&N hauled long coal trains, mostly out of eastern Kentucky, to northern markets: It also had more severe gradients for its northbound coal than the Virginian had for its eastbound coal. Unlike the Virginian, the L&N had no bigger engines than the M-1 2-8-4s (of 1942, 1944, and 1949). These engines put on a real show hauling coal trains from the level of the Kentucky River to the Bluegrass Plateau near Winchester. At Ford, on the river, an M-1 pusher would wait for double headed M-1's from Corbin, each with about 8,500 tons of coal. The pusher assisted the doubleheader up steep Two Mile Creek toward Patio Tower, getting down to seven m.p.h. with all boosters cut in on the 1.07% grade, for nine miles.

Because the booster was applied to the trailing axle of the trailing truck, the increased tractive effort it provided had little effect on the factor of adhesion, which normally went down as the tractive effort went up relative to the weight on drivers. Boosters did not "slip" easily because they made use of "wasted" dead weight that had no effect on the weight on drivers. Nevertheless,

boosters could slip, as evidenced by the fact that one of the six pipes leading downward (on each side) from the K-4's huge sand box, went to feed the front of the powered trailer wheels. The stream of sand dropped on the track just ahead of the powered wheel definitely improved traction.

On the ninety C&O 2-8-4s, the booster, which cut out at 15 mph, added 14,000 lbs to the starting tractive effort of 69,350 Lbs. Of course, if the booster was not cut in, it could not add that boost of power. That's why on some roads prevailing opinion was that boosters were extraneous. S. Kip Farrington, Jr., sportsman and railfan author, was an anti-booster man: "The booster never made much impression on me. It was just one more extravagance to get out of order and was so many times never 'cut in.' One would in fact, be amazed at what little usage boosters received..." Whether C&O locomotive engineers obeyed instructions is not known; nevertheless, C&O prescribed their use in every case where the locomotive was accelerating from a stop to road speed, or had fallen below a certain speed and in danger of stalling, despite wide open throttle. The two-cylindered reciprocating engines, "splash" lubricated, had only forward motion. When "cut in" by the engineer (through compressed air) , their rapid exhaust from a slot in front of the stack added to the impression of power produced. Because data are hard to get as the years pass, one will likely never discover whether there was a disconnect between the mechanical people and the operational people on their usage over the road.

One place to look for solid data on booster usage is in reports of locomotive performance from data gathered on C&O's dynamometer car, DM-1. Luckily one such report has been preserved. C&O's "Engineer of Tests," issuing it in August 1951, recommended an increase in tonnage in both directions following extensive testing of C&O's class K-4 2-8-4s over the scenic and very old (constructed in the 1850s) line across the Alleghenies and Blue Ridge, a line aptly named the Mountain Subdivision. The main finding of the report stated, "Dynamometer car tests indicate that the present straight tonnage rating can be increased ... with no danger of stalling providing full use is made of the booster." "Full use" of course meant in starting and in cutting in when speed falls under 13.5 mph. The real test of the K-4's mettle was when stops were deliberately made on the ruling grade in each direction "with tonnage exceeding the recommended." Lowest permissible speed on westbound ruling grade was 15 mph and on the eastbound 12.5 mph. To attain the summit of momentum grades (such as Longdale Hill) , speed could fall to 8 mph. One can be sure that the booster was used in every situation it was intended for. The K-4s were picked randomly from the Clifton Forge pool of 2-8-4s; however, engines in the 2760 series predominated because they were equipped with Automatic Train Control devices, in use over the Mountain Subdivision. On board for all runs were the "Division Trainmaster and the Road Foreman [of engines]."

As revealed in the dynamometer report, the K-4 tested was a rugged mountain freight hauler. (The 2-6-6-6 type could not be used over the Mountain Sub until near end of world War II because of tunnel clearances. After the war, freight tonnage continued to be handled quite well without need of an articulated and without assistance from a "helper" engine.) Figures from a run up the grade of 2768 from the rolling Piedmont west of Charlottesville to the summit of the Blue Ridge at historic Blue Ridge Tunnel show that on August 8, 1951, 2768 commanded 50 cars, or 1623 tons. The train was stopped and started again without difficulty on the steepest part of the grade (because of curvature) just east of Little Rock Tunnel. Here the ascent of the Blue Ridge was up a nine mile grade that averaged 1.40%. This tonnage being 123 tons above the rating for a K-4 westbound, the tonnage rating was subsequently increased to 1600 tons. On the eastbound run the longest sustained pull was between Augusta Springs and North Mountain station at the summit of Great North Mountain,

"KANAWHA SUBDIVISION" — St. Alban's 500-ton coaling station was located near the wye leading to the Coal River branch (at right). It was torn down after weakening by a serious derailment in August 1956, nine years after this photo. (E. L. Huddleston, collection COHS)

which averaged 1.50%. On August 2, 1951, No. 2763 stopped with 27 cars, 1875 tons, two miles east of Augusta Springs, and started – the booster cut in, of course – with "no difficulty." Because of this, the previous rating was increased from 1750 tons to 1780 tons. One wonders why only a 30 ton increase here and why the tests had not been done years before! (It would only be a couple of years before the Mountain Sub was completely dieselized.)

Other than for piston displacement, principal dimensions for the 2-8-4s of the three Van Sweringen roads were generally the same. However, the C&O engines, from front coupler to end of cab, were slightly longer than the PM and NKP 2-8-4s. The difference resulted from roomier cabs. *Railway Age* observed in its write-up of the C&O 2-8-4s that the Company had consulted officials of the Brotherhoods — presumably the B of LE and the BLF&E — on cab size. This consultation resulted in lengthening the cab. All ninety C&O K-4s had cabs 95 1/8 inches long, whereas the Nickel Plate and

"KANAWHA SUBDIVISION" — On the Kanawha Sub in 1954, 2725 takes eastbound coal toward Handley as 2737 with 140 cars strung out beyond the Coal River wye into St. Albans Tunnel waits for the eastbound to clear before pulling. It will pick up a 2-8-2 pusher for Scary Hill. (Gary E. Huddleston)

Pere Marquette 2-8-4s were 88 3/4 inches long. Three men were expected to ride in some comfort in the cab: engineer, fireman, and head brakeman. Whether the extra space provided more leg room for the engineer or a less cramped "seat box" for the brakeman is unknown. (By way of comparing cab sizes, one finds the length of cab at 80 inches for the standardized road freight locomotives of the United States Railroad Administration.)

Because the Great Depression was past history and world warfare produced a booming economy, the C&O in 1943 could afford the AMC's recommendation that all engine axles be supplied with roller bearings. Previous to this, even C&O's AMC designed passenger locomotives had not had roller bearings. Although carriage maker Henry Timken invented the tapered roller bearing in 1898, it took a long time for the bearings to come to the railroad industry. Even in the booming 1920's Timken (of Canton, Ohio) could not motivate railroads to buy new locomotives with driving axles cradled in roller bearings. Perhaps railroads thought them too expensive, considering that the driving boxes in which

the axles rode were subject to so much stress that necessary maintenance on the boxes overrode the bearings' advantages of not requiring frequent maintenance.

But in 1929 Timken took the ball into its own court. J. Parker Lamb tells about the astounding success of Timken's demonstrator: "... unable to obtain permission from any railroad or builder to allow a demonstration of its bearings on a large mainline locomotive, Timken purchased a stock 4-8-4 from Alco, similar to the engines built earlier for the Delaware, Lackawanna & Western. Officially designated TRBX 1111, but known informally as the Four Aces, it carried the number under its cab window and the Timken name in large letters on the tender. ...the engine was painted dark green and displayed playing card symbols... on its sand dome and headlight number boards. After being fitted with new bearings, it began a nationwide tour during which it consistently impressed railroads with its operating capabilities and the general public with its unusual characteristics. For example, to show how easily No. 1111 could be moved, a photo-op in Chicago's Union Station had three female office workers

"KANAWHA SUBDIVISION" — With solid, barking exhaust, 2704 starts down the Kanawha with westbound New River coal train, July 1955, past Pratt. Handley yard is less than two miles back, (E. L. Huddleston Collection COHS)

from the Pennsy team up on a rope-pull to haul the mammoth machine forward a few feet. This was possible because the rolling resistance of a rollerbearing-equipped locomotive was a mere 10 ounces per ton!" Edwin P. Alexander tells more about the tests of this fascinating 4-8-4, with 73-inch drivers and tractive effort of 63,700 lbs. In *American Locomotives* he writes: "Upon completion the 1111 was first operated in freight service on the New York Central. From there it was tried in both passenger and freight service on thirteen other roads. In these trials some well known trains such as the C&O's "Sportsman" and the New Haven's "Merchant Limited" were hauled by the 1111. On the Pennsylvania it handled twelve passenger cars up the Allegheny mountain grade without a helper and even saved three minutes on the standard schedule. It fully justified the claims for roller bearings and after these service tests totaling 88,992 miles were completed by August, 1931, it was delivered to the Northern Pacific [which purchased it]." C&O also tested the Four Aces on freight, assigning it to long coal trains over the level track work of the Cincinnati Division between Russell and Stevens Yard. Perhaps because the Depression made economies mandatory, C&O did not order its own 4-8-4s in 1934 with roller bearings. Not until the Allegheny 2-6-6-6's of 1941 and the Baldwin built L-2 Hudsons of 1942 would the Advisory

Mechanical committee prescribe roller bearings for locomotives on C&O, NKP, or PM.

By 1943 the AMC wanted the new "Van Sweringen" Berkshires to be among the best equipped of modern power, so cast steel frames (with attachments and cylinders cast integrally), roller bearings, boosters, and air after-coolers guaranteed their modernity. Also, by 1943 Westinghouse Air Brake Company had designed air after-cooler units that were wholly self-contained. This meant that the C&O 2-8-4 front end would have a different look than the NKP and PM engines, which were not equipped with after coolers. Ventilating grids cooled the air compressed by two cross-compound compressors, mounted on either side of the unit. Compressing air generated a great deal of heat (and moisture) in the process. The need for protecting the cooling unit from the elements resulted in the C&O 2-8-4s having a unique and well balanced front end. As I wrote in The Van Sweringen Berkshires (Classic Power 7), "On the front end of the K-4 the purity of the smokebox front was preserved by keeping the headlight and classification lights off it, and the positioning of the headlight midway between coupler and bell was a master touch. A single functional shield protecting air after cooler unit and twin air pumps gave further distinction to the design, for while it left the face of the smokebox completely uncovered, it seemed to divide

"KANAWHA SUBDIVISION" — Navigational locks and dam on the Kanawha provide background for scene at Handley yard about fifteen minutes before the picture of 2704 in action at Pratt. Extra 2728 is entering yard, and 2704 waits to leave for Russell. (E. L. Huddleston, Collection COHS)

along the placid Ohio River between Russell and Stevens, Kentucky, near Cincinnati. The variation in the adverse grades they encountered is illustrated by the contrast in their freight tonnage ratings —from 1,850 over "Mountain Top" (Corey Hill) in eastern Kentucky (assisted by a 2-6-6-2 pusher) to 16,000 down the James River in Virginia on the route from mountains to tidewater. Tonnage ratings were generally set mathematically, based on the track gradient (with the gradient compensated for curvature) and the rated tractive effort of the locomotive. (Because the rated tractive effort could be lower than the actual drawbar pull, as measured by a

dynamometer car, the calculated rating could end up rather conservative, which probably explains why the ratings on the Mountain Sub were revised upward for the K-4 in 1951.) The rated tractive effort did include the total tractive effort, which on a K-4 was 69,350 lbs. (stenciled on the cab) plus 14,400 lbs. for the booster, totaling 83,750 lbs. Whatever the other benefits of a booster, it did help increase tonnage ratings. For example, on the Big Sandy line coal trains were run from Martin, Ky., and from Shelby, Ky., to Russell. K-3 Mikados (2-8-2) were given 9,000 tons down the river, based on tractive effort (with no booster) of 67,700 lbs; the 90 K-4 "Kanawhas"

(2-8-4) were given 10,000 tons, based on tractive effort (with booster) totaling 83,750 lbs. Thus the booster permitted a tonnage increase of roughly 12% over an engine of roughly equivalent tractive effort not so equipped.

Perhaps the greatest moment of glory for a K-4 on the hill-bound Lexington division was in 1948; two K-4s – with 2787 in the lead – hauled the 17-car campaign train of President Harry S. Truman from Lexington to Ashland and beyond. What an impressive sight was this train of heavy-weight coaches and Pullmans, headed by the two big Kanawhas and trailed by the huge, armored "Ferdinand Magellan," with its open platform from which

the President spoke. A doubleheader was run because in climbing the 2.67% of Corey Hill a pusher could not be placed behind the President's car. In addition to "Varnish" on the scenic Lexington Division, K-4's on the main line took long trains of "day coaches," after World War II ended, on weekend baseball excursions from Charleston, West Virginia, picking up along the way, to Cincinnati. The ease of transportation to Cincinnati and the fact that Crosley Field was in easy walking distance from the Union Station made for a great outpouring of baseball fans. During both World War II and the Korean War the K-4's handled many military movements, because of C&O's access to the string of bases in northern Virginia and naval facilities at Hampton Roads. Troop, hospital, and prisoner-of-war trains were given whatever power was available, and K-4's had a record of dependability. (Altogether, about 70 of the 90 K-4's were equipped with steam heat lines and air communication lines needed to haul passenger trains.)

Another interesting passenger movement handled by K-4's is recalled by Joe Slanser of Marion, Ohio. The all-important football rivalry between Ohio State and the University of Michigan merited its own special train every fall (last game of season for both) between Columbus and Ann Arbor. Mr. Slanser recalls, back in 1947 or 1948, riding it to Ann Arbor, with a K-4 on the head end. While clickedy-clacking across the glacial outwash plains of northern Ohio, he asked the conductor how fast they were going, and the conductor obligingly took out his pocket Ingersoll and timed their passage by a couple of mile posts at 70 MPH. The employee timetable in his possession had a chart for converting elapsed time per mile into speed. (As an aside, that speed should not be too surprising since it was a rule of thumb that a steam locomotive could cruise at a speed equal to the diameter of its driver height in inches – 69 inches for the class K-4.)

The Nickel Plate Road (New York, Chicago, and St. Louis) went its own way managerially in 1942, and yet kept buying the AMC designed Berkshires. The Pere Marquette, however, was merged into C&O in 1947, and some of its "Van Sweringen Berkshires" were sent south to serve on the "old" C&O after the PM District dieselized completely early in 1952. C&O's ninety K-4s were all gone from regular service by August 1956. However, numerous C&O "Kanawhas" were preserved from scrapping for public display, and for that matter in the twenty-first century there exist some NKP and Pere Marquette 2-8-4s that have been so well preserved and so lovingly worked on that they are under steam again!

Four safety valves (with bolt threads of standardized size) were housed within protective casing on centerline of boiler. The spring restrained valves were set to lift off seats at 260, 262, 264, and 266 psi. Immediately behind the valve housing is the blow-off muffler and adjacent to it the acorn-shaped exhaust vent for the feedwater heater's cold water pump. H-8 clumps onto turntable at Clifton Forge, 1944. (CSPR, collection. COHS)

Chapter 9

Improving, Maintaining and Repairing C&O Super Power

"The train broke down somewhere beyond Manassas, and I went forward along the tracks with all the other passengers. 'What's the matter?' I said to the engineer. 'The eccentric strap is broken, son,' he said. It was a very cold day. Later I could not forget the face of the engineer and the words 'eccentric strap.' — Thomas Wolfe, "Of Time and the River", 1935

On his way with his father to Woodrow Wilson's second inauguration, young Thomas Wolfe (1900-1938) universalizes a train break-down. Because the Southern-type valve gear was not always reliable — especially in passenger service — a break-down in 1916 was understandable. Failure on the road of valve gear derived, according to A. W. Bruce, from "overheating or from stress concentration." Break-downs could occur even with Super Power — which was still ten years away — despite techniques such as heat treatment of metals and improvements in bearings and in lubrication of the major valve gear types – the Walshaerts and Baker. Inherent in the design and construction of the steam locomotive was the certainty of wear and the need to control wear in the interests of safety and economy, either through repair or replacement. Also, having a locomotive that was "modern" — either through a road's purchase of new locomotives or through rebuilding with the latest appliances or techniques — would forestall breakdowns and expensive repairs.

To the very end, guarding against corrosion and leaks was a top priority due to an open and fluctuating fire, plus fire tubes surrounded by thousands of gallons of water under pressure, As Bruce put it, "Boiler plate

Automatic lubricators with lube oil lines after installation, will force feed oil to sliding-shoe furnace bearers that permit expansion and contraction of boiler and firebox on frame. Photo vividly imparts the great size and weight of a C&O 2-6-6-6 and illustrates one of the improvements Chapelon championed. (Collection COHS)

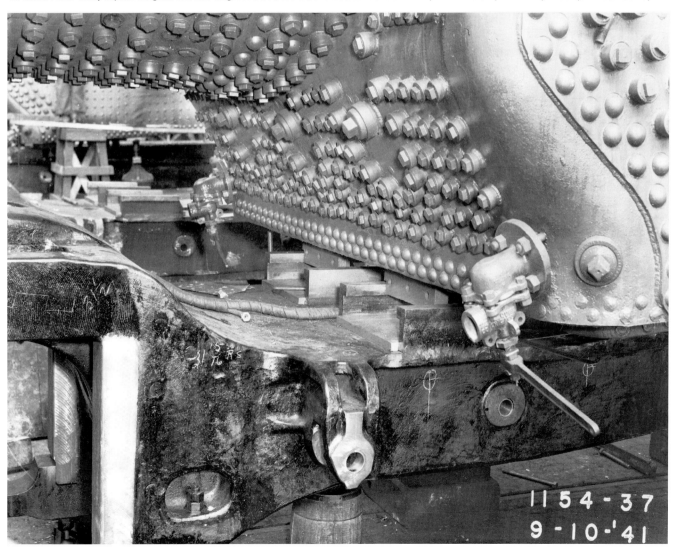

A necessary improvement listed by Andre Chapelon, "water purification treatment," was supplied to boiler feedwater of C&O Super Power, as illustrated by fireman Banks, holding in his left hand a packet of lime and soda ash, which he will pour into the tank before opening the valve on the water spout. Pump house and storage tank are visible on the banks of Big Coal River at Sproul, W.Va , 1949. Compare to photo on page 31 chapter 3. (E. L. Huddleston, collection COHS)

"Before and after" photos of Greenbrier 601 at Charlottesville, Va. , reveal how headlight was lowered and valve gear type changed. TOP LEFT- Left side of 601 (named "Patrick Henry"), in 1938, shows front end similar to "Van Sweringen" Berkshires built about same time. It also has the original Walshaerts valve gear. 601, seen from right (engineer's side (ABOVE) in 1948, displays lowered headlight and Baker valve gear. Two lubricators, side by side, supply valve oil and engine oil to all surfaces not requiring heavier grease fittings. (right side, Joe Schmitz collection; left side, COHS collection.)

and other structural details may fail from embrittlement, corrosion, or fatigue stress due to expansion and contraction caused by temperature variation or to structural flexibility and continued vibration." In addition, the boiling water produced sediments and scale, and the forceful ejection — with wide open throttle — of unburned fuel through the smoke box and up the smoke stack made abrasion and cinder accumulation inside the smoke box a real maintenance problem. Furthermore, the steam locomotive's "backward and forward" power transmission placed huge demands on rod and drive wheel bearings.

Wear from rubbing surfaces and revolving parts was so extensive that lubrication became the most important need in keeping a locomotive running. In his comprehensive history of the steam locomotive, Alfred W. Bruce vividly illustrated the effects of inadequate lubrication: "A properly lubricated driving-axle journal [within the driving box] presents a beautiful blue oily surface. This same surface when dry and unlubricated may become so hot that the surface skin of the journal will rupture in either circumferential or longitudinal characteristic 'heat checks,' or both. Each check has two tiny sharp cutting edges whose effect on the driving-box bearings may be easily imagined. The real damage caused by lack of lubrication must be seen to be appreciated." (With driving axles on a modern locomotive being up to fifteen inches in diameter, there was a lot of

"beautiful blue surface" to admire!) Other "wear and tear" problems included (1) stress on staybolts caused by thin fire spots, expanding and contracting firebox sheets in contact with water under great pressure; (2) grease and dirt accumulating on running gear; (3) steam and water leaks in pipe fittings and connections; (4) metal expansion and contraction due to alternate heating and cooling; (5) wear tolerances exceeding federally mandated safety requirements; (6) locomotive parts incorrectly sized and incorrectly fitted; (7) cinder abrasion within tubes and flues and smoke box.

Excessive and repetitive wear not only affected locomotive performance, it also affected the bottom line costs. Effective control of wear could be exercised by wealthy roads, like those under the Van Sweringen umbrella, through contractual requirements for new locomotives. For example, Alonzo Trumbull, Chief Mechanical Officer of the four Van Sweringen roads, forestalled complaints about ill-fitting parts and leaking connections (in a list of specifications for Pere Marquette 2-8-4s in 1941): "All similar parts of the locomotive and tender shall be perfectly interchangeable in every particular, so that a part taken from one locomotive or tender will replace the same part of another locomotive or tender built from the same drawing . . . " Additionally, "All parts such as boiler, cylinders, cylinder heads, throttle, stand pipe, dry pipe, steam pipe, exhaust pipes, super-

Except for roller bearings and one-piece cast frame, the C&O T-1 2-10-4 of 1930 had about all other "improvements" that would be developed before the end of steam. These included the Worthington open-type feedwater heater, multiple-bearing crosshead and crosshead guides, thermic syphons, type-E superheater, mechanical lubricators (with 24-pint capacity), and over-fire air jets. In fact, the Super Power T-1 pioneered the use of Worthington open-type heaters, multiple-bearing crossheads, and over-fire air jets. (The latter fittings, which enginemen called "smoke consumers," are hard to get data on, for most railroads were evasive about their efforts to eliminate black smoke.) 3004 awaits service at Parsons Yard, Columbus, Ohio, April 1938. (Joe Schmitz collection.)

The 90 K-4 Berkshires (Kanawhas on C&O) purchased between 1943 and 1947 had roller bearings on all engine axles and had General Steel Castings one-piece frames, including cylinders. Thus they had the improvements to modern power that mattered most. They also had all other improvements listed in the caption for T-1 3004. The full-throttled exhaust of 2712 gets sharper as it starts up the "Scary Hill" grade through Milton eastbound over the Kanawha Sub early in 1952. USRA H-5 2-6-6-2 pushes on rear end. (E. L. Huddleston, COHS collection)

heaters, and such other parts as may be designated by the Chief Mechanical Engineer, shall be assembled and tested for accuracy and interchangeability, tightness of joints, or for proper bearing, before final assembling in the locomotive."

Such rigid requirements set forth for the builder by the Advisory Mechanical Committee meant that the chief motive power officials were interested in truly interchangeable parts and precision fits so that parts could be taken out of stock rather than specially machined to fit a particular engine. Precision was especially important to avoid fits that would run hot from being too tight or run loose from not matching. Again, the specifications of the AMC for the Pere Marquette 2-8-4s of 1941 address this issue: "All principal parts of the engine liable to depreciation and renewal in service shall be accurately machined and fitted to gauges and steel bushed templates." Time on a roundhouse spur or backshop bay would be reduced with precise and uniform fittings. And decreased "down time" was the aim of all maintenance and repair.

Also affecting an engine's availability for service were modern devices that, while expensive to install ("retrofit") or to build into the engine when new, would improve performance and decrease maintenance costs. Deciding which improvements were necessary and which were frills was difficult. One locomotive designer was so sure of what these improvements were that he formally listed them. Andre Chapelon, (1892-1978), author of the authoritative *La Locomotiv a Vapeur* (first French ed. 1938, second ed. and trans., 1952 and 2000), spelled out the "techniques which, while apparently expensive, made intensive locomotive utilization possible." They included (using American terminology): (1) solid cast frames with cylinders part of the casting; (2) roller bearings on driving wheel axles and on main rods; (3) Franklin driving box wedges with automatic adjustment; (4) driving wheels with "undeformable rims," namely, the Boxpok, Baldwin disk, or Scullin disk types; (5) automatic (force-feed) lubrication to all rubbing surfaces . . . which in some locomotives may be more than 300;" (6) "water purification treatment" (to control foaming, corrosion, and scaling of the boiler). Typically, on C&O packets of lime and soda ash were added whenever the locomotive tank was filled. Chapelon did not explain why he limited his list to six "techniques." One might assume because the Lima A-1 2-8-4 of 1925 had no "technique" applied except water treatment (the chemicals for which had been available since around 1920, when chemical analysis of water began), that the techniques were not readily available in 1925. That is mostly true, but the first five on Chapelon's list would all be developed by 1929.

C&O Super Power, from 1930 to 1948, variously exemplified all six. Obviously, the first two items on Chapelon's list were quite expensive, and the onslaught of the Depression probably delayed their adoption. For whatever reason, none of the modern power designed by the Advisory Mechanical Committee in the 1930's had roller bearings on the driving axles or cast frames with cylinders integral to the casting. Roller bearings had been marketed since 1930, and Timken Roller Bearing company of Canton, Ohio, had sponsored a fine 4-8-4 to demonstrate the bearings in use, starting in 1930.. However, it was 1937 before American roads and builders placed significant orders with Timken for its tapered roller bearings. 1937 was also about the time that General Steel Castings was able to market its cast steel locomotive beds. These complete frames, made from complex molds in one unit, were marketed under the Commonwealth name. R. G. Henley of the Norfolk and Western early knew the benefits of cast engine beds, for he had made sure N&W's 2-6-6-4s of 1936-1937 had them. In fact, he wrote in the same year of their benefits: "Two cast steel bed castings on a mallet locomotive displace in the neighborhood of a total of 700 major and minor parts."

The AMC's giant 2-10-4s built by Lima for the C&O in early 1930 had solid bearings on all 40 engines, except that on the last two, the leading (pilot) truck was equipped with Timken bearings. Also, while the C&O 2-10-4 made use of impressive castings, they were in three main sections and had to be bolted together. One big improvement on the class T-1 was a 24-pint mechanical lubricator that got its power from the action of a lever attached to the combination lever, which was part of the valve gear. (Later, the T-1 was retrofitted with a second mechanical lubricator.) C&O had pioneered the use of mechanical lubricators in its 2-8-8-2 simple articulateds of 1926, which were not AMC designs. Of course, all subsequent road engines designed by the AMC would have automatic lubricators, usually one on each side. A. W. Bruce stated the these devices did not get general usage until the 1930s.

Not until 1948 did C&O buy Super Power with driving wheels having "undeformable rims." Disk drivers were very rare on freight engines, whatever the road. However, the AMC did equip five out of 25 C&O Super Power passenger engines with disk drivers. The five 4-8-4s (J-3a class) of 1948, Nos. 610-614, were built with the Boxpok design disk drivers instead of the standard spoked type. No expense was spared (or so it seemed) to make engines 610-614, called "Greenbriers" on C&O, the best designed and equipped passenger locomotives on the C&O. They were not, however, the first C&O engines with Boxpok style (that is, composed of two disks fastened together) drivers. C&O's six class F-17 heavy Pacifics of 1914, built with 69-inch spoked drivers, were retrofitted with 74-inch Boxpok drivers in 1934 at C&O's main locomotive shops in Huntington, West Virginia.

Chapelon compiled his list based on the ability of

On a winter morning in 1947 L-1 Hudson 490, completed and inspected, rolled out of Huntington Shops for a steam test run. This poppet-valve 4-6-4 runs effortlessly toward the main line, past Huntington engine terminal, where F-15 Pacific takes on coal for local passenger duty. No. 490, as a class F-19 Pacific, had entered Huntington Shops (seen in background) some months earlier for rebuilding. (CSPR, collection COHS).

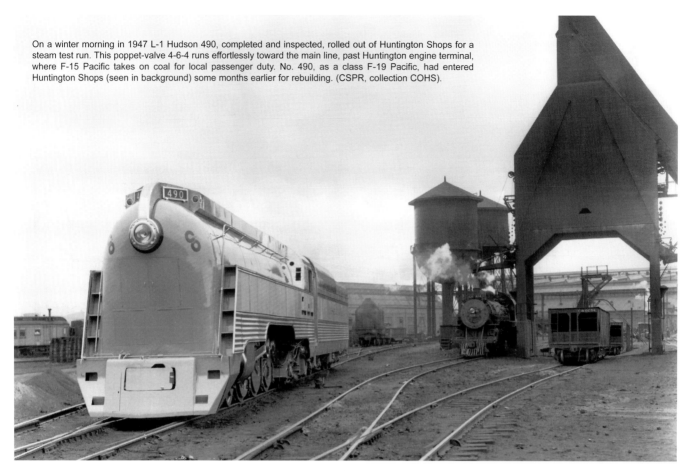

Built as mountain territory passenger engine with 69-inch drivers, the F-17 class was rebuilt for flat-land service with 74-inch drivers of Boxpok design at Huntington in 1934. If the Boxpok application was AMC's choice, then AMC was only mildly interested, for the Committee equipped no other C&O locomotive with this style driver until the five J-3 4-8-4's of 1948. F-17 474 is stopped with no 43 at St. Albans, June 1947. (E. L. Huddleston, collection COHS)

Magnificent photo of a very successful streamlining job taken at Charlottesville a year and a half after its conversion from Pacific to Hudson at Huntington. Some minor changes made in styling (from 490's first appearance) include larger C&O logo up front, wider spacings of mesh in front grill, and number plate just above pilot. (collection Joe Schmitz).

Strip the jacket off 490 and 493 and take a peek! Hudson 494, on grounds of U.S. Army's Fort Eustis north of Newport News, handles a special movement in July, 1952. A lever visible behind the cylinder transfers oscillating movement to the gear box, which times the openings of the steam admission and exhaust valves and which is located on top of frame just behind the cylinder saddle. (collection Joe Schmitz)

each item to decrease maintenance costs and improve performance. Driving box wedges with automatic adjustment, supplied by Franklin Railway Supply Company, did just that. On the market since at least 1930, it is unknown whether AMC had them for the T-1 design in 1930, though the AMC adopted many Franklin specialties for its designs. "Probably no machinery detail of the steam locomotive," according to Alfred Bruce, "has given more trouble than the driving box, owing mainly to overloading and improper lubrication." Each driving box, held in place by vertical walls (pedestals) along the locomotive frame, was subject to great pressures. The Franklin adjustable wedges compensated automatically for the "play" that developed between box and the pedestal sides.

Given Chapelon's reputation as a champion of the reciprocating steam locomotive right to the end, one would expect him to list other major developments in steam technology — late though they might be — which would improve performance and cut maintenance costs. Though not on his list, Chapelon did discuss the Giesl ejector and poppet valves (in the 1952 edition, it should be added.) The Giesl ejector was a carefully researched solution to a fundamental problem of the steam locomotive -balancing the need to draft the fire with the need to

eject as quickly as possible exhaust gases from the cylinders. According to J. N. Westwood's history of modern locomotive designers, Dr. Adolph Giesl-Gieslingen, an Austrian who obtained his doctoral thesis on locomotive front-end design in 1929, designed an exhaust system that increased power and reduced coal consumption. "The arrangement involves seven steam jets one behind the other in a loose fan formation," wrote Westwood, "the steam passing upwards in corresponding fan-like shape. ...The chimney [smoke stack] itself is fan-like to accommodate this [fit] being wide at the top and narrowing downwards. The seven jets present a large entraining periphery to draw the gases from the firebox, and this feature ...ensures good draught while permitting a very low pressure of the exhausting steam." Probably because of the Depression, Giesl's device made little headway in America until 1947 when the C&O (undoubtedly prompted by the Advisory Mechanical Committee) installed the device in the smoke box of a hand-fired locomotive, 0-8-0 no. 191. (The installation in no. 191 took place at C&O's Huntington Shops and might have been in May 1949.) Obviously, the installation required a major overhaul of the exhaust stand, petticoat pipe, spark arrestor, and smoke stack. From what can be

Huge Sellers wheel lathe in Huntington Shops, September 1946, profile contour surface on tires for minimum rail contact. Two of the drivers in foreground belong to T-1 3000; drivers at left to B-1 2951. (CSPR, COHS collection)

Manufactured by Beatty Machine & Mfg. Co. of Hammond, Indiana, this 400-ton hydraulic flanging press in use at Huntington Shops gives shape to metal plate . (CSPR, COHS collection)

learned, the experiment seemed to justify Giesl's claims of improving draft and decreasing back pressure. The fact, though, that C&O (or AMC) supplied the ejector only to a locomotive with very low comparative firing rate suggests that those in the know did not believe the ejector had been as yet perfected for Super Power locomotives, with their very high firing rates and high steam exhaust pressures.

An advance in steam locomotive technology that Chapelon definitely advocated was the poppet valve, which was a European not an American invention. Just as setting the balance between low cylinder back pressure and a strong draft took an ingenious solution, so did working out the timing of steam entrance to and exhaust from the main cylinders. The solution was separate, quick acting admission and exhaust valves to replace the slow acting thimble shaped piston valve. Though an Italian invented the poppet valve, the Franklin Railway Supply Company in the 1930s worked to adapt it to heavy American service. Instead of a thimble shaped valve (whose diameter determined the volume of exhaust that could be discharged), the "Franklin System of Steam Distribution" made use of separate exhaust and admission valves. This prevented the unavoidable overlap that occurred in the act of the piston valve admitting

steam at one end while discharging it at the other. Activating the quick action were cams and tappets, as on automobile engines.

Franklin's Type A valve assembly made use of an oscillating cam shaft to lift the tappets, whereas on the Type B the cam rotated. The advantage of the Type B was a simpler drive mechanism for activating the valves. Both types A and B required less energy for operation than conventional gears. But their main advantage was in reducing wasteful back pressure-that is, exhaust steam which could not be discharged from the main cylinder before the power stroke began. The higher the speed, the more the back pressure. Thus poppet valves were especially effective on passenger locomotives. In fact, all applications of this gear in the United States were on passenger engines.

Widely used on switching, passenger, and freight locomotives even before the advent of Super Power were the Baker and Walshaerts valve gears, which adjusted the valve cut-off and reversed the locomotive through an air-powered cylinder and piston, which the engineer controlled by a relatively small lever or adjusting wheel in the cab. (Even into the 1930s, some steamers in the U.S. still had to be reversed by a large "arm strong" lever.) On both these types, the rods and their

Using what appears to be a Le Blond lathe, operator turns a locomotive piston rod at C&O's Huntington Shops. Piston rods wore mostly on bottoms. (CSPR, collection COHS)

linkages for "timing" the valve events were so complex that railroad slang aptly termed valve gear working as "monkey motion." Parker Lamb in his steam locomotive history has listed the essential parts of both gears: (1) eccentric crank; (2) eccentric rod; (3) reverse link; (4) radius rod; (5) combination lever. The critical part in operating the two types was in the reverse link, which on the Walshaerts was a "single radial slotted rocking link with a fixed central fulcrum" (Bruce) and on the Baker a "peculiar double-bell, crank shaped rocker instead of a link" (Bruce). The Baker gear, widely used on the C&O, was invented by A. D. Baker of Swanton, Ohio, in 1908. The simpler but less reliable Walshaerts was invented around the turn of the century by Egide Walshaerts (1820-1901), a Belgian.

Poppet Valves and the Giesl ejector came so late they had to be evaluated for their potential rather than for their actual utility. This is why Chapelon, perhaps, did not give them their due. His silence on booster engines cannot be explained for the same reason, since booster engines had been used in America since the mid-1920s. in fact, Will Woodard's "recipe" for Super Power included a booster engine on the rear axle of the four-wheel trailing truck of the Lima A-1 demonstrator of 1925. Boosters on the C&O assume great importance because Alonzo

Trumbull, CME of the AMC, supplied all the C&O Super Power freight and passenger locomotives of AMC design with them. (The only exception was the sixty 2-6-6-6 Allegheny type articulateds; space was made for them in the construction of the six-wheel trailing truck, but the weight problem that developed precluded their use).

The booster was a two-cylinder steam engine in which piston rods, eccentric cranks, idler gear, and crankshaft were tightly contained and "splash" lubricated by a pool of motor oil. Valve oil lubricated the pistons. Compressed air moved the idler gear rocker into contact with the trailer axle gear. Boosters were expensive and of no value unless used. Instructions from the Superintendent's Office at Columbus, Ohio, clarify the "Company's" position on their use. In instructions dated April 29, 1948, R. B. Holt, C&O Road Foreman of Engines, stated: Booster must always be used when starting train regardless of the tonnage or number of cars being handled. Before engaging gears , engineers must idle booster engine no less than two minutes in order to warm it up properly. ... booster must not be cut in at any speed greater than 12 miles per hour." (He could have added that high speed boosters on certain class engines could be cut out at speeds up to 35 mph.) The booster's big advantage was in supplying 12,000 to 15,000 lbs.

(depending on the model) of added tractive effort. This additional drawbar pull could be effective in preventing stalling and in starting from a stop in problematical areas. Their only real disadvantage was under utilization.

Andre Chapelon was not the first latter-day locomotive expert to set forth a list of improvements that would make a locomotive truly modern. An unsigned article in Railway Age for November 21, 1931, delineated characteristics of the "modern locomotive." They were: (1) a four-wheel trailer; (2) the Type E superheater (instead of the Type A); (3) thermic syphons; (4) feedwater heater; (5) increase in boiler pressure (made possible by better design and better lubrication methods); (6) a mechanical stoker; (7) limited valve cut-off; (8) booster engine; and (9) solid locomotive bed [frame] casting. Though these improvements were formulated in 1931 -and Chapelon's basic list in 1938- by the time new steam construction in America had ended around 1950, no other significant improvements besides these had come forth to require listing as modern features. C&O Super Power designs eventually had all these latter-day improvements except limited valve cut-off (about which there was disagreement concerning its efficacy). As soon as economic conditions permitted, the Advisory Mechanical Committee in Cleveland adopted the improvements for C&O and the other Van Sweringen roads that asked for them.

The chronology of these improvements reveals that steam locomotive development pretty much stopped about the year 1930. The oldest features chronologically were the mechanical stoker, about 1911, and the superheater about the same time. The stoker, with its powered "screw" feeder, produced much higher firing rates than possible with manual firing. And the superheater, which added "more bounce to the ounce" to the steam, was the most important advance in design of the steam locomotive in the twentieth century. It was easy to overlook because it could not be seen. One had to open the smokebox door and peer inside, looking for its curved tubing behind the cinder screen, stack extension and the exhaust stand. Only one company, the Superheater Company, had mastered the techniques for forging tubing of small diameter which would yet withstand very high exhaust gas speeds and temperatures. According to Bruce, the superheater increased the power output 25 to 30 percent or more "when the same amount of fuel was burned" over the saturated steam engine. (Steam becomes superheated in passing through numerous looped pipes inserted in the hollow spaces of flues, which are the larger of the pipes carrying gases from the fire and not to be confused with the tubes, the smaller of

At Huntington Shops in 1943, two Machinist inspect roller bearings in their races, which have been cleaned of lubricants. (Only one side of twin row is visible.) The flanged tires on this freight engine have been removed from the wheel centers. (C&O Railway Official Photo, COHS collection)

In Huntington's Blacksmith Shop in 1943, smiths do some hot forge shaping with a 1,100 lb. steam hammer. Its sound was ferocious! (CSPR, COHS collection)

the numerous pipes transporting the gases forward.) The type E superheater unit had greater heating surface than the type A. Its tubing was smaller (and thus harder to forge) but fit into many more flues than the type A with its larger tubing.

Next oldest major improvement was the feedwater heater, about 1923, which used exhaust steam to preheat water fed to the boiler. Most of the other techniques and improvements were ready to market in the late 1920s. Roller bearings and solid cast frames with cylin-

ders integrated were ready by 1930, Both were most important in forestalling excessive wear and preventing breakdowns on the road. Yet cash strapped railroads were not ready for them. The otherwise very "modern" C&O T-1 2-10-4 of 1930 was a good example of this. The T-1 had practically all the features listed above, yet as already noted, the forty big engines lacked roller bearings and one-piece cast frames. (Though lacking complete frames in one piece, they did have side bars and crossties-the critical middle section-cast as one piece, a great step forward.)

The AMC was always looking for improvements in steam locomotive technology, particularly as the effects of the Depression lessened. For example, in 1934 C&O shop forces at Russell, Ky., fitted T-1 no. 3008 with patented coils that preheated air entering the firebox through the grates. Eric Hirsimaki, in his history of Lima Locomotive Works, explores the successes and failures of this device.

In the course of maintenance, repair, and upkeep of a steam locomotive, major improvements like most of those listed above could be retrofitted to older locomotives needing them. The life of a steamer was long, and improvements were needed as technology advanced. Of course, modern steam locomotives, like C&O Super Power, had already arrived from the builder with the "modern" features, so if one goes through a collection of photos of the ninety C&O K-4 2-8-4s looking for appliances retrofitted to them, he will not find any of significance. About the only real improvements came about within the chronology of new orders. For example, the first forty 2-8-4s, completed in 1943, had Franklin Precision reverse gears and main air reservoirs mounted under running boards on both sides. The remaining fifty 2-8-4s, coming in 1945 and 1947, had Alco reverse gears and a single air reservoir mounted in the frame just above the main axle driving boxes. Thus the improvements on the C&O 2-8-4s were affected only by changes initiated with new orders, not by retrofits. This was true especially of the T-1 (2-10-4) — which came in only one order and of the H-8 (2-6-6-6) — which had no important changes in orders stretching from 1941 to 1948. Older locomotives would get changes at shopping for programmed repairs, and their looks could be altered in ways that were sometimes hard to figure out the logic of. Some changes, though, made to the older steamers could not be identified in photos, whether of the right or left side of the engine. This was true of C&O Consolidations. Many of these 2-8-0s, built at the turn of the century, were retrofitted at the Huntington Shops with superheaters, which were a significant but hidden improvement.

One enjoyment of studying steam engines is that one can always find anomalies. Thus, one can find a type of C&O Super Power that had significant changes made in the course of shopping at Huntington. These were the J-3 class (4-8-4) of 1935. In 1942 the five engines in this order, at Huntington, had their headlights lowered to the pilot beam from a position in the middle of the smoke box front. They also had their Walshaerts valve gear replaced with the Baker type. Why weren't these things done when the engines were built? One suspects some tension between the wishes of the Advisory Mechanical Committee, who originated the design, and the C&O Motive Power Department in Richmond, Virginia, who had to approve the design. After all, the two brand new

J-3 4-8-4s C&O purchased in 1942 -numbers 605 and 606- came equipped with headlight on pilot and Baker valve gear.

C&O's main locomotive shops, at Huntington, West Virginia, had the necessary equipment to build locomotives from the ground up, but the big complex usually kept busy restoring worn out locomotives and retrofitting them with appliances that offered a better way of doing things or that the government required for safety purposes. There was one interesting exception to not building new locomotives-though technically it was a rebuild. This occurred in 1946 when C&O's most famous and powerful Pacific type of 1926 — the class F-19 — was stripped down and given all new parts and converted into a Hudson type, which by virtue of its 4-6-4 wheel arrangement was considered Super Power. Steam authority Phil Shuster investigated little known details of this modernization. He notes that after no. 490, the first F-19 Pacific to be modernized, was stripped down to the boiler shell, rebuilding proceeded as follows: "New cast steel main frames with integral cylinders and air reservoirs were purchased, new fire box and extended smokebox were added to a rebuilt boiler having less tubes and more flues. A new four-wheel trailing truck with a Franklin E-1 high-speed booster was added, Franklin type A poppet valves were utilized in the cylinder castings, and a trade of feedwater heater equipment was made with the F-17 class [4-6-2], taking Worthington heaters from these Pacifics in exchange for the F-19's Elesco types. Timken roller bearings were added to all rods and axles, including the tender, and the largest cab ever used on the C&O assumed its position behind the [boiler] backhead." Then, said Shuster, a streamlined shroud was applied, the whole conversion taking about five months. (The L-1's did retain arch tubes as support for the brick arch in the firebox. Inclusion of syphons or circulators to the arch support would have added somewhat more heating surface, but making steam was not a problem with the big boilered engine.)

The fact that rebuilt Hudsons (Nos. 490-494) were equipped with multiple bearing crosshead guides (connecting the crosshead with the piston thrust) merits mention because every new road locomotive designed by the Advisory Mechanical Committee of Cleveland from its founding in 1929 came with multiple bearing guides-whether for C&O, NKP, or Pere Marquette. All five F-19 class Pacifics of 1926 came equipped with the alligator type guide. A. W. Bruce in his history of the steam locomotive pointed out that the multiple bearing type "eventually superseded the alligator type" on all large engines built since about 1935. Its advantages were "relative light weight and high in bearing area."

Only the boiler shell was used in construction of the Hudson from the Pacific. Huntington Shops had the facilities for rolling sheets of steel into shapes needed for the new firebox and extended smoke box. The designers already had a big boiler shell to work with. The boilers for the five F-19 Pacifics were "exceptionally large" even for a heavy Pacific, according to historian Don Leach. Keeping the construction process down to five months was aided by the shop's 250-ton overhead crane's ability to lift and carry the smokebox, boiler and firebox assembly onto the already wheeled locomotive frame. As measured by the construction process described above, the Pacific rebuilt to a Hudson had all but one of the "techniques" cited in Chapelon"s book and in the unsigned article in *Railway Age* (1931). From Chapelon's list only disk drivers were lacking, and from Railway Age's only limited valve cut-off. One can conclude that no. 490 and her sisters 491 through 494 (though 494 remained without a streamlined shroud) ended up being very modern locomotives, especially since they had poppet valves, which precious few American steam locomotives had! Of course, the F-19 Pacifics were fine locomotives also, and had been supplied in 1926 with some "modern" features, including mechanical stokers (which some roads thought not necessary for passenger engines), mechanical (force feed) lubricators, and feedwater heaters. (The F-19 Pacifics had come equipped with the Elesco "closed type" heater, whereas the rebuilds-classed L-1 had the Worthington "open" type. The "open" type was more efficient than the "closed" because the steam from the exhaust mixed directly with the cold water; in the "closed" the steam radiated its heat through coils.)

Alterations, retrofits, and rebuildings were the romantic side of locomotive upkeep, repair, and utilization. For these changes did not just preserve the status quo. As exemplars of modernization that were well designed and clearly in evidence, they introduced a certain panache into locomotive styling. However, wear exerted its insidious influence in ways that could only be controlled through replacement of parts that required lots of muscle power but that little affected the appearance of the locomotive. Those readers who knew steam as the predominant form of railroad motive power can recall how a steam locomotive gave evidence of its needing "repair work" by such crude reminders as leaks at steam seals (such as front end multiple throttle valve) made more visible in cold weather, and banging and clanking main rods and side rods, caused by worn and loose bearings.

Keeping an engine running involved a technology that never advanced very far beyond basic needs for lubrication of moving parts and tightening of those parts. Even maintaining the best Super Power produced in the 1940's never got beyond techniques and tools that had been around since the first World War. When a steamer was new, it ran "tight" and thus noiselessly. (This writer recalls well following new 2-8-4, 2740. on his bike as the engine arrived at the Russell engine terminal via the runaround track; lateral motion was so well controlled and adjusted that the there were no groans from driver box hubs or flanges binding on the sharp curves. Its silence in motion was a golden characteristic.) Of course, a steamer could be adjusted too tight.

Records of the United States Railroad Administration disclose that both C&O and Norfolk and Western complained (when asked to rate their new power) that their new USRA designed 4-8-4s of 1919 were "tight." This must have been a temporary condition, for both roads got excellent service from their heavy Mountain types until the 1950s.

Truly, adjustments to the moving parts of a steamer were regular and integral to locomotive operation. These adjustments were so taken for granted that the AMC, the locomotive builders, and the Interstate Commerce Commission established dimensional wear limits beyond which machining was required. For critical locomotive parts, like main rod brasses, for example, the ICC decreed that "the bore of main rod bearings shall not exceed pin diameters more than 3/32 inch at front or back." Loose brasses resulted in banging and clanking main rods, of course, but with tight brasses (a condition on new or newly shopped engines) there was a danger of overheating. General practice was to let engines wear to approximate clearances rather than to expend many shop hours achieving precise clearances. Nowadays a fully automated procedure would achieve those precise clearances.

More rugged was the work required on the tubes and flues in the boiler. Their leaking at the ends was caused by expansion and contraction and corrosion and scale build-up. Only close inspection would reveal their condition. To assure that these inspections took place, the Bureau of Locomotive Inspection of the Interstate Commerce Commission laid down Rule 10; to wit, "Flues [and tubes] to be removed at least once every four years and a thorough examination shall be made of the entire interior of the boiler. After flues [and tubes] are taken out, the inside of the boiler must have the scale removed and be thoroughly cleaned. This period for the removal of flues [and tubes] may be extended upon application if an investigation shows that conditions warrant it."To provide a convenient record of these extensions and dates of last removal, C&O's Mechanical Department published a booklet with this information.

Inside the shops, force was often more important than micrometer precision in mating parts. Smithsonian curator William Withuhn illustrates this point in an anecdote about shop men of the Pennsylvania Railroad at Fort Wayne, Indiana, and their failure to cope with "some minor adjustment" to a heavy PRR Pacific (class K-4) that had been retrofitted, experimentally, with Franklin Type A poppet valves. Situated near the cylinder saddle was a gear box which transmitted the motion of the combination lever to activate the oscillating cam shafts on both sides of the engine; inside, the box was akin to a

A Machinist operator uses a Milling Machine to tandem finish cut outside dimensions on new intermediate side rods in 1945. Shavings accumulate as liquid cools cutting teeth. (CSPR, COHS collection)

small version of a Walshaerts valve gear. (The valve box was similar to that used on C&O 4-6-4 no. 490 and her sisters.) In order to make the adjustment to the gear box, the representative from Franklin Railway Supply who was on the scene requested help from the local shop men. They showed up, in Withuhns words, with a "little wooden shop wagon, loaded with the usual array of hammers, mauls, bars, Stillson wrenches, and ten-pound end wrenches, common to a steam roundhouse. The Franklin representative "took a horrified look at the smallest tool on the cart, a three inch Stillson. ...'My God, is that the smallest thing you have?' The representative had to go out to his own car and use his own set of socket wrenches on the complex gear box. The point is, no one at Fort Wayne appreciated the precision fits of the Franklin gear."

The impression should not be left that for men who worked on Super Power steam locomotives, more brawn than brain was required. It was rather the fact that so many parts were so large they had to be supported by jib cranes and press forced into place or expanded by heat to loosen. Sheer muscle power and the leverage afforded by wrenches were the keys to assembling and disassembling. (One wonders when powered torque wrenches were required for use in shops that worked on steamers.) Most auxiliary appliances on a modern steamer had "nut and bolt" connections that did require precision fits and adjustments that socket and specialized wrenches were capable of. For example, Franklin Railway Supply Company in 1945 issued a fifteen page "Shop and Terminal Maintenance Guide" for its Franklin Type F-2 Precision Reverse Gear. A list of 207 parts covered the compressed-air operated piston assembly, to which was attached a booster-latch mechanism. The gear assembly did not include the revolving reach rod from the cab nor the extension from the piston rod to the valve gear. The list did include all necessary nuts, washers, and cotter pins.

Upkeep of modern locomotives like C&O Super Power was not that much different from upkeep of other steam power. The very way steamers were put together was a handicap. Usually whenever writers today describe how a locomotive was disassembled for repairs and inspections, they use the term "stripped." There was no easy access to the major areas of "wear" on the locomotive -e.g., inside the boiler, inside the firebox, and to the driving boxes that held the bearings for the driving wheels. Also adding to the costs and difficulty was the need for periodic "safety first" inspections of the inside of the locomotive that could not be made without extinguishing the fire. One big advantage of the steamer was that parts could be renewed by borrowing from other locomotives. Thus parts not otherwise kept in stock could be supplied and machined to fit as needed. Also, often parts did not need replacing; they only needed renewing. For example, retired C&O machinist Alan Hickman explained to this writer that because locomotive pistons wore much more on the bottom than on the top, they were built up with bronze metal and then "trued" on a lathe.

Where did the inspections and repairs take place? The most critical places were on the cab of the locomotive and the inspection pit under the locomotive right after a run. The fitness of a locomotive for service was its performance in service. Thus the locomotive's engineer, at the end of his run, left on the cab a "Daily Locomotive Inspection and Repair Report" (C&O form L-24). When the locomotive entered the engine terminal area at the end of its run, an inspector from the Mechanical Department also prepared a report noting problems that would prevent the locomotive from making a fast turn-around time. This writer recalls as a teenager observing these men in action, performing checks like draining a pet cock on a main air reservoir (an action not necessary with modern self-draining reservoirs) or — while underneath the engine — using a ball-peen hammer to test the soundness of metal parts. The problems that the inspector and engine crew had noted could usually be handled as a "running repair" by the roundhouse force, consisting at the minimum of a journeyman machinist and pipe fitter.

If a problem developed on the road that could not wait until the run was completed, the engineer and fireman could use tools kept on the locomotive (on C&O in bunkers in the tender on either side of the coal supply). As listed in an older C&O booklet on "Progressive Examination of Locomotive Firemen," they included "hammer, [cold] chisel, [15 in.] monkey wrench, [special] wrench to take down main and side rods [in case transmission is disabled, frame broken, etc.], grate shaver [shaker], fire racks, broom, dope bucket, dope hook ["dope" was "waste" saturated with oil for solid bearings], scoops, and torches." The Advisory Mechanical Committee had its own list of supplies listed in AMC specifications for new locomotives, and they duplicated mostly the preceding list, with a with a Prime Alemite air operated grease gun and 18-inch pipe wrench being significant additions in terms of items needed for improvised repair work.

In the cab of a locomotive, on the roof above the fireman's seat box were posted two ICC sanctioned forms, one an Annual Locomotive Inspection and Repair Report and the other a Monthly form completed the first month after the annual inspection These "Forms" would be one record of when the engine would be due its next 30-day required inspection plus information on other tests and renewals. For the Monthly inspection, the engine hostlers would "drop the fire" on the inward move at the engine terminal. This entailed shaking grates in a front to back rocking motion at the cinder pit, and then moving the locomotive to an empty roundhouse stall. Surprisingly, even after dumping the fire and cleaning the inside of the ash pan, enough saturated steam remained in the boiler to power the locomotive's move into the roundhouse After the boiler was drained, it was thoroughly washed out by high-pressure water nozzles, cleaning also included arch tubes, Nicholson thermic syphons or water circulators depending on class of locomotive. There were as many as thirty-five washout plugs to be removed for a 30 day inspection and boiler wash.

It is often assumed the federal government mandated "class" repairs. The ICC was interested only in safety inspections and in keeping track of critical wear limits. It was up to the railroads to schedule the repairs and to conduct "preventive maintenance." Only the main shops at Huntington could provide the space, the skilled workmen, and facilities (like cranes) for stripping down a steam locomotive and putting it back together again. On the C&O, numbers designated the classes, "5" being the least involved and "1" the most extensive. A procedure required in all five classes was removing the thick steel tires from the driving wheels and either "turning" them (grinding them to conform to gauged surface contour) or supplying new tires. For its Eastern General Division C&O had a classic shop building at Clifton Forge, Virginia, to handle the least involved class repairs, with a similar building (attached directly to two roundhouses) at Russell, Kentucky, for the Western General Division. For its Northern Region (originally called the Pere Marquette District) C&O used the main shop building at Grand Rapids, Michigan, acquired with the Pere Marquette merger. (This building was not long used for steam repairs after the merger because the Northern Region was fully dieselized by 1952.)

It was appropriate that the C&O's main locomotive shops, a jewel among such heavy repair facilities, worldwide, should be at Huntington, West Virginia, a city that Collis Huntington, C&O's founder, picked as its western terminus and named after himself. The shops were built on a scale that could handle the biggest of engines and handle them in quantity and expeditiously. The scheduling of Class 3 repairs (required about every four or five years) at Huntington is instructive. According to *Railway Mechanical Engineer*, Class 3 repairs at Huntington took only twenty-one working days: "The boiler jacket and lagging (heat insulation) were removed on the first day. The boiler was not removed but miscellaneous boiler work (including descaling tubes) took 16 days; hydrostatic testing was done on the seventeenth day. Lagging and jacket were replaced on the twenty-first day. Meanwhile, side rods and wheels had received separate attention and were replaced on the eighteenth day. Valve gear work was finished on the nineteenth day, and pistons, main rods, and brake rigging were finished on the twenty-first day. The tender was refurbished separately and finished on the twenty-third day. Many additional operations were proceeding simultaneously, of course, such as the 24 items sent to the machine shop, including cylin-

ders, crossheads, valves, and pistons; injectors; lubricators; brake cylinders; main and side rods; and air pumps." For doing this work employees were assigned by skills into various crafts; namely, machinists, boilermakers, blacksmiths, electricians, pipe fitters, and tin smiths.

The work in the Huntington Shops, organized by areas, included (1) the erecting shop; (2) machine shop; (3)boiler shop; (4) pipe and tire shop; (5) blacksmith shop; (6) electrical department; (7) smaller units such as carpenters, painters a chemist, and storekeeper department.

The capability of the shops to handle the biggest of "Mallets' and a sizeable number of them at one time is well supported by statistics on the number and size cranes in the Shops (as cited in Railway Mechanical Engineer, May 1931): seventeen traveling cranes ranging from a 250-ton capacity Industrial Brownhoist to several fifteen-ton capacity. All of these cranes are modern high-speed cranes which will permit the handling of parts with the least possible delay. A large number of smaller capacity cranes, mostly of the jib type, have been installed throughout the shop for the purpose of handling work to and from machines without the necessity of calling on the overhead cranes. The majority of these smaller cranes are equipped with two-ton electric hoists."

Working in an environment where heavy steel appliances or component parts had to be removed from the engine and then taken apart (typically with pneumatic wrenches) required the workers' attention to "safety first" rules. This was especially true of removing and attaching "brake rigging, spring rigging, super heaters, and [the frame's] bottom binder," according to Allen Hickman, retired machinist from Clifton Forge. Galloway and Wrenn made clear the need for "safety first" in their description of safety hazards at the shops of the Southern Railway at Spencer, North Carolina. They cited as examples "rapidly spinning machines and metal shavings sprayed from parts being machined." Carelessness could be fatal. Allen Hickman spent most of his long career operating a Bullard turret lathe, a large machine tool capable of fashioning from steel some 140 different locomotive parts, according to the 1944 *Locomotive Cyclopedia*. Conversing with this writer about the difficulty of physically removing safety valves from the boiler shell and the need for special wrenches to do so, Mr. Hickman told of a fatal error in removing the valves preparatory to a hydrostatic pressure test of a C&O locomotive boiler. This particular worker fitted solid threaded caps over the opening left by removal of the safety valves (usually three in number). One of these caps, incorrectly cross threaded, blew off and killed the worker. (Safety valves cannot be used for the test because the test pressure on the boiler is 25 percent above the working pressure.)

C&O machinest's helper C.J. Swoope heating locomotive tire at Clifton Forge, VA shop January 1951. Inspection has revealed surface defects. After tires are turned or new ones supplied, "shrink fitting" on wheel centers will tighten them again.

Machine Tools
Eugen L Huddleston

Say "tool" to home owners and they'll think of hammers, saws, planers, wrenches, levels, drills – those items needed to make home repairs. Mention "tools" to those more creative around the home and more in need of precision fits and invisible fastenings and they will think of advertisements in magazines like Tauton's Fine Wood Working (whose typical article is "Mortise and Tenon Basics.") Mention tools to a steam locomotive Machinist and he'll think of tools which are so complex, so accurate, and capable of doing any job that they acquire an extensive vocabulary of technical terms (like mandrel, spindle, chuck, arbor, jig and tram) and an identity of their own, based usually on the manufacturer producing the specialized machine tool. A lot of adjectives apply when you see them in operation-finesse, polish, geometrical perfection. Operating them becomes an end in itself because of the skill required to set an operation and to carry it through. This was certainly true when Super Power locomotives were being made, but today of course computers program the operations.

Machine tools were so essential to steam locomotive repair, maintenance, and construction that at its high point in 1926, the Altoona Works of the Pennsylvania Railroad, which repaired and built cars and locomotives, had a total of 4,500 machine tools. There would never have been a steam locomotive without machine tools. John Wilkinson's invention of the boring machine in 1775 enabled James Watt to bore a true cylinder and make his first successful steam engine. A machine tool is defined as a power-driven machine used to shape metal. Machining as operation is summed up well in Galloway and Wrinn's book on the Southern's Spencer Shops: parts smoothed, straightened, or changed in size.

According to *World Book*, there are two chief machine tool operations: metal removal and metal forming. Metal removal is mostly achieved by cutting away. The cutting machine most people know about is the lathe. It's basic for turning metal into round shapes. A "turret lathe" has several different cutting tools mounted on a revolving tool holder, called a turret. Machines that drill holes include the drill press and boring mill, which typically enlarges and finish a hole already drilled. On the milling machine, metal is removed by a rotary multiple tooth cutter. The work piece is secured to a table whose motion relative to the cutter is controlled in any combination of longitudinal, transverse, or vertical "feels." A planning machine makes smooth, flat surfaces like a hand planer, only the surfaces cover much more area and usually the cutter remains stationary while the surface being planed moves back and forth. These, and shapers, slotters, and grinders are the basic metal removing machines so necessary in Super Power engines' projecting a look of precision and pleasing angles.

Metal forming operations involved the heaviest machine tools. These tools were used to rebuild the F-19 Pacifics into L-1 Hudson at Huntington in 1946-47. They were also used for replacing major components on older C&O locomotives,

and there were plenty of those around. (Even in 1948 C&O's "fleet" of Consolidations went back to 1909 or before.) The AMC, in designing C&O's Super Power, tried to design parts that were interchangeable or that could be easily fashioned from dies and templates. Thus, though Huntington had forging machines, they would not be widely used on Super Power for hammering hot metal into required shapes. For main and side rods, valve gear, brakes, springs, and other heavy work, Huntington had a 100-ton hydraulic forging press, and in its blacksmith shop had a 1,100 lb. steam hammer (often called a drop hammer). Another heavy kind of tool was the flange press, which-using a die to form the shape-could stamp a metal sheet into any shape, like that cover on the steam dome. The "press brake " to bend cold rolled sheet steel to form boiler and cylinder jacket or to form boiler steel plate for firebox repairs.

At the other extreme from these noisy machines that hammer or bend hot metal into shape were hand tools that the boilermaker, machinist, blacksmith, pipe fitter, or electrician used in the course of work, such as the sledge hammer, ball peen hammer, blacksmith's hammer, and the beetle. Among wrenches were the Stillson wrench, spanner wrench, box wrench, Reed strap wrench, and wrenches machined "at home" such as; recessed open hex wrenches of varying sizes for removal and installation of hexagonal nut castings on bottom of safety valves and valve setting pressures. Barrel wrenches were forged with a hexagonal shape to remove large and small nuts for running gear repairs. For reaming, "scraping out", or shaping metal or wood were the broach, chisel, auger, fluted mill cutters and awl. For checking tolerances to thousandths of an inch, the machinist could use a micrometer or vernier caliper. To assure accuracy in maintaining snug fits, the machinist fit his machine tool with patterns, dies, jigs, or templates. The AMC wanted to cut the cost of replacement parts for its Super Power engines. It thus demanded in its specifications that the builder use jigs, etc. This was made clear in the AMC's specs for the order of fifteen Pere Marquette 2-8-4s in 1941 under the heading "gauges, templates, and jigs": "All principal parts of engine liable to depreciation and renewal in service shall be accurately machined and fitted to gauges and steel bushed templates."

There were (and are) of course specialized variations in the basic machine tools. One is the vertical turret lathe, which like a boring mill can finish the inside of a circular form but which can finish the outside also. Artist and retired machinist Allen Hickman of Clifton Forge, Virginia, for twelve years operated a "Bullards" in the Clifton Forge shops. His vertical turret lathe, made by the Bullard Company would "turn" the inside and outside of brass driving-box bearings (called crown brasses) at the same time. (Obviously, the Clifton Forge locomotive shops worked mostly on locomotives with solid bearings, even to the late 1940's, for the Alleghenies and

Berkshires at Clifton forge-with roller bearings-were outnumbered by the Mikados, Mallets, Consolidations and 4-8-2s and 4-8-4s without roller bearings.)

The main reason for specialized machine tools was to save money. Repairing steam locomotives was the most expensive item in their operation. Because of this high cost the railroad company was very much aware of time. After all, time is money. Mining childhood memories, I can illustrate how the Company so carefully measured time. On summer mornings I could hear loud and clear the steam work whistle give a single short blast from the power plant at the Russell Locomotive Shops to announce that it was 6:55AM and time to put up tools or shut them down. Then at 7AM promptly came a longer blast announcing the end of third trick and the start of first. C&O management's focus on time led to time studies at the newly enlarged Huntington Shops in 1931 concluding that specialized machine tools operated in groups could save time and thus money. The point here is that for modern steam repair basic machine tools had been largely supplanted by special duty tools, like the Bullard vertical turret lathe (described above), the Morton keyway cutter, the 90-inch driver wheel lathe, the double head rod boring mill, Coleman vertical boring and turning mill, the Cincinnati 32-inch back geared shaper, and many others. The McCabe pneumatic flanging machine performed many uses in firebox work; forming of door sheets and knuckle sheet, a 90° rolled-radius bend on top of tube sheet riveted to the crown sheet.

Machinist and Boilermaker hand tools by Ingersoll Rand and Wiedeke Co. included air hammers and air motors using special tools that created a work of art by skilled craftsmen. Air hammer and air motors of various sizes and weight were used extensively for boiler and tender tank repairs. Air hammers accommodated an assortment of forged tools and dies for tube and flues, staybolts, hot and cold rivet work. Air motors powered cutter tools to cut out old boiler tubes and flues, self-feed tube rolls rolled new tubes and flues tight into tube sheets, fluted reamers reamed mud ring and staybolt holes for new rivets and staybolts.

Special shop made Inspectors Hammers included; Air Reservoir Hammer for hammer testing non-welded air reservoirs, Staybolt Hammer for testing rigid staybolts and Machinist Inspectors Hammer, to inspect running gear, safety appliances and couplers.

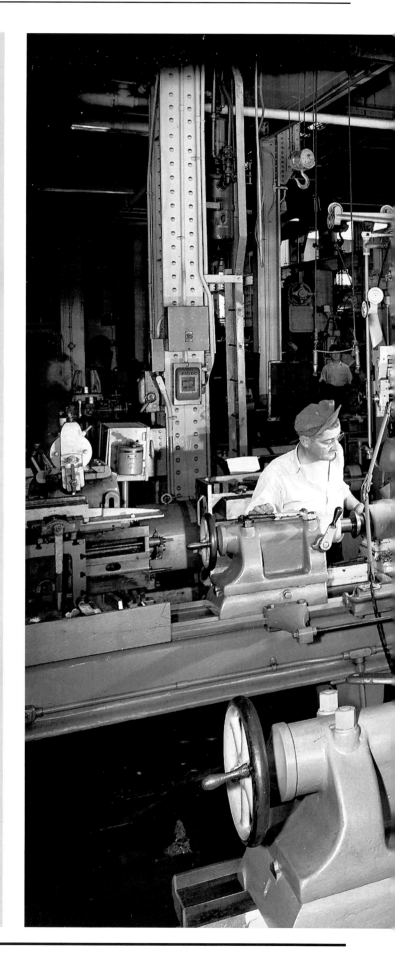

RIGHT - Stoker repairs were often the results of a foreign piece of metal or object that jammed the tender conveyor screw. After inspection, screws were straightened and worn conveyor screw flights welded with a hard-facing alloy material. Engine lathes are used to complete a finish cut to Standard Stoker Co. dimension specifications. (CSPR, collection. COHS)

"The K4's could lug coal drags, hotshot merchandise, and even heavy varnish; they rode like Pullmans... the 2-8-4's could do it all and in a most efficient and impressive manner."
— Curt Tillotson, Jr., *Classic Steam Trains of the South*.

C&O #2731 brings No. 90, the Expeditor up the Ohio Valley toward Russell. - Photo by Eugene L. Huddleston

Chapter 10

C&O Super Power Suitability

"In May 1937, I again was called into the Assistant Shop Superintendent's office [in Huntington] and advised that the Advisory Mechanical Committee in Cleveland, Ohio, had some special work and I was to report to the Chief Mechanical Engineer on May 15th for a three month period. The Advisory Mechanical Committee was composed of personnel from the four railroads the Van Sweringen brothers controlled. ...The committee performed all engineering and design work for the four [roads] with the idea of standardizing whenever possible. It was the most pleasurable detail I [ever] had, as the Cleveland Exposition was held on the lakefront that summer."
— *"The Main Line: The Life and Career of Larry Howard Booth" (manuscript, May 1996)*

Discovering the suitability of AMC designed Super Power to C&O's needs involves the input of C&O motive power officials, for only they were close enough to C&O operating people to know their preferences in motive power. After all, while the AMC traveled a lot by office cars, they probably seldom rode them all the way from Cleveland to Richmond. Getting input is hard, for most of the men involved are gone from the scene, and few apparently left memoirs. One who did was Larry Howard Booth, originally of Richmond, Va., whose ambition to be a graduate mechanical engineer was thwarted by the Depression but who was able to rise through the ranks in the Mechanical Department beginning with machinist apprenticeship at C&O's main locomotive shops in Huntington. By his retirement he had been Superintendent of Motive Power on C&O and after the C&O-B&O merger, Assistant Chief Mechanical Officer for the Chessie System.

Other than what is quoted above, Booth had little to say about his first contact with the AMC. His second contact, in 1941, was as C&O's equipment inspector for the 2-6-6-6s under construction at Lima Locomotive

"Washington, Cincinnati, and Western" is more appropriate than "Chesapeake & Ohio" in view of C&O's premier passenger trains the "George Washington," "F. F. V.", and "Sportsman". This was true up until World War II, when the "Sportsman" between Newport News and Norfolk to Detroit became an important conduit from South to North. At Washington, where streamlined Hudson 492 poses in 1948, a passenger could connect with important Pennsylvania Railroad trains for points up the Atlantic coast. And at Cincinnati the same passenger could have come in on NYC or B&O trains from Chicago and St. Louis to travel to Washington. Hudson 302 is in metropolitan Cincinnati area (specifically the C&O bridge in Covington, Kentucky) near end of its run with no. 43 (Newport News to Cincinnati F. F. V.) circa 1944. (C&O Ry. photo)

At Washington, streamlined Hudson 492 poses in 1948.

Works. While he has nothing to say about his work or the AMC's, he does make meaningful comments about AMC executives: (1) Daniel Ellis' interest in Booth resulted in an indirect offer for Booth's promotion inside the AMC that he turned down; (2) Booth concluded while in Lima that "Lima Locomotive Works was a playground for all the top mechanical officers from Cleveland, Ohio"; and (3) though he became "friends" with the AMC's Ellis, Trumbull, and Hauer, he formed a special relationship with Mike Donovan, "who became my father confessor and mentor."

Booth's two contacts with the AMC do reveal hitherto unstated facts about the AMC – that it "performed all the engineering and design work" for the C&O and that the AMC considered Lima, Ohio, a "playground." Presumably Booth, a man whose memoirs indirectly display his own moral probity and high ethical standards, cast a critical eye at what he perceived – rightly or wrongly – as padded expense accounts and moral transgressions of the AMC executives in using the word "playground."

If, as Booth suggests with the words "performs all", the AMC controlled development of C&O motive power, who on C&O decided when new power was needed? Because the standards for engineering new locomotives were independent of C&O management, the AMC alone could handle those decisions. However, only the C&O people knew what the road needed and when it was time

for new power. Learning the process by which C&O formulated its needs would be valuable. Booth's memoirs are of no help here even though Booth mentions locomotive orders that he was involved in one way or another; namely, the PM 2-8-4 of 1937; C&O 2-6-6-6 of 1941; C&O 0-8-0 order of 1943; C&O steam-turbo-electrics of 1947, and C&O's conversion to diesels. Booth typically says "orders were placed" or "C&O purchased." As for diesels, Booth does point out their "reliability," their "efficiency," and the "minimum of maintenance" required. Little wonder Booth was more communicative about diesels, since he received promotion to Master Mechanic of the Chicago Division, after the decision was made in 1950 to dieselize that entire division.

The only known source for learning how and why C&O made its locomotive purchase decisions is an article in the C&O employees' magazine for February 1949 titled "Power Builders" by George McCann. Because the article mentions no officers' names or positions beyond "president", "operating supervisors", and "chief mechanical officers", one learns little about the process beyond the theoretical. The aforementioned officers, McCann wrote, hold a conference and decide what kind of engines they will order – freight, passenger, or switching "in light of economy and future benefits." Their decision also "may be prompted by an expected increase in traffic or the need to replace obsolete equipment." (It is ironical that this article appears after the very last steamers

"History and geography worked to establish patterns involving distance, ruling grade, and type of service." Illustrating these contrasts are J-3a 613 passing Ellerson, Va., depot (TOP) and by T-1 No. 3025 about two miles north of Sciotoville, Ohio, both in 1949. They contrast historically by Ellerson being associated with attempts by Union forces during the Civil War to cross the Chickahominy River and Virginia Central (as the Piedmont Division was known then) Because they were built some 75 years apart, the grades and curves on the Northern Sub were much less severe than on the Piedmont. Homemade pilots, like that on 3025, seemed the norm. (The pilot from T-1 3008, after scrapping, runs today on consolidation No. 33 of the Ohio Central Railroad) (3025, E. L. Huddleston; 613, J. I. Kelly)

History and geography worked against an efficient line through the hills of eastern Kentucky. Locating engineers had a tunnel planned near Olive Hill on the extension from the Ohio to Lexington and Louisville, but Collis Huntington ruled out the tunnel, not wanting to "build a monument to engineers." Limited to 1850 tons, a westbound freight pulled by a 2-8-4 and pushed by a 2-6-6-2 climbs the 2.67% grade in 1951. (E.L. Huddleston)

for the C&O had been ordered.) They also recognize that these engines "will have to meet special requirements peculiar to their service and the territory where they will serve." And at this point the conferees call in the Advisory Mechanical Committee!

McCann, labeling the AMC "engineering experts," dramatically has the conferees beseeching the AMC to "give us an engine, modern, powerful, economical that will satisfy demands of traffic and our operations." McCann points out that the AMC must know how much tonnage the engines will haul, the speeds they must maintain, and steepness of the grades. Further, they "must know how heavy and how high these engines may be built," and "where such information is not available, committee investigators [will] take to the road, observing these locomotive features in question in actual operation."

From reading Booth's memoirs, one learns that C&O motive power officials often jealously protected their own authority, so deciding to order motive power and suiting the proposed new engines to C&O's needs must have involved office politics. To examine the complex and overlapping organization, one has only to look at the personnel charts in the 1944 (or 1948) C&O "station" book for the Executive, Operating, Engineering, and Motive Power Departments. The saving factor in all this complexity was the C&O's strong tradition of excellence in motive power design and use. This tradition made for an *esprit de corps* in C&O's management, and to a certain extent in the Advisory Mechanical Committee whose leader, Alonzo Trumbull, promoted excellence at all levels.

To demonstrate the tradition of excellence one can point to such "firsts" in C&O's motive power development as: (1) C&O's first Pacific type locomotive (class F-15) appeared in 1902, just a few weeks after Missouri Pacific received its first 4-6-2, making these two roads the first to receive this important new passenger design. According to Brian Hollingsworth, the "size and power" of the 27 C&O's F-15 Pacifics "set a new standard." (2) In 1903 C&O received two big 0-8-0s (class C-8), the first 0-8-0s designed specifically as switchers. (3) Beginning 1903 C&O had built by Lima for use (mostly) in the New River coal fields the largest fleet of Shay geared locomotives of any Class 1 railroad (classes C-9 and C-10). (4) C&O's H-2 Mallets of 1911 marked a great advancement in articulated locomotive design, for these 2-6-6-2s had a combustion chamber 6 1/2 ft. long, making possible lengthening the boiler without lengthening the boiler tubes beyond 24 ft. The advantage of this was that the firebox would not have to rest upon the drivers; an outside bearing radial trailing truck would wholly bear the weight. (5) 1911 also saw two other pioneering designs. C&O and Alco produced the first Mountain type (4-8-2) ever built (class J-1) and, based on its design, the heaviest and most powerful Mikado type yet built (class K-1). Both types were highly successful in service. (6) In 1914 appeared the first of an order for a series of heavy Pacifics that would culminate in the famous F-19 class of 1926. The F-17 (470-475), the first of this line, was the most powerful Pacific type yet built. (7) In 1923 Alco and Baldwin (1926) built for C&O a fleet of 2-8-8-2s — a new type of articulated locomotive (class H-7) that according to R. A. LeMassena were the most powerful engines "on the continent" at time of their construction. Innovations which pioneered standard practice included Elesco feedwater heater, cast-frame trailing truck, and twin stacks. Hitherto, single expansion, simple articulateds had been only experimental.

The success of C&O's "Simple Simons" made possible development in America of the most powerful steam locomotives ever built — single expansion simple articulateds. (8) When they were built — 1924 to 1926 — C&O's K-3 Mikados (2-8-2) comprised the largest and most powerful fleet of Mikados to that time, and 2-8-2s, after the end of World War I, had become the most popular type locomotive built in America. By the 1930s only Mikes owned by Frisco and Great Northern exceeded them in speed or rated tractive effort, but neither hauled the tonnage in one train that the 100 K-3s hauled.

The tradition of excellence conditioned C&O motive power officials to look for the best. And C&O's history, its geography, and operations developed patterns affecting motive power selection. These patterns involved distance, ruling grade, type of revenue. Measured by the impact of history alone, C&O would be called "Huntington's Road" after Collis P. Huntington, C&O's founder and transcontinental railroad baron. Conversely, if geography alone established patterns, the C&O might have been called the "Washington, Cincinnati, and

History and geography determined that a major terminal on the C&O would be at Clifton Forge, Va. Claudius Crozet, brilliant engineer, took the Virginia Central to the base of the main summit of the Alleghenies at Jackson River station west of Clifton Forge. And the Richmond and Allegheny Railroad came all the way from Richmond to the base of the Alleghenies via the James and Jackson Rivers (which joined just south of Clifton Forge). In this 1936 scene, all engines face east. Brill car, No. 9050 (in back), will go toward Richmond on the Richmond and Allegheny route, and big Mountain type 544 and Greenbrier 604 will take different sections of the "Sportsman" over the Mountain Sub, which was Crozet's route west. (COHS collection.)

"The road ended up with some natural rock tunnels in the remoteness of New River Gorge that would eventually make selection of very large locomotives difficult." One of those tunnels, bypassed in the 1930s by a big fill, is behind the photographer, who in April 1956 pictured extra 1644 in the rain as it blasted east up the New, coming and going. Blue Hole, an 800 ft. unlined tunnel, is still there today, dark and empty. (E. L. Huddleston)

Western," which was more accurate about where the road went than "Chesapeake & Ohio" at least from the viewpoint of passenger traffic. Both forces working together made the C&O what it was. Huntington, skillfully juggling the demands of finances, traffic sources, and engineers while overseeing construction of the road, knew the importance of reaching the Ohio River and rightfully named the new city that arose at that spot after himself. After all, it was the first railroad to connect ocean ports on the lower Chesapeake Bay with the Ohio Valley.

The patterns resulting from grades and distance of runs over the new line formed two important yard sticks for motive power selection. The fact that Huntington was a "hands on" executive meant that his ideas about traffic and construction costs would mark the line's economic development. (Huntington foresaw the road as part of a transcontinental and wanted to keep construction costs down in a period when rock removal was very expensive!) Geography would mark the road's physical development by confronting locating engineers with waterways that would "make easy the way" for heading west, in the words of George Washington, who had foreseen the practicality of the route that Huntington's road would eventually follow. What developed then was a crossing of the Appalachians the easiest of any road south of New York state. That yard stick permitted selecting locomotives that could haul long trains of high tonnage over a single summit. But because of Huntington's restrictive ideas about construction costs, the road ended up with some natural rock tunnels in the remoteness of New River Gorge that would eventually make selection of very large locomotives difficult. These tunnels produced clearance problems until the road had the money to engage in line improvements during the Depression, of all times.

The length of runs from one terminal to another, called "divisions" by railroaders, was another yard stick affecting locomotive performance. These divisions made for runs that were too short for efficiency. Locating engineers did not have much choice about terminals because

"1644, eastbound, passes abandoned west portal of Blue Hole Tunnel, at left out of picture."

options for establishing division points in mountainous country were few. However, mountain country had its advantages that is, the mountain country west of Hinton for hidden under the talus slopes of hill sides were thick seams of bituminous. Huntington did not foresee the great rise in coal traffic out of West Virginia. He thought instead of C&O's part in a transcontinental route by way of New Orleans, which of course did not develop. Yet hauling coal eastward and westward out of Appalachia would establish the most significant yard stick for measuring locomotive needs.

While the selection of division points worked

against efficiency in locomotive deployment, a historical development in C&O's physical plant worked to permit efficient use of the road's locomotives; it involved establishing two yard sticks: one for the Appalachian crossing and the other for lines on either side of the Allegheny crossing. When C&O was extended west over the Appalachian ranges (the Blue Ridge, the Alleghenies, and the Appalachian Plateau) to the Ohio, its line from Richmond came over a direct route to western Virginia but a very mountainous one; namely, the Piedmont and Mountain divisions. The historic line thru Charlottesville and Staunton involved steep grades and stiff curves. If ever C&O was to develop as a coal road, it would need a better way of moving loaded coal cars toward the coast. Fortunately, that way came when the Richmond and Allegheny Railroad went bankrupt. Built on the tow path of the James River and Kanawha Canal and following the flood plain of the James and Jackson into Clifton Forge, Va., the railroad dropped over 1,000 feet in altitude from Clifton Forge at the base of the Alleghenies to the level of the ocean at Richmond, thus offering an alternative route to tidewater. (Geographers' labeling Richmond a "fall line" city meant that the city had been built at the point where the downward flow of the James gave way to the level gradient of ocean tidewater.) The only disadvantage of this route was its twisting course.

(One can see that modern highway builders take little stock in building new highways in river valleys, which flood and which offer an indirect route from point A to point B.) The railroad along the James was completed in 1881 and acquired by C&O in 1889. The fascinating account of how this road was intended to connect with a planned competitor of C&O's extending to Toledo is told in C&O Chief Engineer Harry Frazier's *Recollections* (1938).

C&O enjoyed the same good fortune in attaining a low grade line to the West all the way from Huntington to Cincinnati. C&O had come to Huntington by way of a mostly river-level route from the base of the Alleghenies near Ronceverte where the main line joined the Greenbrier River. The new road crossed the Alleghenies at the state line very near the socially high toned spa at White Sulphur Springs, a route that would attract rail travelers to the resort. Engineering this crossing of the summit had involved two long tunnels and a great fill over 400 ft. in height. Once White Sulphur was reached, the path to the Greenbrier could be kept to a maximum .57% grade. C&O then followed the Greenbrier and the New west, both providing water level passage through the Allegheny Front, and thus penetrating this barrier at its lowest point from southern New York State to its end in Alabama. Additionally, the Teays "river" valley provided a

Just past "A" Cabin at Alleghany, Va., in June 1947, 1628 has the first half of its long train over the apex of the vertical curve that marks the summit some thousand feet back. Its pusher is in the middle of Alleghany Tunnel. Steam escaping under 1628 is the rail washer. (E. L. Huddleston)

"What developed then was a crossing of the Appalachians the easiest of any road south of New York state." This was mainly result of the proximity of the Greenbrier and New-Kanawha Rivers to C&O's route west. But geography also had its problems. The Alleghany Subdivision is only 80 miles long. (The first terminal west of Clifton Forge was of necessity at Hinton, where the Greenbrier flowed into the New.) Another impediment to efficiency was a 50-mile pusher district, where some 30 miles in the middle of this district required no pusher. In the 12 miles of .57% adverse grade against 140 car coal trains up Howards and Dry Creeks, pushers were definitely needed, as shown by 1613 and 1621 in 1951 near Tuckahoe, W. Va. (Observe the "block" sized coal ahead of 1613 and the New York Central coal cars off NF&G Railroad ahead of 1621.) — (both, E. L. Huddleston)

Spectacular New River Gorge gave C&O a low grade passage through the Allegheny Front. Norfolk and Western and Virginian, C&O's competitors, needed pushers to climb across the Front, via Flat Top Mountain, whereas C&O cut through it. Hawks Nest Overlook, 585 ft. above the New (dammed up at this point), looms in background of both photos of 2-6-6-6s headed upriver circa 1950. (Bridge showing in 1607 photo (BELOW) is just out of sight in 1659 photo (ABOVE)) (both, E. L. Huddleston)

The .40% grade for the first six miles east of Hinton definitely required helpers, like 1628 (in 1947) leaving Avis Yard, Hinton. It will shove fifty miles to Alleghany, turn, and return "light" to Hinton. Pockmarked rock cliff above the two coal cars is the "Avis Limestone." (E. L. Huddleston)

shortcut from the Kanawha Valley (extension of the New) to the Ohio in a westward direction.

The 160 mile segment of the C&O main line along the Ohio River from Huntington to Cincinnati was built to such high standards of engineering that it became a race track for C&O's premier passenger trains terminating in the Queen City. The Cincinnati Division would become important too for manifest freight — namely, the "Kanawha Dispatch" service — and westbound coal moving to the B&O, Pennsylvania, New York Central, Southern, and Louisville and Nashville. Let Harry Frazier, who had a long and distinguished career with C&O, tell of locating this line from Ashland to Covington (across the river from Cincinnati): "The senior Mr. Huntington, alive to the better possibilities for his C&O investments, if a railway from Ashland to Cincinnati was built, and having acquired the charter rights of prior companies, ordered surveys started on this line down the Ohio River in 1882. I was sent there as an instrument man on the locating party making that survey. Col. C. B. Childs was the Chief Engineer. Our work in making this survey was done with unusual comfort. We lived in a house boat on the Ohio River. [There were no roads down the Valley.] The survey was started at Ashland, and the men in charge of the boat would drop it down with the current to about the place that we would probably have lunch, and further along in the afternoon when it was time to quit we would find it conveniently near. ...Col. Childs was appar-

ently an austere man. Having been Provo-Marshall under [Union General] Ben Butler at New Orleans, it was easy to think that he could be a bit rough and he was, at times; but under all that fierce exterior was a kindly heart which he was always afraid somebody would discover. ... he made a location down the Ohio River from Ashland to Cincinnati that has been above criticism ever since, if not always above high water. The line was placed above ordinary high water, but to have located it above the great inundations that follow each other at long intervals, would have been ...out of the question as a business proposition then and now." The reason the line was "above criticism" was its gentle curves and level gradient.

Harry Frazier was to C&O engineering what George W. Stevens would be to C&O traffic development. Frazier's greatest accomplishment was construction of the Richmond viaduct, which, paralleling the James through the city, permitted the former R&A roadbed to keep the same level gradient that the tow-path of the Canal provided west of the city.

Hinton, West Virginia, comes into focus in understanding the C&O's motive power tradition because both Frazier and Larry Booth discuss it as operating point. Hinton, as a division terminal, was poorly located, yet the New River "valley" was so narrow that it was Hinton or nowhere! The same situation relative to location existed in the relatively short distance — 73 miles — to the next crew change point, at Handley (though eventually after

C&O Super Power Suitability

Though the New River Subdivision of the Hinton Div. was only 73 miles, the company got good day's work out of the Allegheny 2-6-6-6 Super Power and its crews because it was upgrade all the way (drop in lower New River was over 80 feet to the mile) and it had four pick-up points for east and westbound coal. A major point was Quinnimont, where in December 1949, 1615 (RIGHT) makes an eastbound pick-up and 1640,(ABOVE) which will pick up at Meadow Creek, blasts past QN cabin near twilight with long train trailing around curve at left.. (Same church shows in both views.) (both, E. L. Huddleston)

receipt of Super Power, through manifest runs were made to Russell.) In his *Recollections*, Harry Frazier wrote of General Manager Stevens naming him General Superintendent of C&O lines from Clifton Forge to Cincinnati in the early 1890s. The western general division comprised the Huntington and Cincinnati Divisions with headquarters at Hinton and Covington, Ky., respectively. (As traffic grew, the Huntington Division was divided into the Huntington and Hinton divisions.)

Quoting Frazier's memoirs during this period illuminates the rapidly developing motive power yard sticks, before the separation of motive power into mountain and level land service but after a distinction between passenger and freight power: "Freight trains were moved then in convoys; that is, four or more sections to a schedule number, and more freight trains were moved over the single track between East Sewell [New River assembly yard west of Hinton in oldest C&O coal field] and Clifton Forge than are moved today on two tracks, the tonnage was less than now, and overtime, more than occasionally, was something fierce. ...We had train wrecks then, yes, lots of them, and finding the wrecking crew ineffi-

cient at Hinton, my first official act as Superintendent was to put James Brightwell in charge of that crew. ...having shown unusual capacity as an emergency wrecker...The power at that time consisted of light ten-wheelers (4-6-0) on through passenger trains, with G-3 and G-4 consolidations (2-8-0) on freight trains between Clifton Forge and Hinton. West of Hinton eight-wheelers (4-4-0s) were used on passenger trains, with G-1 and G-2 consolidations on freights. The 70 and 71 brand new (4-4-0s) were brought over from Virginia and were the show locomotives moving the F. F. V.'s between Hinton and Huntington. (The F.F.V., established in1890 with an orange color motif, offered the first through service of any road between Washington and Cincinnati.)

At the time Frazier made this observation about motive power at Hinton, American types and Ten Wheelers were "done for" as mainline haulers in the move toward ever bigger, ever more powerful, and more reliable motive power. Consolidations (2-8-0), which would increase in great numbers until "class G-9" was reached, were the standard freight power for crossing the Allegheny summit and moving coal and merchandise on

the level parts of the system, east and west of the Alleghenies. But suddenly in 1910-1911 came a revolution in freight and passenger engines (like the appearance of the Pacific (4-6-2) had done in 1902 for passenger power). Then developed a policy whereby the newly invented Mallets took long trains over the Alleghenies and Mikes took equally long trains over the "level" divisions. And as passenger trains grew in weight and length the new Mountain type (4-8-2) took over from Pacifics for the mountain haul. It was the policy also not to mix engines in each category of service.

Hinton comes up again in elucidating C&O's motive power tradition, for not only had Harry Frazier served there but some forty years later Larry Booth as well. Booth relates how in October 1943 he was told that the Master Mechanic of the Hinton Division needed a new Assistant Roundhouse Foreman and that he had been recommended for the job. Noting that arrangements were then made for an interview at Hinton, Booth continues: "Hinton was the division point between the Hinton-Huntington divisions and the Clifton Forge division. All locomotives east and west were cut off here and exchanged for the heavy Mallet locomotives to traverse Allegheny Mountain eastbound or vice versa for Mikado high speed freight locomotives westbound. The same was true of passenger locomotives. Hinton was consid-

ered to be the hot spot on the railroad and it was assumed whenever anyone was transferred to that station, they were on the way up. Hinton was a town of approximately 6,000 people, mostly railroaders, and was situated on the side of a mountain above the railroad and the New River." Yes, he was on his way up, for after four years at Hinton, Booth was named General Roundhouse Foreman at Huntington.

In setting the scene at Hinton in his memoirs Booth oversimplifies the dual service policy followed in dispatching freight and passenger locomotives at Hinton. This is probably because of a forty year lapse in memory between working at Hinton and writing about it. "Mallet" locomotives were sent westbound, as well as eastbound, out of Hinton because the New River had great rapids that made for adverse grades on the mainline of the Hinton division heading up the river. These "Mallets" (not actually Mallets but H-7 and H-8 simple articulateds) ran to Handley, the terminal west of Hinton in the Kanawha Valley. The "Mikado high speed freight locomotives" were actually K-4 2-8-4 Kanawha Super Power types. (C&O employees mostly called the K-4s "big Mikes".) The K-4s hauled the main sections of manifest trains all the way to Russell and back to Hinton. Otherwise, articulateds prevailed on the New River. "Mountain territory" passenger engines (4-8-4 and 4-8-2)

The versatility, or flexibility, of the 90 C&O 2-8-4s, 2700-2789, is illustrated with 2731 (PAGE 142) in fast manifest service, 2743 in coal drag service, and 2760 in passenger service. 2760, with mail-express No. 103, heads down New River while 2743 leaves Kanawha Valley at St. Albans with 160 empties for Danville. 2731 brings no. 90, the Expeditor, up the Ohio Valley toward Russell. Its rapid run along the 128 mile division justifies Harry Frazier's praise of the line's engineering: "Col. Childs ...made a location down the Ohio River from Ashland to Cincinnati that has been above criticism ever since, if not always above high water." (all, E. L. Huddleston)

never went west of Hinton. "Level land" westbound passenger engines (4-6-2 and 4-6-4) ran without change from Hinton to Cincinnati and back or to Detroit and back. (An exception to the Hinton-Detroit run were the five L-1 Hudsons, rebuilt from the F-19 Pacifics.)

Four classes of C&O locomotives could thus handle the east to west and west to east freight and passenger traffic over the main line from Richmond to Cincinnati. The low-land, high-land assignments established a pattern, as ever bigger power was received, whereby older main line power moved to secondary and branch line duties and to segments of the railroad being leased-in particular the L&N tracks between Lexington and Louisville and the Orange to Alexandria tracks of the Southern. In every case the secondary, branch, and leased divisions had clearance or weight restrictions that prevented C&O from using its heaviest and latest power on them.

C&O lines accessing its major coal fields were not necessarily secondary. They handled coal traffic in such volume that they were built to main line standards. But the main reason they were treated like "main" lines is the distances in getting to the coal field. This is not true of the New River field, which mostly adjoins the main line and is accessed only by very steep grades. But it is true of the Kanawha, Coal River, Logan, and Big Sandy fields. (The Hocking Valley field was of little importance after 1930.) The fascinating history of development of these fields is covered in the TLC book Chesapeake & Ohio, Coal, and Color. The C&O, mostly under leadership of George Stevens, had to hustle to get to these fields before competitors. All these fields involved divisional runs out of Russell and Handley, simply to get near the coal field in question. This meant C&O's biggest "level land" power could take long trains to and from assembly terminals for each coal field. Remember, N&W's main line went through the center of its bonanza coal field, the Pocahontas. C&O's main line was over seventy miles away from its bonanza field, the Logan.

From the industrial district of Detroit to the wilds of the New River Gorge, class L-2 Hudsons displayed their versatility. No. 307 blasts away from South Fayette with mail-express no. 104 in June 1950. Now, in background would be the majestic Rainbow highway bridge. (E. 1. Huddleston)

But getting to the coal mines themselves required something less than Super Power. It should be remembered that there was no "flood loading" then. Different grades of coal were loaded under separate tracks at the mine head, and tracks leading up the hollows to the mines were definitely secondary. Thus the big power — including Super Power Kanawhas — that came into the assembly terminals could not be used to serve the actual coal mines. C&O discovered that its 2-6-6-2s were well designed to supply the mines and pull the loads. That is the reason C&O purchased World War I era Mallets in 1949.

The Norfolk and Western, C&O's chief competitor, mostly supplied its mines with 2-6-6-2s, almost identical to C&O's, and with 2-8-8-2's, including its "souped up" models, Y-6 and Y-6 a and b. Because N&W's large coal mines were generally quite close to the main line , due to the compactness of its major coal field, N&W was able to place its 2-8-8-2s in pools with road engines, Doing this, the road sacrificed heavy over-the-road power for smaller articulateds offering convenience and efficient utilization. If the mines were part of a field some distance away from the mainline, 2-8-8-2s were used because of heavy grades usually involved. In both cases Mallet compounds were utilized as road engines and mine shifters. But there was a sacrifice in doing this. The Y-6, essentially a World War I design, could meet the clearance and axle load requirements of coal branch lines, but for taking long trains over N&W's three major Appalachian grades, it had comparative low tonnage ratings, and helpers were required on all three grades. N&W wanted something approaching a Super Power design for its main line mountain area grades; in the class A 2-6-6-4 it already had Super Power for the "flat land" hauls.

Lewis Jeffries, in his N&W: *Giant of Steam* tells how "it was thought a more powerful locomotive than even the A or Y6 was needed to increase the speed of the heavy freight. So what evolved was a locomotive (classed Y7) that was to be as big as clearances would allow . ...From early 1936 to July 1937, a 2-8-8-2 single expansion articulated was being designed. Some ...known specifications are the 112-inch maximum outside diameter boiler, ...drivers sixty-three inches, tractive effort 153,000 pounds, grate area 130 square feet. ..." Perhaps what stopped development of this huge locomotive with a high drawbar horsepower potential was realization that 63-inch drivers, besides being difficult to balance, would not have the speed potential of Super Power .

In studying the influence of the Advisory Mechanical Committee on the C&O motive power tradition, one should not forget that C&O's very last order – going to Baldwin rather than Alco or Lima -- was for the World War I era 2-6-6-2 Mallets (1300-1309, class H-6) and for thirty improved USRA 0-8-0 switchers (late in 1948) that were soon sold to N&W. Because Mallet mine shifters are essentially switchers, one concludes that the Advisory Mechanical Committee never offered C&O a new design for any kind of switcher. This would indicate that the AMC was interested only in road engine design or that the 2-6-6-2 and 0-8-0 (class C-16) were so well suited for the tasks for which they were employed that new designs were not needed.

For the four categories of road engines discussed in this chapter, the AMC designed Super Power, replacing or supplementing existing C&O power, in every case improved performance and availability. For freight power the H-8 2-6-6-6 replaced the H-7 2-8-8-2; and the K-4 2-8-4 replaced or supplemented the K-3 2-8-2; for passenger power, the J-3 and J-3a 4-8-4 replaced the J-2 4-8-2; and the L-2 and L-2a 4-6-4 replaced the F-17 and F-19 4-6-2. (Actually, the L-2 Hudsons supplemented the F-19 Pacifics in the sense that the F-19 engines were rebuilt to L-1 Hudsons. The F-18 Pacifics were not replaced as main line passenger power in the sense that they hauled the named trains over leased Southern Railroad tracks between Orange, Va., and Washington, D.C. that would not allow the heavier L-2 and L-2a Hudsons.) Despite the complications explained herein, the four-part matching works fine, except for the C&O T-1 2-10-4.

While there were 2-10-2 Santa Fe types on C&O in the 1940s – some leased and some acquired from Hocking Valley (in 1930) and some from the Pere Marquette merger – none was in the C&O motive power tradition of main line power. Rather, the T-1 was literally in a class by itself and was designed from ground up to do a particular job. This job was unique in terms of C&O geographic and historical development. How this design came about for hauling long trains on a new main line route on C&O from the Ohio River to Toledo has been told elsewhere in this book. The design met requirements mandated by ruling grades, clearances, bridge loads, curvature and yard and siding capacity. The success of the T-1 has been told in books from *C&O Power* to *The Allegheny, Lima's Finest* – how the men who operated them were crazy about them and how design was so well adapted to need.

The unique nature of this line to the "Toledo Docks" is that since its completion, "mountain area" motive power was assigned to coal trains on this route and "level land" power assigned to passenger trains, notably the "Sportsman," a first-class, well patronized train running between Newport News-Norfolk and Detroit. In 1930 the T-1 took over the long haul from C&O 2-6-6-2 Mallet compounds and H-7 simple articulateds that had dominated through the first years. The T-1's 160 cars became the standard for maximum train length on this line from 1930 to 1952. (Though the H-8 Allegheny type, which supplemented the T-1's beginning about 1943, could have hauled more, siding and yard track length kept tonnage to 160 cars also). As for power for the "Sportsman", first the F-17 and F-19 heavy Pacifics held sway and then the L-2 and L-2a Hudsons (4-6-4). The ambiguity of

Tops in "beauty, dependability, and performance" were the L-2 and L-2a Hudsons. In April 1950 Class L-2 no. 304 leaves Detroit (Ambassador Bridge to Canada in background) with the "Sportsman" bound for Toledo and points south to Hinton and beyond to Newport News-Norfolk. (Elmer Treolar)

the line from Limeville to Columbus and Toledo being both "mountain area" and "level land" is resolved in that the Pacifics and Hudsons hauled relatively light tonnage and the 2-10-4s and 2-6-6-6s had heavy tonnage. For the former engines the line was level; for the latter it was mountainous. The severity of a grade is relative to the tonnage on it.

For engines C&O ordered from 1930 to the end of steam – as already noted – the AMC let C&O use its own pre-1930 designs for 2-6-6-2 mine shifters and 0-8-0 switchers. Also, AMC had little to do with selection of, and maintenance procedures for, the three fireless switchers purchased in 1949 from Porter for chemical plant work at South Charleston, WV , because the Committee's main concern was road engines and because the AMC had been or was about to be abolished. Also, because turbine engineering was not its forte, the AMC obviously kept hands off the attempts by Westinghouse electric and Baldwin Locomotive to build

three steam-turbo-electric locomotives for C&O around 1946.

How does one rank the AMC designed Super Power's adaptability? Recalling that the ranking is a guessing game rather than a real inquiry, we propose that first ranking go to the T-1 2-10-4s of 1930 for reasons cited above. Second would be the ninety C&O Berkshires received from 1943 to 1947 (plus several that came to C&O via the Pere Marquette merger of 1948). Most of these engines had steam heat and were as capable of hauling passenger trains as freights. They handled through manifests over the Mountain Subdivision and over the Lexington Division between Ashland and Lexington. (Admittedly tonnage on these two lines, whether coal or manifest, was relatively light, though grades were formidable.) Their tonnage rating over the James River line was 16,000 tons eastbound and 14,000 tons westbound down the Cincinnati Division. (Because of siding limitations, K-4s were not

Undoubtedly the most numerous standardized modern steam locomotive in the United States was the eight-wheel switcher, designed by the United States Railroad Administration in 1918 and as improved somewhat in the 1920s. The Van Sweringen roads adopted this switcher, but the Advisory Mechanical Committee had no part in its original design. Typical is C-16 no, 190, built in 1930, at work at Handley. The USRA 0-8-0 was also the last steam engine built new in the U.S.-by N&W in December 1953. (E. L. Huddleston)

used down James River.) C&O rightfully called these 2-8-4s Kanawhas, for that river saw them running in profusion along its banks. But C&O's 2-8-4s could have also been named Guyandottes, for that river led to a bonanza coal field in Logan county, and probably as many K-4s ran along its banks as ran along the Kanawha. (For that matter, they could have been called "Big Sandys," for in their heyday the 2-8-4s made long divisional runs from Russell to Martin, Shelby, and Elkhorn City on the Sandy and its tributaries.) Third in this arbitrary ranking of adaptability to C&O's needs would be the L-2 and L-2a Hudsons. (Where to place the less heavy L-1 Hudsons is a bit more of a quandary.) Speeding over ninety mph up and down the Ohio or running without change from the confines of the New River Gorge past the wind swept plains north of Fostoria to the Penobscot Building overlooking Detroit's Fort St. station, the 300 class 4-6-4s showed the world what "class" is made of, in terms of beauty, dependability, and performance.

Fourth is the awesome Allegheny 2-6-6-6. Despite this machine's potent power, C&O management seemed too conservative to utilize it fully. Handicapping the H-8 Allegheny type was its comparatively low calculated tractive effort (110,200 lbs.) usually determining tonnage ratings rather than actual performance. Another problem was the Allegheny's great weight preventing use

on the Huntington Division (Russell to Handley) until a new bridge was built over the Big Sandy at Cattletsburg in 1947. By late 1951 tests with DM-1 showed too late how the 2-6-6-6's could have conquered Scary Hill without helpers. Thus, C&O apparently got little more out of these locomotives – in terms of tonnage hauled – than it could have gotten from a second order of T-1 2-10-4s. Because they utilized two sets of three coupled axles, the H-8s were much better riders than the T-1, were much easier on the track, and could run like a deer with passenger equipment. Everyone who has read the Hundman and TLC books covering the Allegheny type knows how dynamometer tests of the H-8s revealed time and again how the engines were being under utilized in terms of drawbar horsepower and drawbar pull (as opposed to calculated tractive effort). However, lest we tend to put down the H-8 in favor of the T-1, we should consider that the H-8 could go up the .70% grade to the Sciotoville bridge without a helper whereas the T-1 needed a helper. There's also a tendency to compare the T-1 with the H-8, forgetting that the H-8 was intended to supplement the T-1 in Ohio but to replace completely the H-7 "Simons" in the mountains, where the 2-8-8-2s plodded along, wasting burnt coal and slowing other traffic and filling up employee time cards with overtime. The Allegheny truly fulfilled the Super Power promise of power at speed.

Fifth place goes to the Super Power that best represented in looks what the public saw when they attempted to picture Super Power. While the big boilered Greenbrier (otherwise known as Northern) 4-8-4s could accelerate from standing a passenger train faster than a C&O 2-8-4, the class K-4 freight engines probably could have held down modern mountain area passenger service equally well were it not for the tradition that caused C&O to separate level land from mountain power. Perhaps there would have been better utilization if the Greenbriers had been given dual-service assignments. As it was, they were restricted to mountain area passenger trains, only getting freight assignments after they were displaced from regular passenger service in the shift from steam to diesel power. Also, unlike C&O's level land Hudsons, the J-3 4-8-4s were mostly limited in terms of divisional mileage they accumulated. But, again, they were, as Super Power, stronger and peppier than the improved J-2 (4-8-2) Mountain types designed by the USRA in World War I, which were fine engines by any road's standards.

"The historic line through Charlottesville and Staunton involved steep grades and stiff curves." July 1948 J-3a no. 610, at the portal of Little Rock Tunnel, climbs the slope of the Blue Ridge range with the heavyweight "Sportsman" westbound over a nine-mile grade averaging 1.40%.
-- (J. I. Kelly)

The J-3 (and J-3a) Greenbrier type had a reputation as a real mountain territory passenger engine, and No. 604, the Edmund Randolph, lives up to that reputation in the summer of 1951 as the engineer of the "Sportsman" applies the brakes on the downgrade leading into the pleasant white colonial station at White Sulphur Springs, just around the curve. (E. L. Huddleston)

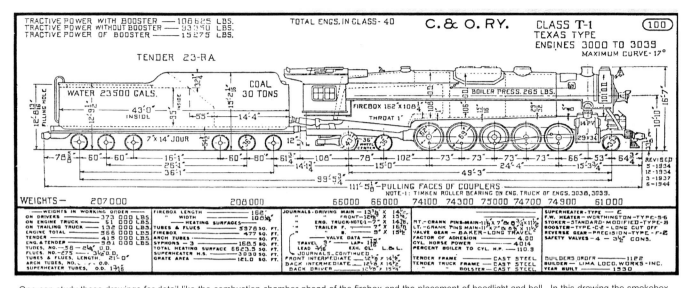

One can study these drawings for detail like the combustion chamber ahead of the firebox and the placement of headlight and bell. In this drawing the smokebox door (in profile) does not match the flatness of the actual door.

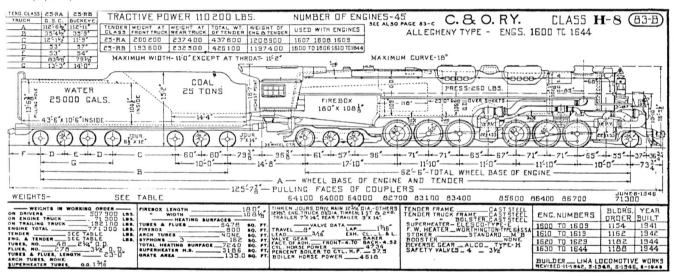

Drawings like these gave railroads practical data on the dimensions and specialties of each class of locomotive. On C&O they were bound between thick canvas covers and found wherever there was a roundhouse office.

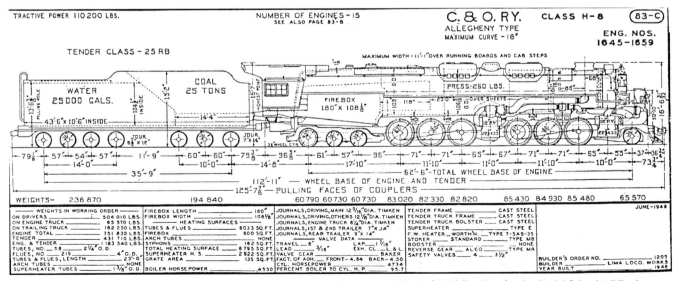

Typical of such drawings, this one included seemingly unneeded detail-like the rain gutter on the back of the H-8's cab roof-and omitted defining detail-like the injector under the cab and the reverse gear under the running board.

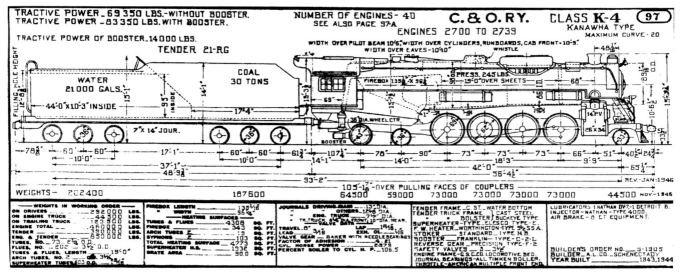

Most C&O Super Power freight and passenger engines came equipped with Nicholson Thermic Syphons. But only the order of Kanawhas (2700-2739), represented here, had them showing in the locomotive drawings (inside the outline of the firebox).

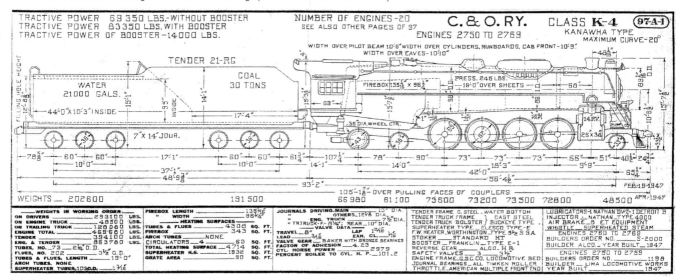

This diagram offers confusing data. 2-8-4's nos. 2750-2759, built by Lima Locomotive Works, belong with Lima 2-8-4s, 2740-2749, omitted here. Kanawhas 2760-2769 are part of an order to American Locomotive for 2760-2789. (See next drawing.)

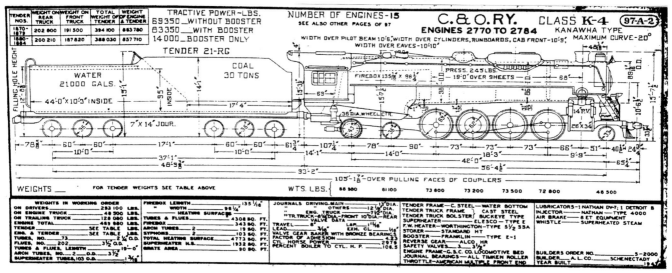

Alco builder's order no. S-2000 included Kanawhas 2760-2789 (1947). Yet 2785-2789 are not covered by this drawing, presumably because the last five would have their own diagram sheet. 2785-2789 pioneered in having all-welded boilers

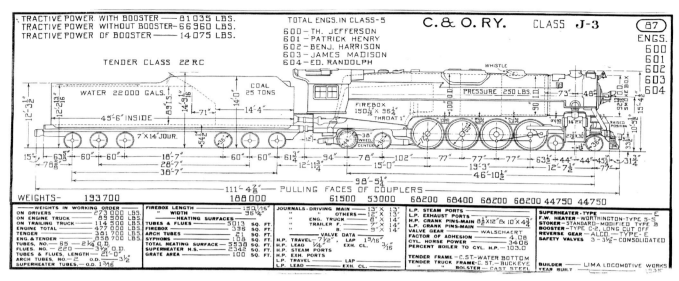

All these locomotive drawings have a provision for noting revisions-in the lower right corner of the drawing area itself. This drawing has no dates noted, for it was prepared at the time of initial construction..

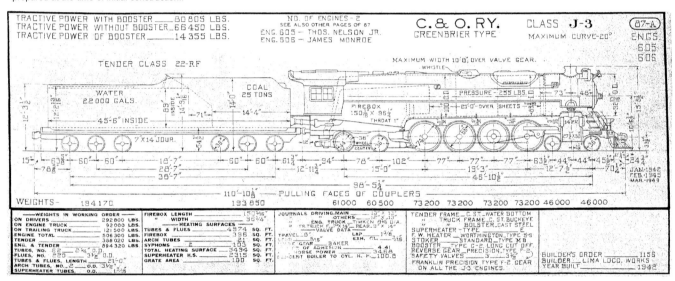

An accurate looking side elevation of the main frame of these C&O locomotives is probably the main weakness of these drawings. A strong point of most is depiction of detail on top of the boiler.

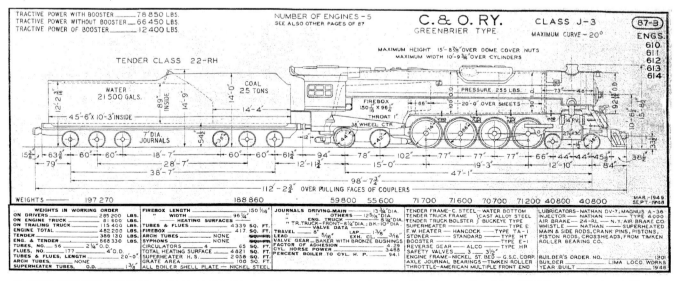

Beginning about 1947 GSC Corp. cast one central air reservoir in locomotive frame above the driving boxes. Greenbriers 610-614 were so equipped. Though drawing does not have this feature, it does show steam dome inside sand box.

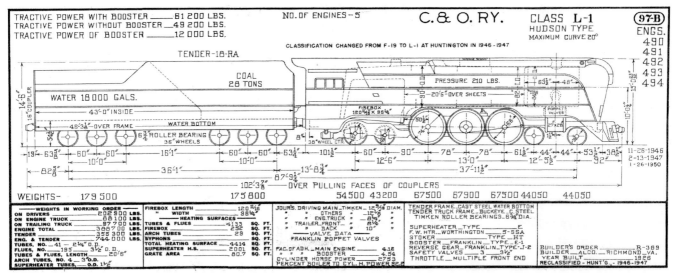

Disclosed by "dotted" outline of firebox is absence of combustion chamber, indicating that, in rebuilding, Hudsons 490-494 made use of boilers of F-19 Pacifics unchanged, though fireboxes might have been renewed.

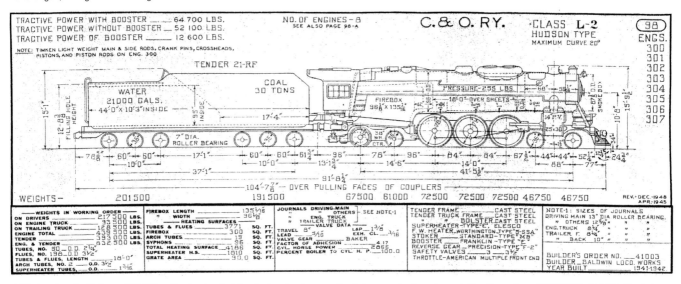

This drawing of Hudsons 300-307 omits showing that they had main air reservoirs below running boards much like Kanawhas 2700-2739. Detail below running boards is usually left out of drawings.

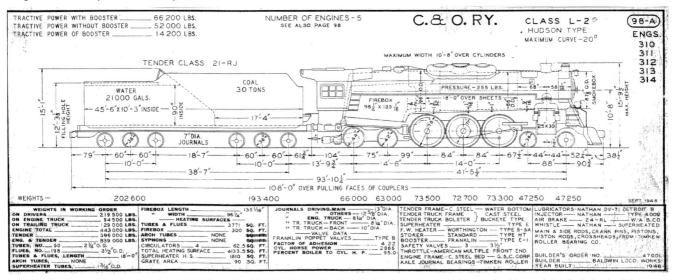

Only indication in this drawing that these 4-6-4s have Franklin Type B poppet valves is shape of valve area above main piston. A detail missing in all these drawings is "dotted" outline of shape of ash pan under firebox.

accidents, 44
air after cooler, 29, 49, 115
air pumps, 35, 45, 55, 74, 106, 115, 137
Alco reverse gear, 61, 133
Alemite lubrication, 75
Alleghany, Va., 150
Alleghany Corporation, 7, 88, 104
Alleghany Tunnel, 150
Alligator crosshead, 48
American Locomotive Company (Alco), 3, 14, 23, 67, 104
articulated trailing truck, 5, 32
Ashland, Ky., 28, 68, 72, 75, 76, 80, 84, 90, 116, 119, 153, 156, 159
Atkins, Philip, 24, 51
automatic stoker, 14
auxiliary air reservoir, 72
Avis, W. Va., 99
axles, 33, 34, 43, 54, 60, 64, 70, 72, 78, 111, 114, 123, 124, 125, 133, 160

B-1 class, 66, 128
B-2 Class, 66
B-3 Class, 66
back pressure, 13, 38, 47, 69, 70, 82, 101, 129
Baker valve gear, 13, 42, 57, 61, 74, 81, 123, 133
Baldwin Locomotive Works, 3, 25, 51, 59, 61, 67, 95, 159
Barboursville, W. Va., 103
baseball excursions, 119
Beebe, Lucius, i, 3, 5, 11
Berkshires, 4-9, 18-25, 29, 37, 48, 64, 69-71, 103-106, 110, 115, 119, 123, 124, 140, 159
Bernet, John J., 25, 29
Big Bend Tunnel, 99, 101
Big Sandy Division, 66
Big Sandy Subdivision, 105
Black, William G., 24, 25
black smoke, 60, 61, 124
Blackburn, J. B., 29
Blue Hole Tunnel, 149
boiler maximum outside diameter, 12
booster, 3, 4, 13, 26, 35, 43-50, 54, 61, 69, 72-78, 83, 104-107, 111-119, 130-133, 136
booster engine, 26, 74, 75, 83, 111, 130, 131
Booth, Larry Howard, 143
Box-Pok drivers, 61, 64
Boyd, Jim, 69
Bruce, Alfred W., 63, 123
Bullard turret lathe, 137

C-16 class, 66
Cane Fork, W. Va., 107, 116
CB&Q 2-10-4, 6
CB&Q Texas type, 6, 18
Chapelon, Andre, 77, 122, 125, 131
Charlottesville, Va., 27, 123
Chessie, 13, 20, 25, 56, 63, 64, 70, 82, 84, 143
Chessie Safety Express, 63, 64
Chicago Division, 144
Cincinnati Div., 12, 50, 69, 70, 81, 115, 153, 154
cinder abrasion, 123
cinders, 13
circulators, 48, 54, 55, 64, 71, 95, 133
class 3 repairs, 137
clearances, 4, 9, 13, 18, 28, 34, 67, 104, 106, 113, 134, 158
Clifton Forge, Va., 12, 138, 148, 150
Clifton Forge Division, 155
Coal River Subdivision, 11, 62, 104, 112-117, 122, 157
coils that preheated air, 133
Columbus, Oh., 99, 124, 130
combustion chamber, 5, 6, 18, 37, 48, 55, 59, 95, 110, 147
compound articulated, 88
Comstock, Henry, 99
Consolidation type, 69
Corey Hill, 118, 119
Cornell University, 4, 24, 98

corrosion and leaks, 121
cost cutting, 57
Cotton Hill, W. Va., 98
Covington, Ky., 11, 143, 153, 154
crank pin, 34, 54, 60, 61, 74, 75, 78
crown sheet, 46
customized design, iii
cylinder bore, 12, 106, 111

Daily Locomotive Inspection and Repair Report, 136
Danville, W. Va., 11
Delta type trailing trucks, 13
Detroit, Michigan, i, iii, iv, 9, 26, 27, 69, 75, 77, 81, 107, 143, 157-160
Detroit mechanical lubricator, 77
disk drivers, 125, 134
Dixon, Thomas W., iii, iv, 13, 16, 18, 35, 38, 53, 56, 62, 66, 69, 70, 101
Ball, Don, 11
Donovan, Mike, 23, 29, 30, 144
drawbar horsepower, 5, 18, 47, 158, 160
driver diameter, 3, 14, 53, 70
driving box wedges, 125, 128
Drury, George, i, 3, 5, 36
dynamic augment, 43, 44, 51, 61, 70
dynamometer car, 4, 12, 35, 38, 47, 94, 95, 113, 118

E8 passenger diesel, 67
eccentric rod, 74, 75, 130
King, Ed, 40, 95
Alexander, Edwin P. , 115
eight-wheel switchers, 21, 111
Elesco feedwater heater, 147
Elk Run Jct., W. Va., 116
Elkhorn City, Ky., 117, 160
Ellis, Daniel, 23, 25, 144
engine oil, 74, 77, 78, 123
erecting shop, 137
Erie Railroad, 99
evaporative heating surface, 48, 54
explosion, 44, 45, 46, 101

F. F. V., iii, 17, 53, 56, 67, 69, 79, 81, 83, 84, 143, 154
F-17 class, 13, 14, 17, 125, 126, 133, 147, 158,
F-18 Class, 13, 53, 158
F-19 class, 13, 19, 56, 63, 69, 82, 84, 126, 133, 134, 139, 147, 157, 158
factor of adhesion, 13, 35, 47, 51, 53, 64, 104, 112
Farrington, S. Kip, 10, 41, 67, 112
firebox, iv, 2, 3, 12, 18, 26, 33, 34, 46, 48, 49, 54, 60, 61, 70, 71, 72, 75, 77, 87, 95
firebox siphons, 5
first Pacific type, 147
flangeless drivers, 33
four wheel trucks, iv, 3, 6, 17, 69, 95
Franklin Precision reverse gear, 59, 81, 133
Franklin Railway Supply Company, 6, 31, 34, 61, 128, 129, 136
Frazier, Harry, 150-156
fuel economy, 38
Fuller, Homer, 70
Fulton, Va., 15, 45

G-9 Class, 11, 21, 154
gas area, 37, 95
George Washington, iii, 53, 56, 67, 69, 70, 72, 75, 81, 116, 143
Giesl ejector, 128, 130
Glass, H., 23
GP7 diesel, 7
grate area, iv, 2-6, 11, 17, 37, 71, 72, 78, 87, 95, 158
grate shakers, 46, 74, 91, 136
grease guns, 74, 78
Great Depression, iii, 3, 6, 11, 18, 51, 78, 103, 114
Greenbrier type, 30, 162
Greenup, Ky., 46, 69

H-5 class, 66, 124
H-6 class, 12, 13, 20, 21, 66, 158
H-7 class, 21, 35, 42, 43, 147, 155, 158, 160
H-8 class, 12, 17, 19, 21, 23, 37-39, 44-46, 77, 78, 87, 90-94, 98-101, 120, 133, 155-160
Hancock exhaust steam injector, 61, 62
Handley, W. Va., 12, 19, 28, 65, 86, 90-96, 99, 104, 107, 114-118, 154-160
Hauer, Ed, 29, 57, 60, 71
Hawks Nest, W. Va., 81, 98, 152
headlight, 24, 35, 49, 55, 57, 59, 60, 106, 110, 114, 115, 116, 123, 133
Henley, R. G., 125
Henry, Robert S., 27
Henry Ford Museum, 101
Hickman, Allen, 137
high speed booster, 130, 133
Hiltz, Vince, 59
Hinton, W. Va., 12, 58
Hinton Division. 154, 155
Hirsimaki, Eric, 7, 29, 30, 32, 133
Hitch, Clyde B., 23
Hocking Valley Railroad, 14
Holland, Kevin J., 18
Hollingsworth, Brian, 84, 147
Hudson type, 3, 18, 133
Huntington, Collis P., 137, 146, 147
Huntington Division, 28, 31, 91, 96, 154, 155
Huntington Shops, 17, 35, 63, 84, 95, 101, 126, 128, 129, 130, 131, 133, 137, 140
hydraulic flanging press, 129
hydrostatic lubricator, 77

increase in boiler pressure, 84, 131
interchangeable parts, 125
Interstate Commerce Commission, 134

J-1 class, 13, 17, 43, 47, 48, 49, 50, 51, 147
J-2 class, 14, 17, 51, 53, 56, 158, 161
J-3 class, 17, 19, 30, 52-58, 60, 62, 64, 70, 74, 77, 104, 110, 125, 126, 133, 145, 158, 161, 162
James River Subdivision, 15, 63, 101, 104, 116, 110, 118, 150, 159, 160
jib cranes, 136
Johnson, Ralph, 25, 43, 44, 51, 59, 61, 63, 64, 95,

K-1 class, 147
K-2 class, 15, 104
K-3 class, 10, 12, 13, 15, 19, 24, 35, 36, 101, 103, 104, 110, 118, 147, 158
K-4 class, 13, 15, 17, 19, 28, 29, 49, 60, 69, 70, 71, 72, 77, 82, 102, 103-119, 124, 133, 134, 155, 158, 160, 161
Kanawha Subdivision, 28, 96, 102, 107-110, 112-118
King, Ed 40, 95,
Kanawha type, 109
Kratville, William, 63
Kuhler, Otto, 27

L-1 class, 17, 19, 57, 59, 60, 67, 78, 82, 84, 126, 133, 134, 139, 157, 158, 160
L-2 class, iv, 2, 17, 19, 31, 55-57, 64-79, 82, 84, 104, 111, 115, 157-160
Lamb, J. Parker, 5, 6, 18, 114
LeMassena, Robert A., 8, 64
Level land power, 96, 111, 157, 158
Lexington Division, 119, 159
Lima, Oh., 3, 6, 19, 28, 30, 61, 91, 144
Lima A-l, 3
Lima Locomotive Works, iv, 2, 3, 4, 24, 25, 28, 29, 30, 46, 47, 59, 78, 87, 94, 95, 104, 133, 144
Limeville, Ky., 32, 38, 40, 42, 44, 92, 94, 95, 99, 159
limited cutoff, 32, 79
Little Rock Tunnel, Va., 56, 113, 161
Little Wright Watchman, 44
Logan, W. Va., 116, 157
Logan Subdivision, 103

Longdale Hill, 113
Louisville, Ky., 8, 19, 111, 146, 153, 157
low water alarm, 46, 72
Lucas, Walter, 53

M-1 class, 19, 54, 63, 112
Magellan, Ferdinand, 119
main air reservoirs, 133
main rods, 6, 14, 60, 64, 74, 78, 125, 134, 137
Mallet, 3-6, 11-14, 19-21, 33, 56, 66, 69, 88-91, 116, 125, 137, 140, 147, 155-158
Martin, Ky., 97, 116, 118, 160
maximum evaporation, 95
McCann, George, 144
mechanical lubricators, 72, 77, 124, 125
mechanical stoker, 4, 5, 131, 134
Mikado type, 3, 106, 147
milling machines, 135, 139
Milton, W. Va., 49, 124
momentum grade, 113
Mountain power, 96, 161
Mountain Top, Ky., 118
Mountain type, 2, 5, 13, 14, 17, 69, 134, 147, 148, 155, 161
multiple-bearing crosshead, 124

N&W Class A, 47, 95
N&W Y-6, 158
Nathan mechanical lubricator, 74, 77
National Association of Manufacturers, 6
Nelson, Joe, 34, 44, 46
New River Subdivision, 24, 65, 90, 96, 98, 154
New York, Chicago, and St. Louis, 119
New York Air Brake Co., 30, 59
Newport News, Va., 11, 19, 45, 46, 54, 55, 56, 57, 69, 88, 127, 143, 158, 159
NewYork Central, iv, 2, 3, 4, 5, 18, 25, 54, 67, 106, 115, 151, 153
Nickel Plate Berkshires, 18, 104
Nock, O.S., 11, 95
North Mountain, Va., 48, 105,
Northern type, 2, 8
nosing & yawing, 43, 54, 70
NYC H-10 Mikado, 4
NYC Mohawk, iv, 2
NYC Niagara, 64

office cars, 29, 143
Office of Defense Transportation, 8, 29, 60
Olive Hill, Ky., 146
operating territory, 12, 57, 99
Orange, Va., 158

over-fire air jets, 60, 61, 124
Pacific type, 3, 13, 14, 17, 133, 147,
Parsons, Oh., 42, 43, 75, 124
passenger diesels, 67
passenger power, 17, 67, 69, 70, 72, 155, 158
Peach Creek, W. Va., 13, 66, 103, 107, 116
Peninsula Subdivision, 45, 46
Pennypacker, Bert, 42, 43, 47
Pere Marquette, iii, iv, 7, 9, 12, 19, 24, 25, 26, 27, 35, 56, 66, 70, 78, 98, 104, 107, 110, 11, 113, 116, 119, 123, 125, 133, 137, 139, 158, 159
Pere Marquette Berkshires, 25
Philadelphia, Pa., 3, 6, 19, 28
Piedmont Subdivision, 145, 150
piston rods, 130,
piston thrust, 34, 48, 60, 133
placement of steam dome, 106
poppet valves, 6, 7, 29, 57, 59, 67, 69, 75, 82, 84, 128, 129, 130, 133, 134
Potomac Yard, Va., 66, 116
Powell Hill, 42, 44, 87, 99
Prime grease gun, 136
Probert, L. C., 25
programmed repairs, 133
PRR K-4, 82
PRR Q-2, 48
Pullman-Standard , 58

Purdy, Charles, 47

Quinnimont, W. Va., 154

Raceland Car Shops, 33
rebuilt Hudsons, 59, 133
Reed, Brian, 54, 60
Rehor, John A., 89
Richmond, Va., 29, 31, 143
Richmond and Allegheny Railroad, 148, 150
riding quality, 5, 43
Riel, Halsey W., 45
roomier cabs, 113
Rowland, Ross, 65
running board, 62, 64, 105, 133
Russell, 12-21, 28, 29, 33-42, 44-49, 59-65, 71, 72, 76, 79, 81-93, 95, 99-110, 115-118, 133, 134, 137, 140, 142, 154-157, 160

safety first, 136, 137
safety valves, 72, 120, 137, 139
sand box, 48, 55, 58, 99, 111, 112, 116
Santa Fe Texas type, 47, 50, 51, 54, 66
Scary Hill, W. Va., 49, 91, 94, 111, 114, 124
Sciotoville, Oh., 38, 40, 42, 93, 145, 160
Scullin disk drivers, 125
Security circulators, 64, 71
sediment and scale, 58, 125
Sellers wheel lathe, 128
Shay geared locomotive, 147
Shelby, Ky., 107, 116, 118, 160
Shuster, Philip, 47
side rods, i, 33, 43, 60, 74, 78, 84, 134, 136, 137, 139
Simons, 147, 160
simple articulated, 6, 13, 19, 35, 38, 66, 88, 91, 95, 99, 125, 147, 155, 158
Smith, J. Edgar, 29
smoke consumers, 60, 61, 124
smoke stack, i, 13, 38, 42, 75, 91, 99, 116, 123, 128
smokebox, 18, 24, 35, 37, 45, 46, 48, 49, 55, 59, 71, 75, 115, 116, 131, 134
smokebox door, 45, 46, 49, 55, 116, 131
solid cast frames, 110, 125, 132
Solomon, Brian, 3
Southern valve gear
speedometer, 44, 69
splash lubrication, 77
spoked drivers, 125
Sportsman, 10, 41, 52, 53, 54, 56, 69, 75, 81, 85, 112, 115, 143, 148, 158, 159, 161, 162
St. Albans, W. Va., 94, 104, 112, 114, 126, 156
stack tempo, 101
Stagner, Lloyd, 47, 57, 79
stalling, 45, 111, 112, 113, 131, 132
Standard Maintenance Equipment Instructions, 24, 30
standardized design, 7, 14
steam dome, 48, 55, 58, 72, 106, 110, 111, 116, 139
steam heat, 61, 69, 103, 119, 159
Stevens, George, 157
Stevens, Ky., 65
stoker, 4, 5, 14, 51, 67, 69, 72, 74, 77, 76, 91, 131, 134, 140
streamlined jacket, 5, 59, 64, 79, 82
streamlining, 19, 57, 60, 79, 127
Stutz Bear Cat, 2, 3
Super Power definition, 2
Superheater Company, 64, 131
Superintendent of motive power, 25, 27, 143
switchers, 2, 11, 13, 20, 21, 56, 66, 111, 147, 158, 159

tandem main rod, 60, 78
Teays Valley, W. Va., 111
tender classification, 94
Terminal Tower, Cleveland, 7, 29, 98
Texas and Pacific 2-10-4, 5, 6, 18, 33

Texas type, 5, 18, 32-51, 104
Thurmond, W. Va., 21
Timken roller bearings, 60, 78, 133
tires, 128, 53, 131, 137, 138
Toledo Subdivision, 42, 44
tonnage rating, 3, 47, 91, 113, 118, 158, 159
tonnage ratings, 47, 91, 118, 158
torque wrenches, 136
tractive effort, 3, 5, 11, 14, 35, 38, 47, 50-55, 64, 69, 70, 75, 79, 91, 94, 104, 111-119, 131, 147, 158, 160
transportation ratio, 55
traveling cranes, 137
Trumbull, Alonzo, 24, 28, 29, 34, 57, 60, 71, 87, 98, 104, 110, 123, 147
tubes and flues, 5, 37, 46, 48, 55, 59, 123, 134
turbo-generator, 63
turntable clearance, 37
turret, 72, 74, 77, 137, 139, 140
type E superheater, 37, 124, 131, 132

United States Railroad Administration, 3, 11, 14, 17, 28, 33, 114, 134, 160
USRA, 17, 25, 33, 34, 66, 106, 124, 134, 158, 160, 161

valve oil, 74, 77, 78, 123, 130
Van Sweringen, M. J., 23
Van Sweringen brothers, 7, 18, 29, 143
Vauclain, Samuel, 6
Virginian Railway, 6, 66, 87

Walbridge, Oh., 21, 34, 42, 43
Walshaerts valve gear, 9, 55, 123, 129, 133, 134
War Production Board, 51
Washington, D. C., 158
washout plugs, 137
water purification treatment, 122, 125
weight on drivers, 3, 33, 35, 51, 53, 65, 70, 106, 111, 112
Westinghouse Air Brake Co., 11, 29, 115
whistle, i, 47, 56, 75, 76, 116, 140
White Sulphur Springs, W. Va., 52, 56, 99, 150, 162
Withuhn, William, 37, 84, 134
Woodard, William G., 25
World War II, 3, 7, 19, 38, 47, 53, 56, 67, 103, 103, 119, 143
World War I, 5, 13, 14, 16, 28, 147, 158, 161
Worthington feedwater heater, 25, 55, 62, 63, 64, 124, 133, 134
wrecks, 43, 44, 154

Young, Charles D., 8
Young, Robert R., 19, 53, 56, 66